FRANCISCO DE ZURBARÁN

Books in the RENAISSANCE LIVES series explore and illustrate the life histories and achievements of significant artists, rulers, intellectuals and scientists in the early modern world. They delve into literature, philosophy, the history of art, science and natural history and cover narratives of exploration, statecraft and technology.

Series Editor: François Quiviger

Already published

Albrecht Dürer: Art and Autobiography *David Ekserdjian*
Aldus Manutius: The Invention of the Publisher *Oren Margolis*
Andreas Vesalius: Anatomy and the World of Books *Sashiko Kusukawa*
Artemisia Gentileschi and Feminism in Early Modern Europe *Mary D. Garrard*
Benvenuto Cellini and the Embodiment of the Modern Artist *Andreas Beyer*
Bernard Palissy and the Arts of the Earth *François Quiviger*
Blaise Pascal: Miracles and Reason *Mary Ann Caws*
Botticelli: Artist and Designer *Ana Debenedetti*
Caravaggio and the Creation of Modernity *Troy Thomas*
Descartes: The Renewal of Philosophy *Steven Nadler*
Domenico Ghirlandaio: An Elite Artisan and His World *Jean K. Cadogan*
Donatello and the Dawn of Renaissance Art *A. Victor Coonin*
Erasmus of Rotterdam: The Spirit of a Scholar *William Barker*
Filippino Lippi: An Abundance of Invention *Jonathan K. Nelson*
Francis I: The Knight-King *Glenn Richardson*
Francisco de Zurbarán and the Fabric of the World *Jeremy Robbins*
Giorgione's Ambiguity *Tom Nichols*
Hans Holbein: The Artist in a Changing World *Jeanne Nuechterlein*
Hans Memling and the Merchants *Mitzi Kirkland-Ives*
Hieronymus Bosch: Visions and Nightmares *Nils Büttner*
Isaac Newton and Natural Philosophy *Niccolò Guicciardini*
Jan van Eyck within His Art *Alfred Acres*
John Donne: In the Shadow of Religion *Andrew Hadfield*
John Evelyn: A Life of Domesticity *John Dixon Hunt*
Leon Battista Alberti: The Chameleon's Eye *Caspar Pearson*
Leonardo da Vinci: Self, Art and Nature *François Quiviger*
Lorenzo Ghiberti: Designer *Scott Nethersole*
Lucas Cranach: From German Myth to Reformation *Jennifer Nelson*
Machiavelli: From Radical to Reactionary *Robert Black*
Michelangelo and the Viewer in His Time *Bernadine Barnes*
Paolo Veronese and the Nobility of Painting *Tom Nichols*
Paracelsus: An Alchemical Life *Bruce T. Moran*
Petrarch: Everywhere a Wanderer *Christopher S. Celenza*
Piero della Francesca and the Invention of the Artist *Machtelt Brüggen Israëls*
Piero di Cosimo: Eccentricity and Delight *Sarah Blake McHam*
Pieter Bruegel and the Idea of Human Nature *Elizabeth Alice Honig*
Raphael and the Antique *Claudia La Malfa*
Rembrandt's Holland *Larry Silver*
Robert Hooke's Experimental Philosophy *Felicity Henderson*
Rubens's Spirit: From Ingenuity to Genius *Alexander Marr*
Rudolf II: The Life and Legend of the Mad Emperor *Thomas DaCosta Kaufmann*
Salvator Rosa: Paint and Performance *Helen Langdon*
Thomas Nashe and Late Elizabethan Writing *Andrew Hadfield*
Titian's Touch: Art, Magic and Philosophy *Maria H. Loh*
Tycho Brahe and the Measure of the Heavens *John Robert Christianson*
Ulisse Aldrovandi: Naturalist and Collector *Peter Mason*

FRANCISCO DE ZURBARÁN

and the Fabric of the World

JEREMY ROBBINS

REAKTION BOOKS

For David

Published by Reaktion Books Ltd
2–4 Sebastian Street
London EC1V 0HE, UK
www.reaktionbooks.co.uk

First published 2026

EU GPSR Authorised Representative
Logos Europe, 9 rue Nicolas Poussin, 17000, La Rochelle, France
email: contact@logoseurope.eu

Printed and bound in India by Replika Press Pvt. Ltd

A catalogue record for this book is available from the British Library

ISBN 978 1 83639 175 3

COVER: Francisco de Zurbarán, *Veil of Veronica*, *c.* 1635, oil on canvas. Photo Anna Danielsson/Nationalmuseum, Stockholm.

CONTENTS

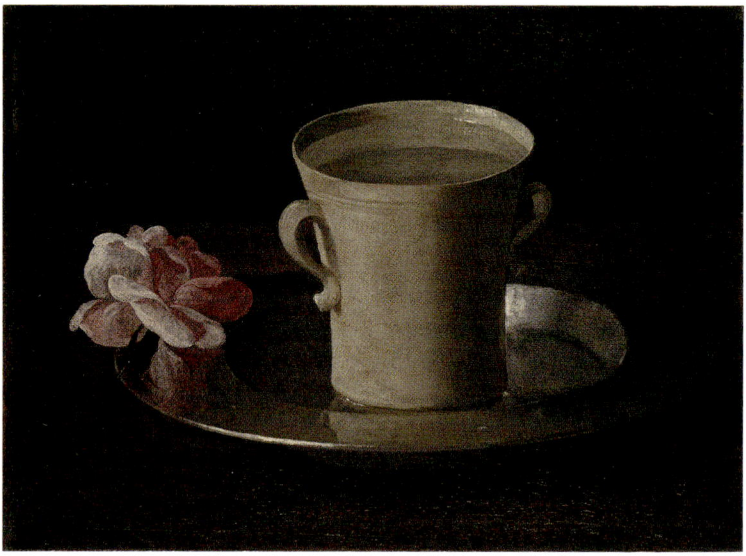

Introduction

Francisco de Zurbarán's exquisite *Cup of Water and a Rose* of circa 1630 shows a white ceramic cup against an almost black background (illus. 1). Turned so its graceful handles are not presented face on and with two striations encircling it below the rim, the cup is full of water and sits on a small pewter or silver plate, a pale pink rose resting on the plate's left edge. Possibly initially part of a larger composition, this still life as a still life nonetheless typifies Zurbarán's work, for although this consists overwhelmingly of figure painting – not least of saints, friars, monks and martyrs – his entire oeuvre expresses what one might term a 'still-life aesthetic'. Life in Zurbarán is stilled. In contrast to the dynamism of Rubens's compositions or the bravura brushstrokes of Diego Velázquez that produce, for example, the illusion of a spinning wheel spinning, Zurbarán's work, including his figures, is defined by the absence of movement, by an absolute stillness. Therein lies the uniqueness and power of his artistic style and vision.

Zurbarán renders objects such that they not only exert tremendous presence but embody a monumental sense of being, in and for themselves. The singularity that he captures seems as much an inner as an outer quality, each object self-contained, indeed almost self-absorbed. This is an aesthetic quality, a striking artistic skill, and an embodiment of a particular attitude towards reality. It is the nature and effects of these in themselves and in

1 Francisco de Zurbarán, *Cup of Water and a Rose*, *c.* 1630, oil on canvas.

the artistic and spiritual contexts of early modern Spain that are the focus of this book. The evocation in pigment of the materiality of all things, the intense rendering of what I am calling the 'fabric of the world', is perhaps most evident in one of his work's remarkable features, the clothes that his figures wear. What is compelling is less the clothes as clothes, but what constitutes them, the fabrics and materials in all their colour, hang, heft, their weaving and stitching. Zurbarán's clothes never define the body; they drape, fold and fall around it. Whether white, black or brown if religious habits, or fabulously coloured if the clothes of female saints, the taffetas, brocades, fleeces, damasks, wools and linens have a presence that arrests the eye. And the objects so carefully placed in his works – baskets, fruit, pectoral crosses, books, thuribles, croziers, bowls, writing tools and so on – are just as materially present, each evoked in its singularity, each as if it had a life of its own. A fellow painter in Zurbarán's Seville, the theorist Francisco Pacheco, wrote of the danger of what we would now call still-life objects in narrative paintings. He cites a *Last Supper* by Pablo de Céspedes. Céspedes found that people fixated on a pitcher in this work and ignored the human figures, clearly the carriers of the Biblical story. Infuriated, he had the pitcher painted out.[1] That such 'stupid things', 'trifles' and 'irrelevances', as they are called in Pacheco's discussion, might capture the eye over Biblical or religious figures is a risk Zurbarán's work consistently runs.

Spanish culture was acutely preoccupied with the incommensurability of the human and the divine. For Zurbarán's contemporaries, the two were utterly distinct, yet utterly folded together.[2] Christianity had long recognized that God was beyond human comprehension, beyond therefore word and image, unencompassable by either, and in a period that saw a remarkable intensification of engagement with mysticism, not least through the lives and writings of Teresa de Jesús (St Teresa of Ávila) and Juan de la Cruz (St John of the Cross), mystics, artists and writers had to struggle with how to convey in word and image experiences of the divine that took place beyond word and image. Zurbarán developed his own highly distinctive exploration of the tension between the human and the divine and by his intense focus on material reality paradoxically enables its transcendence, thereby also conveying the eternal through the temporal in a more impactful way than any other Spanish artist. It is here that the play of immanence and transcendence that characterizes his work is at its most mesmerizingly intense. In terms of the binary opposites that so shaped Spanish thought and culture – appearance-reality, material-spiritual, temporal-eternal, outer-inner – we see Zurbarán's art expressing one term through its precise rendering of the opposite: through appearances, reality, through the material, the spiritual and so on.

In exploring these qualities I will place Zurbarán's work in its artistic, devotional and spiritual contexts, the last two often either ignored or treated cursorily in discussions of the artist despite their centrality to early modern religious life and thus to the lives of his first viewers, and will argue that both his artistic strengths and also, strangely, his artistic weaknesses resonated in very specific ways with the spiritual values of his major clients, those from religious orders. We know more about Zurbarán's career than his life. We have contracts for certain commissions, witness and notarial statements from a lawsuit that he brought over his transatlantic trade, and documents covering aspects of his personal life; but we don't know what he thought or believed, or what he looked like. (Suggestions that he portrayed himself in the *Crucifixion with a Painter* remain just suggestions (see illus. 56).) His success and some documented comments aside, we don't know what contemporaries thought of him. In the two most important art treatises Pacheco doesn't mention him, and Antonio Palomino, writing at the start of the eighteenth century, treats him only briefly, in stark contrast to Velázquez to whom he devotes the longest and most detailed account of any artist in the biographical section of his work. There is no evidence of what he thought about art other than his art itself, the more than 290 works that make up his oeuvre in the most recent catalogue raisonné.[3]

In looking at Zurbarán I will take a broadly chronological approach, following him from his birth in the Extremaduran town of Fuente de Cantos in 1598, through his apprenticeship in the cosmopolitan city of Seville, where he eventually settled and captured the market, running a workshop and engaging in the transatlantic art trade, to his final move to Madrid in the late 1650s, where he died in 1664. Some chapters, however, will focus on subjects that he painted across his career such as the Virgin Mary (Chapter Six) or on the artistic qualities across his work that resonated profoundly with contemporary spiritual practices, Chapters Four and Five forming the heart of my examination of the distinctive features of the artist who best encapsulated not only Sevillian but Spanish spirituality. Zurbarán's work is obviously engaged with the art and religion of his time, often in distinctive ways, but perhaps because it is overwhelmingly religious, there is something of a tendency to implicitly view him as a less reflective artist than, say, Velázquez, so Chapter Seven examines the ways in which his images engage innovatively with image-making and image use.

Zurbarán is an artist whose use of colour is extraordinary, whose rendering of surface makes inanimate objects vibrate with life, and whose manner of painting reveals a distinct ontological ethos with no apparent visual hierarchy, no category distinction between objects and people in the same composition, each having as much presence as the other, both embodying a profound introversion, for Zurbarán's world is a world of detached singularity. Together, these make his depiction of the transitory world powerfully his own.

ONE

Seville in a Time of Decline

Zurbarán was born in Fuente de Cantos in Extremadura in western Spain, but his career was largely centred on Seville, the city where he trained from 1614–17 and where he took up residence in 1629. Seville was a cosmopolitan city, culturally and socially distinct from Madrid, the seat of the court, and it is those differences that made it a city unlike any other in Spain that I want to explore first, together with the challenges that it faced as its fortunes declined across the seventeenth century. Spain itself declined politically and economically across the same period and its position as the dominant Western power was ultimately and successfully contested, by France in particular, but Seville's decline was accelerated by several natural disasters. After considering these I will then explore what little is known about Zurbarán's apprenticeship in Seville and what the limitations of apprenticeships were at this time in the city, for these pose some interesting interpretative challenges for Zurbarán's oeuvre. Before he definitively moved to Seville, the artist lived and worked in Llerena in Extremadura, and the years of independent practice there are largely a frustrating blank since only one work remains from then prior to his 1626 commission for the Dominicans in Seville. The purpose of the chapter is to set Zurbarán in the context of the city that shaped his life and work, and whose spiritual life and yearnings he would so clearly and uniquely capture.

THE 'FATAL CENTURY'

The youngest of six children, Zurbarán was baptized on 7 November 1598 in Fuente de Cantos, a town of around 2,650 people.[1] Luis de Zurbarán, his father, was a shopkeeper and he and his wife, Isabel Márquez, were comfortably off with several properties.[2] In January 1614 the fifteen-year-old Francisco was apprenticed to Pedro Díaz de Villanueva, a 'pintor de imaginería' (figurative painter) in Seville.

Seville was fabulously wealthy and richly diverse, a mercantile city full of luxury goods and materials centred around its highly visible aristocrats, merchants, friars, monks and clergy (illus. 2). As one Sevillian poet declared, it was 'not a city, but a world . . . part of Spain, but better than the whole'.[3] Its fortune had been made in 1503 when it was granted the commercial monopoly of trade with the newly 'discovered' America. This made it in effect the 'capital of the Atlantic world'.[4] Its population expanded dramatically from 65–70,000 at the start of the sixteenth century, to a peak of 130,000 around 1580, making it one of the largest cities in Europe.[5]

The most eye-catching aspect of this mercantile city was the gold and silver that flowed into it from the New World and that was a major contributor to the rise of Spain as a dominant European power. A common metaphor applied to Seville was that it was the 'stomach of Spain and the world', distributing widely the 'universal sustenance' that it twice-yearly ingested from the New World.[6] The volume of precious metal that arrived was prodigious, an estimated 16,886,000 kilograms of silver and 185,000 kilograms of gold between 1503 and 1660, though these figures should perhaps be at least doubled to take account of loss through fraud.[7]

The twice-yearly fleets between Seville and Spanish America meant that the city was home to an international body of merchants and bankers, making it one of the most cosmopolitan cities in the Spanish empire, and certainly in Spain. Important local industries included textiles and silk weaving; tobacco, given that Seville was its point of entry from the Americas; pottery; and one of the country's most important mints, again due to the city being the entry point for precious metals.[8] Sevillian artists also began to send art for speculative sale to Spanish America, and Zurbarán would actively engage in this market.

Two things are worth highlighting about this city of trade. First, for an artist defined by his fabulous ability to depict textiles, the city provided excellent opportunities to see at first hand any amount of luxury fabrics. Second, and as a consequence of having wealthy Flemish, Genoese and Florentine merchants as well as many aristocratic families, artists had ready access to art from beyond Spain, whether actual canvases or prints – the latter a major source of inspiration to Sevillian painters, especially Zurbarán.

The city was also the most significant religious centre in southern Spain, its archbishopric the second richest in the country.[9] Lacking the court and not a vice-regal centre, its artistic and cultural life was dominated by the church, as obviously was its spiritual life whose fervour and intensity was manifested in religious processions and public devotions, not least to the Immaculate Conception. Spain itself was an intensely religious society and the seventeenth century saw a sharp rise in those entering the Church, whether through vocation or for security in what was a period of economic crisis. At the end of the sixteenth century there were 91,000 clergy, secular and regular (that is, in religious orders), in Spain, amounting to 1.1 per cent of the population. This rose to 160,000 or 2.5 per cent of the population by the 1660s.[10] Reflecting this trend, the number of monasteries in Seville grew significantly. A contemporary chronicler writing under '1649' in a work published in the second half of the century stated that it had 45 monasteries, 28 convents and 118 main churches.[11] This contrasts with an estimate for the start of the

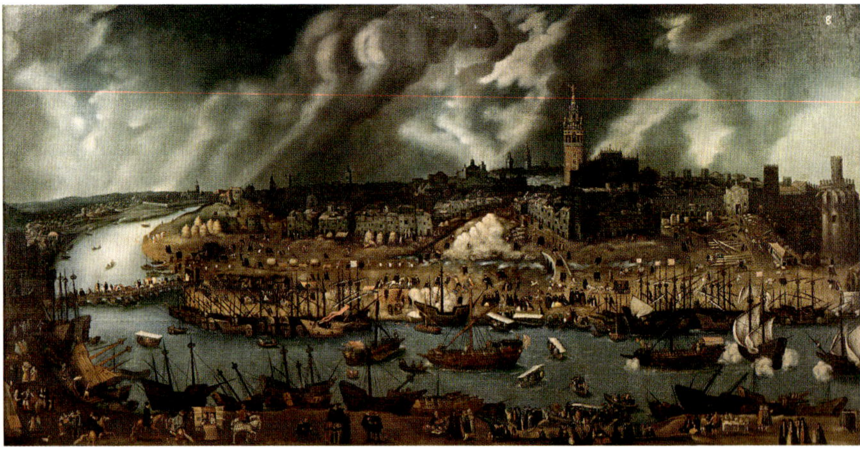

century of 33 monasteries and 27 convents.[12] Alongside the resurgence in confidence of the Church following the Council of Trent (1545–63), this increase in foundations led to significant expenditure on religious art – Zurbarán's career is shaped by this, his core clientele being religious orders in Seville, wider Andalusia and Extremadura.

Although Seville was a city of immense wealth and opportunity, it was also heavily marked and shaped by the opposite. The use of enslaved labour was a reality in smaller cities and towns such as Llerena and Fuente de Cantos, where Zurbarán's father owned enslaved people, but in Seville it was a dominant feature of life.[13] The city was actively engaged in the trade in enslaved people and a recent estimate suggests that in the early seventeenth century 'around ten to fifteen percent of its population was enslaved or newly freed, the majority being people of color.'[14] Sevillian artists such as Francisco Pacheco, Francisco de Herrera the Elder, Velázquez, Alonso Cano and Bartolomé Esteban Murillo owned enslaved people, sometimes as workshop assistants, the best-known being Juan de Pareja, who became an independent artist once freed by Velázquez. This is a reminder

2 Alonso Sánchez Coello (attrib.), *View of Seville*, late 16th century, oil on canvas.

that 'sixteenth- and seventeenth-century Spanish visual culture cannot be disassociated from enslaved labor.'[15] Poverty and destitution were endemic and the poor and destitute a focus of charity for the Church and for groups such as the Hermandad de la Santa Caridad (Brotherhood of Holy Charity), to which Zurbarán would eventually belong. Such brotherhoods were institutions whose members were engaged in a form of spiritual investment, active Christian charity through giving or more hands-on work with the poor or the sick, but also thereby endeavouring to ensure their own salvation. Among the wealthy, such forms of spiritual investment were also very much focused on commissioning works to decorate churches, chapels and altars, for, as Amanda Wunder has shown citing the terms of a contemporary chronicler, Sevillians placed more trust in 'divine methods' than 'human ones' when addressing the many problems the city faced.[16]

A series of natural disasters in the seventeenth century had a cumulative impact on the population, not least the poor. The city's river, the Guadalquivir, regularly flooded, for example, but the flood of 1626 was particularly devastating, covering almost one-third of the city.[17] Across the century there were sharp declines in crop production (cereals, wine, oil), so that when currency devaluation led to a dramatic increase in the price of bread this led in turn to a week-long bread riot in 1652 that was violently suppressed, the leaders executed, their heads put on display.[18] The desperation behind these riots was itself a result of the city's worst disaster, the 1649 plague that killed around 60,000 people, nearly half the population.[19] Its effect can be further gauged from the figures for the foundling hospital that normally looked after thirty to forty infants but in 1659 had some 340.[20]

In the light of this, it is understandable why the seventeenth century was described as a 'fatal century' for Seville.[21] And that is before mentioning Seville's worst disaster in terms of its prosperity, indeed its existence as a trading port – the silting up of its lifeline, the Guadalquivir. This was due in part to the nature of the river itself, but was also a result of the increase in the tonnage of transatlantic ships. A further significant factor was the vested interests of various parties – Seville itself; Cadiz, the city's main rival with its deep port but vulnerability due to its exposed position; and the Duke of Medina Sidonia, who had the lordship of another significant port, Sanlúcar de Barrameda – which resulted in a failure to make decisions over engineering proposals to address the problem.[22] The result was that by the mid-seventeenth century Seville's trade monopoly was already nominal only.[23] The city lost this monopoly in 1680 when Cadiz was made the Atlantic trade port, but administration remained in the city until the Casa de la Contratación de Indias (House of Trade with the Indies) was also moved to Cadiz in 1717.[24]

In terms of its literary life, this had flourished in the sixteenth century, but when Philip IV came to the throne in 1621, his favourite, the Count-Duke of Olivares, exploited his 'Seville connection' to draw writers and intellectuals away to the court in Madrid.[25] That said, and despite Velázquez leaving the city to serve the king, as Seville entered its century of crisis and decline, it was also entering an astonishing period of artistic creativity. The three great Golden Age artists – Zurbarán, Velázquez and Murillo – all trained there.

APPRENTICESHIP

Zurbarán began his apprenticeship in Seville in 1614. No works by Díaz de Villanueva, the artist to whom he was apprenticed, are known. In fact, virtually nothing is known about him except that he had a brother, Jerónimo Velázquez, together with whom Zurbarán signed contracts in 1631 and 1636, with Velázquez to construct *retablos* (reredoses) in Seville and Llerena for which Zurbarán would provide the paintings.[26] The apprentice agreement set out standard obligations. Díaz de Villanueva was to train Zurbarán without withholding any aspect of his art from him. He was to provide bed and board, but Zurbarán's father had to provide shoes and clothes. If Zurbarán became ill, Díaz de Villanueva had to cover the costs, but if the illness lasted more than a fortnight, Zurbarán's father was required to step up. Any money that Zurbarán earned by working on feast days was to remain with Zurbarán. The apprenticeship was for three years from the date of the agreement, 15 January 1614.[27]

The only unusual thing here is Zurbarán's age at the start of his apprenticeship since he was at the upper end of the standard apprentice age in Seville.[28] (Diego Velázquez, for example, was twelve when he began his six-year apprenticeship with Pacheco.[29]) This has led to speculation that he had had some prior training. At the start of the eighteenth century, the artist and theorist Antonio Palomino claimed that Zurbarán had initial training in Extremadura with 'some disciple of the Divine Morales and then went to perfect himself in Seville in the school of Doctor Pablo de las Roelas'.[30] Though he makes no mention of his actual master in Seville, and 'Pablo de las Roelas' seems to be an error for Juan de Roelas, these undocumented assertions are revealing whether true or not. Luis de Morales (1510/11–1586), who had been based in Badajoz in Extremadura, was an artist of 'austere and plangent devotional images',[31] notable among other things for their intense, dark backgrounds akin to those so often employed by Zurbarán (illus. 3). Juan de Roelas, an artist and priest of Flemish origin who worked in Seville from 1603 to 1616, helped introduce naturalism into Sevillian art – something that Zurbarán, Velázquez and others of their generation would make their own – and in his work 'he knew how to humanize the divine and introduce earthly aspects clearly and directly that were easily

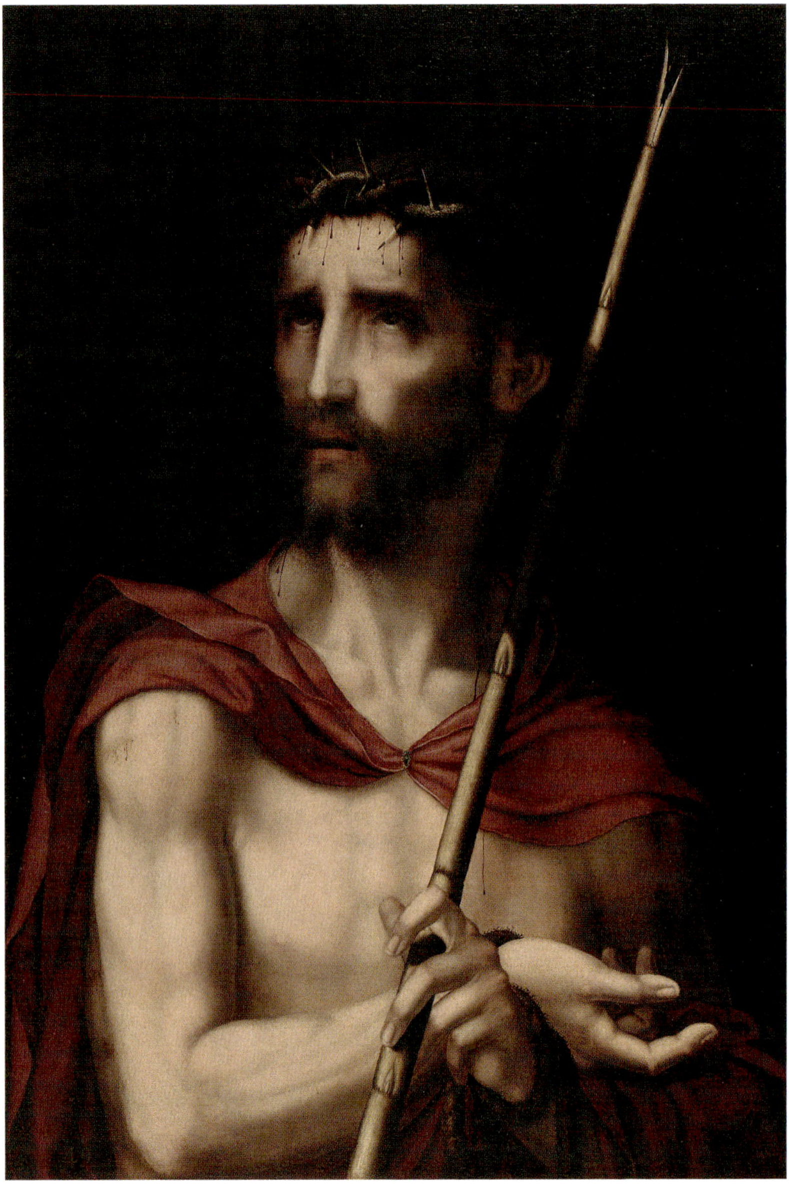

3 Luis de Morales, *Ecce Homo*, 1560–70, oil on wood.

understandable to all.'[32] The mention of Roelas, therefore, seeks 'to justify the evolution of Zurbarán's style towards the naturalism of Caravaggio', with whom Palomino closely identifies Zurbarán, as we shall see.[33]

If nothing is known about Díaz de Villanueva, and thus about his influence on Zurbarán, much is known or inferred about Pacheco's influence on Velázquez. In large part this is because much of Pacheco's largely dry, stilted and often-lifeless work remains, as does his extensive treatise, the *Arte de la pintura*, published posthumously in 1649, and because Pacheco played a central role in Seville's cultural life. He was friends with intellectuals, writers and clerics, not least Jesuits; he engaged in polemics over the most appropriate way of depicting certain sacred subjects; and from 1618, he examined art for the Inquisition to ensure its orthodoxy.

Pacheco's work was very different from the work of the young Velázquez, for Velázquez, like Zurbarán, embraced naturalism in his Sevillian work, but unlike him depicted lower class, working people as independent subjects in genre paintings and *bodegones* (still lifes). When he moved definitively to Madrid in 1623, he ceased to depict such 'lowly' figures and to paint *bodegones* as he sought to become a 'consummate court artist'.[34] As a court artist he was free to paint non-religious subjects, and almost exclusively chose to do so; whereas Zurbarán, dependent on the Church and religious orders as the dominant client base in Seville, almost exclusively painted religious subjects. What we see here is the shaping of careers by the client market. This determinist view, though true, also hides choices that Zurbarán could and did make. Velázquez's early work as an independent artist in Seville shows that there was a client base, however small, interested in *bodegones* and genre subjects, in the depiction of working people as the sole protagonists of works of art. Zurbarán's decision not to depict such figures was therefore an active artistic choice on his part.

While his figures are never fully idealized, throughout his career poor or working people appear only occasionally in an incredibly small number of works, and only when the subject matter required them. Even here they are secondary figures, witnesses in the *Adoration of the Shepherds* (1638; see illus. 23) or recipients of charity in *Fray Martín de Vizcaya Distributing Bread* (1639) and *St Thomas of Villanueva* (*c.* 1660). Although it remains possible that his early, lost work treated such figures, his known work suggests otherwise. Interestingly, Murillo, also overwhelmingly a religious artist, would, like Velázquez, paint many works depicting poor and working people as sole protagonists, albeit often in a more sentimentalized fashion. But this major segment of Seville's population did not interest Zurbarán.

It is clear that Zurbarán's training had its shortcomings, the most evident of which is sometimes seen in his depiction of space and architecture.[35] More specifically, the 'ineptitude of the perspective' in various examples of his paintings reveals an insecure knowledge of perspective, something of a characteristic in artistic training in Seville.[36] Velázquez, for example, acquired a full knowledge of perspective only after his first stay in Italy (1629–31), from which he returned 'greatly improved in the art of perspective and architecture', as a contemporary artist and theorist commented.[37] Zurbarán tended to avoid the overt depiction of spatial recession, as did the early Velázquez, but unlike Velázquez, this avoidance ran throughout his career. To obviate the need to depict perspectivally the recession from foreground to background Zurbarán favoured using architectural features, most noticeably a column, partially to block the visible transition from one to the other. In some works, though, his clumsiness in rendering space is disconcertingly apparent, *St Bruno and Pope Urban II* often cited here (illus. 4).

It has been suggested that his so-called breaches of the period's perspectival rules and norms were deliberate and purposeful, so

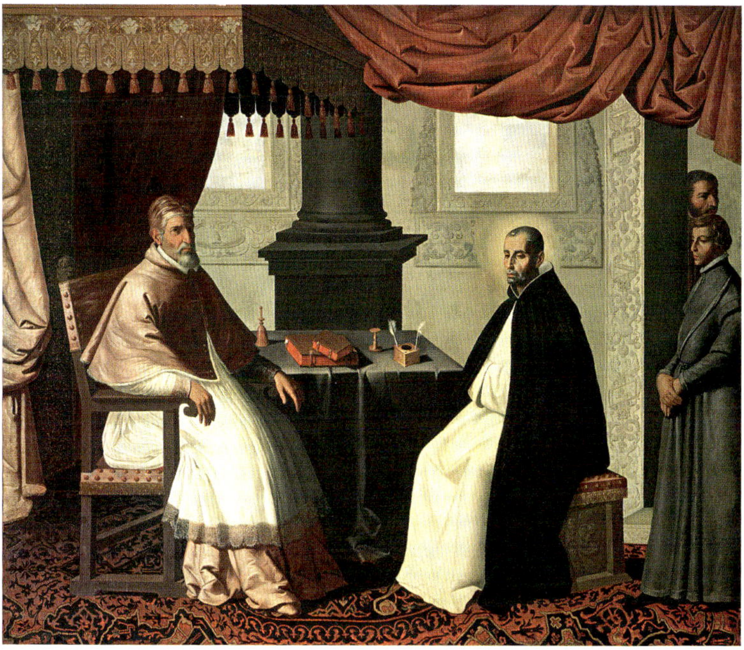

as to give prominence to objects and their symbolic import and that, along with such things as the disconnect between the elements in his composition and the favouring of the front plane for the key figure, these are not signs of ineptitude but rather a means of creating in the viewer 'an unease, an intellectual tension and . . . a feeling of passivity' akin to the 'psychological effects produced in the person having the vision' depicted.[38] This makes them not so much things that Zurbarán could not do, but rather things he chose not to do, an example of what Marcia Hall, writing not of Zurbarán but of European sacred art of the period, refers to as 'making strange'; that is, 'the way the painter makes the familiar unfamiliar that arrests viewers' attention and causes them to pause'.[39] While a suggestive interpretation, I am unconvinced that all such breaches are deliberate. This aside, the unique way that

4 Francisco de Zurbarán, *St Bruno and Pope Urban II*, c. 1655, oil on canvas.

Zurbarán places things in space is a defining aspect of his style and a major factor in his work's impact.

LLERENA

Zurbarán's three-year apprenticeship ended in 1617 without him being formally examined by the painters' guild, as Velázquez successfully was that same year. In itself this was not that unusual. Herrera the Elder – whose inability to complete a commission for the Franciscans in Seville would lead to Zurbarán being brought in in 1629 to do so – had not undergone examination, for example, and in the absence of documentary evidence Murillo possibly did not either.[40] In Herrera's case the guild eventually forced the matter in 1619 and he was ultimately required to undergo examination.[41] The issue would raise its head for Zurbarán in 1630, as we shall see.

Why Zurbarán did not undertake examination in 1617 is unclear, but that same year saw him marry María Páez in Llerena, where he then lived and worked for the next decade. Llerena was a prosperous town in Extremadura with a population of 7,644 in 1591 and of 6,038 in 1631, a decline echoed elsewhere in Extremadura due to a falling birthrate, grain shortages and crises in the transhumance on which Extremadura depended.[42] The town had two churches and seven monasteries, was the seat of the Priory of San Marcos de León of the Order of Santiago, the elite military order that Velázquez sought to join towards the end of his life, and the location for a tribunal of the Inquisition.[43]

His time in Llerena leaves archival traces but just one work, a *Virgin of the Clouds* (*c*. 1619–20?) now in Badajoz. María Páez was older than Zurbarán, and together they had three children: María, Juan and Isabel Paula, the two daughters outliving him and Juan, who become a painter, dying in the plague that engulfed Seville in 1649. After his wife died in 1623, Zurbarán married again in

Llerena in 1625. Beatriz de Morales, who had property in the town, was a widow and older than the artist. They had one child, Jerónima, who died young.[44] When Beatriz died in 1639, Zurbarán married for a third time in 1644, this time in Seville where he was now living. Leonor de Tordera was a younger widow and would outlive Zurbarán, but none of their six children (Micaela Francisca, José Antonio, Juana Micaela, María, Eusebio and Agustina Florencia) would.

Although only one painting from the period remains, there is documentary evidence of the type of work that he produced in and around the Extremaduran town: a drawing for a fountain in Llerena (1618); a painting of the Virgin for Llerena's city gate to Villagarcía (1619), possibly the work now in Badajoz;[45] gilding and decorating a processional float in Fuente de Cantos, and gilding and painting the reredos for the altar of Our Lady of the Rosary in the same town (1622); a sculpture of a crucifix for the town of Azuaga (1624); a painting in the town of Montemolín (1625).

The significance of some of this work and its commissioners will be picked up in the next chapter. What stands out is its eclectic nature, which has resulted in Zurbarán being described at this point in his career as an 'artisan painter'.[46] Regardless of the designation's validity, what is clear is that the quality of his art and the size of his workshop must have been such to enable him to grasp the opportunity when it arose and to seize the market in Seville seemingly from nowhere, or at least after a decade away from the 'great Babylon of Spain'.[47]

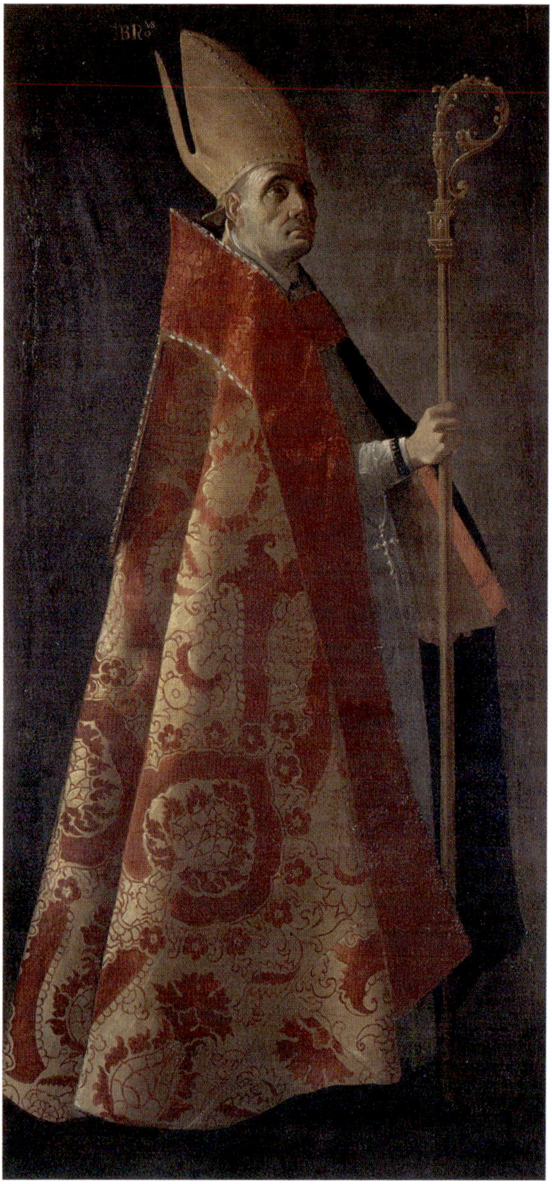

TWO

Zurbarán Takes Seville

In the second half of the 1620s, Zurbarán took Seville by storm. Not until the late 1650s would his life undergo as dramatic and radical a change as it did at this point. Across a five-year period he produced a significant number of works for powerful religious institutions and was invited to set up residence in the city – which he did, though not without controversy. I will focus on aspects of these commissions that exemplify his style, because, while this will evolve, its essential characteristics are all present in his work for the Dominicans, Mercedarians and Franciscans in the 1620s. I will also use these commissions to outline areas that are common to his practice: his use of prints, his workshop, the nature of contracts and the affinities between his aesthetic and that of contemporary sculpture. At the same time, we will encounter the pursuit of pictorial orthodoxy in early seventeenth-century Seville as well as the impact of reform on artists, for the opening decades of the century saw significant expenditure by churches and orders on art. The nature of reform on spiritual life and practice will then be picked up in later chapters.

5 Francisco de Zurbarán, *St Ambrose*, *c.* 1626–7, oil on canvas.

DOMINICANS (1626)

In a contract signed in January 1626, Zurbarán agreed to produce 21 paintings within eight months for the Dominican monastery of San Pablo el Real in Seville.[1] His entry into the Sevillian market may have been facilitated by Lorenzo de Cárdenas, a member of one of Llerena's noble families and *asistente* (governor) of Seville from 1626 to 1629.[2] San Pablo el Real was the most important Dominican monastery in Andalusia. It had been founded in 1250 by Ferdinand III of Castile – the Catholic monarch who captured the city from the Muslims in 1248 and who would be canonized in 1671 – and had around two hundred friars.[3] The contract was for fourteen paintings on the life of St Dominic, and seven images of the four doctors of the Church plus saints Bonaventure, Thomas Aquinas and Dominic. Of these 21 works, only five remain: the *Miraculous Cure of the Blessed Reginald of Orléans* (illus. 6), *St Dominic in Soriano* and the single figures *St Gregory*,

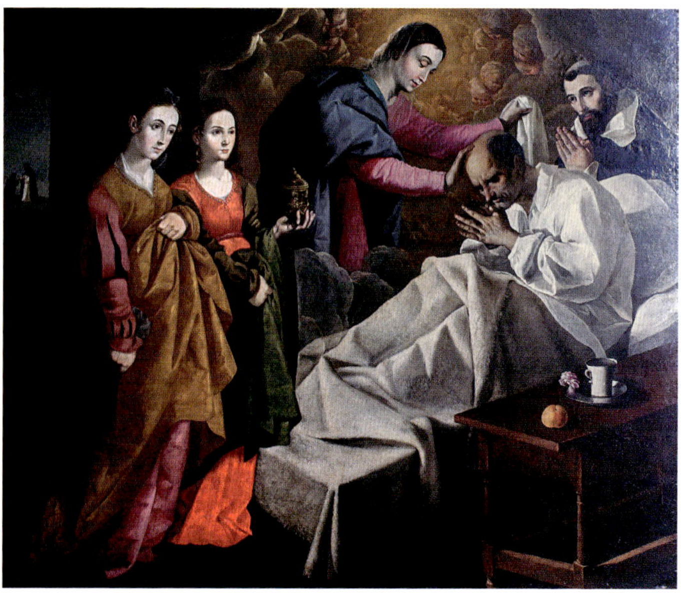

6 Francisco de Zurbarán, *Miraculous Cure of the Blessed Reginald of Orléans*, *c.* 1626–7, oil on canvas.

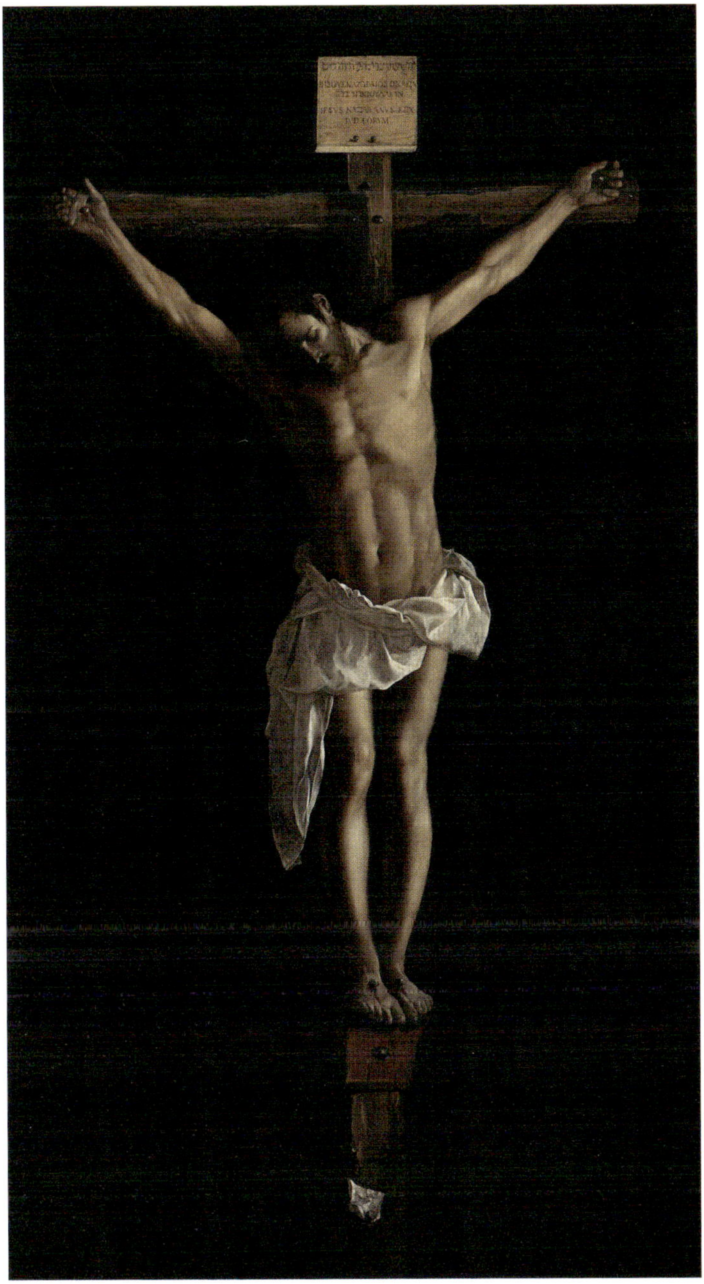

7 Francisco de Zurbarán, *Crucifixion*, 1627, oil on canvas.

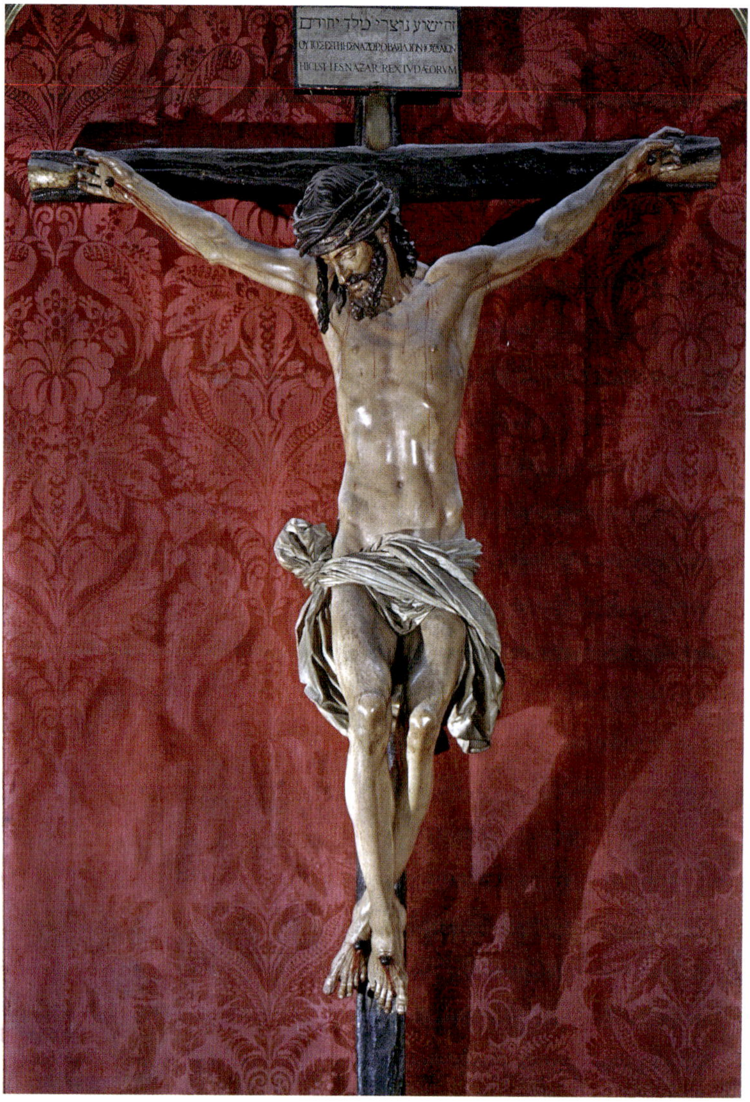

8 Juan Martínez Montañés, *Christ of Clemency*, 1603–6, polychromed wood.

St Jerome and *St Ambrose* (illus. 5). The two narrative works have a certain compositional gaucheness but are early manifestations of two distinct features of Zurbarán: beautifully attired female saints, here draped in simple fields of quiet colour; and exquisite still-life elements, in this case an apple next to a white cup and rose on a pewter or silver plate, all on an obliquely placed table. The three church doctors, in turn, are lavish displays of his skill at portraying fabrics, copes, rochets and mozzetta creating plays of crimsons, burgundies, reds and whites.[4] Palomino describes Zurbarán depicting bodies from life, but clothing by using mannequins, and the heavy folds and gatherings that characterize his drapery may be the result of using mannequins that tended to be less than life-size and glue-stiffened fabric (*tela encolada*) when modelling it.[5] Here such heaviness may well be due simply to the type of fabric depicted.

It was a work not mentioned in the contract and that hung in a chapel off the sacristy of the monastery's church that made the greatest impact. Zurbarán's first signed and dated work, here on the *cartellino* 'affixed' to the bottom of the cross, the 1627 *Crucifixion* (illus. 7) is the earliest surviving of his Crucifixions, he and his workshop painting perhaps as many as fifty over his career.[6] Palomino claims that those who saw the 1627 version in its poorly lit location believed it to be a polychrome sculpture.[7] Polychrome sculpture was a distinctive art form in early modern Spain, and the sculptural qualities of Zurbarán's monumental, static figures with their heavy drapery have a real affinity with such sculptures, normally made of wood and painted to appear as life-like as possible. Zurbarán himself was contracted in 1624 to make and polychrome a crucifix for the monastery of Nuestra Señora de la Merced in Azuaga, east of Llerena, so such an affinity may be the result of directly creating these distinctive forms.[8] (Sculptors and painters usually worked together to create such an image, so Zurbarán may have subcontracted the carving to a sculptor.[9]) The Azuaga contract uses the standard term for polychroming a sculpted figure's flesh, '*encarnación*'. This, by directly evoking the 'being made flesh' of the Incarnation, emphasizes the desired lifelikeness of the end results.

In his comments about the *Crucifixion*, Palomino is obviously setting up a *paragone*, the competitive comparison between painting and sculpture that occurs in early modern art writing, painting's superiority shown here in people believing that what they were seeing was a polychrome sculpture. Such sculpture aimed at incredible realism so as to place the viewer as though in the actual presence of the subject, as can be inferred from the contract for Juan Martínez Montañés's *Christ of Clemency* (1603–6; illus. 8) stipulating that the polychromed sculpture should depict the crucified Christ

> alive, prior to his dying, with his head inclined to the right looking at any person who might be praying before him, such as if Christ himself was speaking to them, lamenting that what he is suffering is for the person praying, and thus his eyes and face should be slightly severe and his eyes completely open.[10]

Zurbarán's Christ is dead, but no less tangibly real. Palomino's anecdote that people believed it to be a sculpture highlights something that we will see across this book; namely, that Zurbarán's art is an art of presence, a presence monumentally stilled, the stillness here being that not only of a corpse but of a 'sculpture'. The profound affinities between polychrome sculpture and Zurbarán's figures can be seen if one compares the solidly sculptural habits in his two Carthusian cycles (*c.* 1638–9 and *c.* 1655) with Martínez Montañés's sculpture of *St Bruno* (1634) or contrasts them with the habits depicted in the paintings of Vicente Carducho and Eustache Le Sueur for the Charterhouses of Santa

María de El Paular and Paris, respectively (1626–32, 1645–8). The affinities between polychrome sculpture and Zurbarán's sculptural fabrics and still forms worked both ways, Pedro de Mena's celebrated sculpture of *St Francis* (1663, Toledo Cathedral) clearly recalling the figure in Zurbarán's versions of *St Francis According to the Vision of Pope Nicholas V* (*c.* 1640–45).[11]

The *Crucifixion* for the Dominicans is also very much a product of the Seville of its time, for the issue of whether to show one nail through both feet or each foot separately nailed was the subject of learned debate in the city as artist and theorist Pacheco pursued pictorial orthodoxy in the wake of the Council of Trent. The reasons for preferring four nails were set out in two letters of 1619 and 1620 by Francisco de Rioja and Pacheco. They rest predominantly on the authority of certain patristic writings and mystical revelations, but also importantly on 'ancient' artistic examples.[12] Martínez Montañés's *Christ of Clemency* was an early example of the use of four nails, in this case the feet being crossed, whereas Pacheco's *Crucifixion* of 1614 has the feet nailed uncrossed to the suppedaneum (foot-support). The use of four nails became standard in Seville, and Pacheco's uncrossed feet are followed in Crucifixions by former pupils Velázquez (*c.* 1632) and Alonso Cano (*c.* 1646), as well as in examples by Zurbarán. Zurbarán's Crucifixions offer a number of variations – Christ dead or still alive, feet side by side or crossed and each one nailed; Christ alone or with another figure and so on. In terms of Christ's physique, Zurbarán will move from the more pronouncedly modelled and solid, as in his 1627 *Crucifixion* for San Pablo el Real, to the more gaunt and attenuated (*Crucifixion with a Painter*, *c.* 1655–60). In all, the forceful realism and presence of the nailed feet stand out, and that force and realism would be one entry point to a meditative engagement with the image.

CALCED MERCEDARIANS (1628)

Zurbarán's 1628 contract with the Calced Mercedarians was significant in terms of his growing focus on Seville rather than Llerena, for it required him and his team to be based in the monastery at the Mercedarians' expense while he produced 22 works on the life of St Peter Nolasco.[13] A sign of his ascendancy is the fact he was paid almost four times what he had been for his work for San Pablo el Real.[14]

Zurbarán's ability to undertake large commissions depended on a successful workshop. His second marriage in 1625 to Beatriz de Morales has been seen as providing him the means to run one of sufficient size to accept his first major commission in Seville from the Dominicans.[15] Studies of his workshops are at an early stage. Several individuals have been identified as members of his workshop in Llerena: Manuel Rodríguez, Juan Guerra and Diego Muñoz Naranjo.[16] Once he was in Seville, a document listing his household identifies, along with Muñoz Naranjo, three others who may have been members of his workshop there – Antonio Flamenco, Alonso Ramírez and one 'Francisco' – all four described as '*críados*' (servants), a term that could apply to workshop assistants.[17] Muñoz Naranjo was to have a long association with the artist and testified for him in a 1640 lawsuit.[18] This lawsuit reveals further assistants; namely, José Durán, Alonso de Flores and Ignacio de Ríes.[19] Other identified assistants and collaborators are Bernabé de Ayala, Miguel and Francisco Polanco, Juan Luis Zambrano and Juan de Zurbarán, his son.[20] Many will have trained under him, as Palomino also claims Jerónimo Bobadilla, Antonio del Castillo and José de Sarabia did.[21] As well as being essential for delivering large-scale commissions, Zurbarán's workshop would be central to his engagement with the transatlantic art market.

The Mercedarian commission may have been the result of a recommendation from the Commendator of the order in Azuaga following Zurbarán's sculpture for them.[22] Furthermore, if his work for the Mercedarian monastery in Villagarcía, close to Llerena, mentioned by Palomino but otherwise unknown, dates to his time in Llerena, then he had further contact with the Mercedarians to recommend him to Seville.[23] Given the scale of the Sevillian contract, it has been suggested this may have been preceded by a 'test piece', the powerful *St Serapion* (1628) that hung in the mortuary chapel (illus. 9).[24] Like the 1627 *Crucifixion*, this is another masterpiece that embodies Zurbarán's distinctive aesthetic: an avoidance of virtually all signs of pain and suffering, with no reminder here of Serapion's martyrdom through disembowelment;[25] the use of dark backgrounds to foreground the subject; and the stillness and calmness of his figures and of his compositions. The integrity of the martyr's habit speaks to the absolute integrity of his spirit, and the powerful sense of realistic presence exists in tension with the work's *trompe l'œil cartellino* that signals such presence is the result of the artist's skill. We will return to both these features of Zurbarán's work.

As with many commissions for religious orders, the paintings were to celebrate the life of the order's founder, in this case, to coincide with Nolasco's canonization in 1628, and were to hang in the smaller of the monastery's two largest cloisters. The Mercedarians were established in 1218 following an appearance of the Virgin, and they were granted permission to found a monastery in Seville by Ferdinand III after he took the city, its actual foundation dating to his son's reign.[26] Several of the works show Nolasco present at the conquest of the Muslim cities of Valencia and Seville by the Christian kings of Aragon and Castile, respectively. The cycle thus celebrates the saint, and by extension the order, as recipient of both royal and divine favour. The order had built a larger monastery at the start of the seventeenth century, part of widespread (re-)building work by religious orders in Seville at the time, Zurbarán meeting the need for artistic embellishment of the public and private areas of these new monasteries, chapels

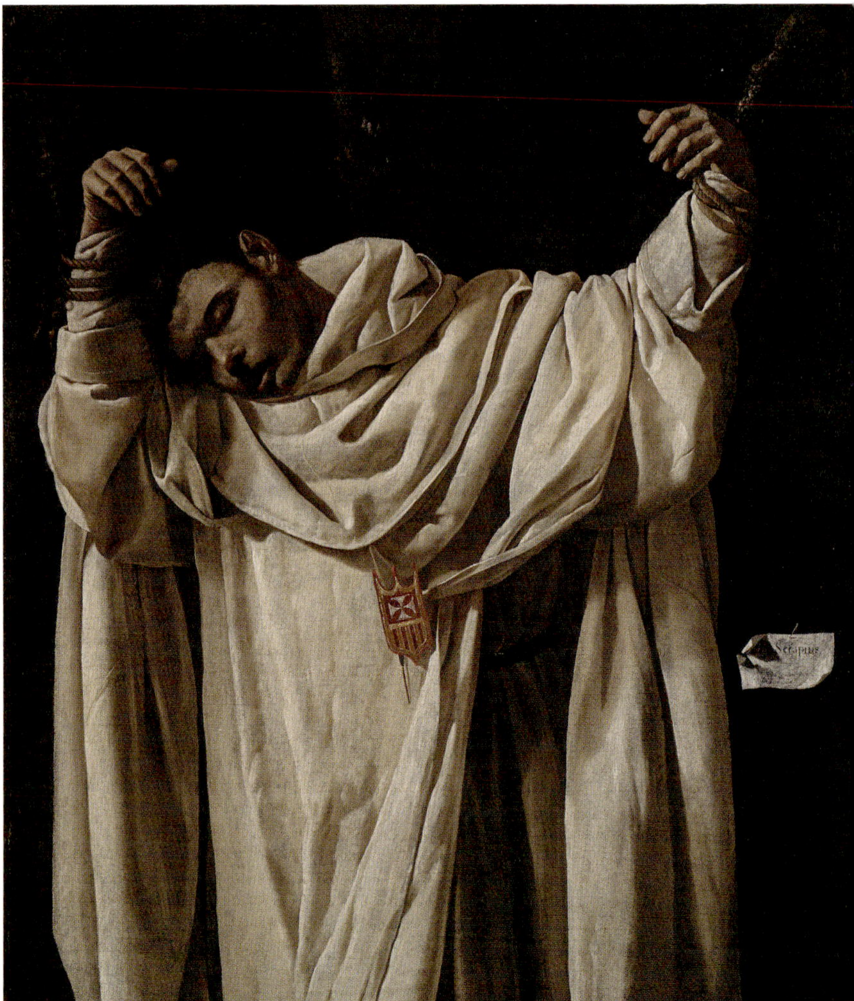

9 Francisco de Zurbarán, *St Serapion*, 1628, oil on canvas.

and colleges. One of the reasons for such building and the commissioning of art were the reform movements of the sixteenth century that saw many orders split as some sought to return to their orders' more 'austere' beginnings. In the case of the Mercedarians, like other orders before them, they split into Calced and Discalced (reformed) branches, the Discalced being established in Seville in 1604. The Discalced were granted papal approval in 1623 and, following the building of a new church (1628–36), Zurbarán would work for them as well.[27] The Mercedarians were instituted to redeem captives, their friars ultimately taking the place of captives if financial means were lacking. Following the order's reform, there was a sharp increase in redemption missions in the seventeenth century.[28] This is a mark of both the renewed zeal of the order and the realities of the Mediterranean, which saw Muslims and Christians capturing and ransoming each other, failed ransoming or exchanges perpetuating enslavement on both sides.[29] The order's redemptive work had itself been depicted in paintings by Pacheco and Alonso Vázquez in the 1600s for the largest cloister of the Calced Mercedarian monastery.

The 1628 contract specifies that Zurbarán was to 'place in each work the figures and other things that the father Commendator orders', while that of 1639 for the monastery of Guadalupe mentions a separate document, or *memoría*, setting out each canvas' subject.[30] This is a reminder that artists did not necessarily have compositional free rein, and indeed the San Pablo el Real contract stipulated that if something did not please the prior and the person he appointed to assess the finished canvases alongside him, Zurbarán had to redo the work(s).[31] A contract might specify the degree of involvement by the artist, as did that for a *retablo* in Llerena that required its paintings 'all be by the hand of the eminent painter Francisco de Zurbarán' and be signed by him.[32] A *retablo* was standardly a multi-work form, usually with a number of tiers and channels (left to right) in which paintings and sculptures were placed. If a contract was for a new *retablo*, it often covered both its construction, painting and/or gilding and the paintings to be placed in it, and was drawn up between the commissioner and both the artist and the sculptor/'master assembler architect', as Jerónimo Velázquez is variously called in contracts alongside Zurbarán.[33] Finally, a contract would set a completion date. In the case of the Mercedarian commission, the contract was signed by Zurbarán on 29 July 1628 and he agreed to finish the 22 works by the end of August 1629, the Mercedarians being able to appoint another artist at his expense to finish the work if he failed to do so.[34]

Of the 22 canvases for the cloister, only six by Zurbarán remain, several with workshop participation.[35] There are a further four canvases attributed to Zambrano, with an anonymous work possibly linked to the cycle recently discounted as probably mid-century.[36] It is not clear whether the full cycle was completed, a suggestion being that other works, including the full-length images of illustrious members of the order that Zurbarán painted for the monastery's library, were painted in lieu.[37] These portrait-like images are a virtuoso display of variations on a very limited theme and palette, for each friar is dressed in the voluminous white habit of the order, with its distinctive shield sometimes visible, as in the case of *Fray Pedro Machado* (illus. 10), and standing against a very dark background, minimal shadow and usually a small table with biretta and closed book or inkstand on it the only spatial demarcations. The painting of the habits was deemed a 'wonder' by Palomino, who praised the fact that while all are white, one can be distinguished from another, their lines, colour and form such that they gave the lie to reality itself.[38] This is an early celebration of perhaps Zurbarán's most characteristic trait, his consummate skill in portraying fabric.

Of the paintings on the life of Peter Nolasco, *St Peter Nolasco's Vision of St Peter* is the standout work (illus. 11). Zurbarán signs and dates many of his canvases, but it is tempting to read a particular degree of pride in those where he did so very visibly and legibly as here, where name and date – 1629 – are painted prominently below the edge of Nolasco's habit and on a slant that echoes the work's dominant diagonals. Nolasco was devoted to his namesake and wanted to go to Rome to see the apostle's relics but was unable to. One night, alone in the choir after prayer, he hears a voice saying 'Peter, as you haven't come to see me, I have to see you,' but sees nothing. This is repeated a second night, and on the third he feels that St Peter is rebuking him and goes to the chapel of the Virgin to ask her what the meaning is. When he raises his eyes to look at her image, he sees instead men raising a cross upside down with the elderly St Peter nailed to it. Peter speaks to him and the vision vanishes, leaving the altar's actual image of the Virgin visible again.[39] There are many aspects of Zurbarán's depiction of this vision that stand out: the pronounced tenebrist setting; the elegance of Nolasco's arms that seem to frame the vision of St Peter, on whose face he calmly gazes; the naturalism evident in St Peter's missing teeth and his bulging forehead as he hangs upside down; the orangey clouds all around St Peter that the painter uses time and again to demarcate the heavens. But it is two things, typical of Zurbarán's work, that I want to highlight: one visible, one not.

The first is his use of diagonals to both separate and unite what Teresa de Jesús refers to as the *acá* (here) and *allá* (there); that is, earth and heaven. Here that metaphysical distinction is represented by the two saints, the diagonal of St Peter's cross being echoed in the kneeling Nolasco's back, a smaller counter diagonal being sketched by the space between Nolasco's open arms that seems to breach the distinction between *allá* and *acá*. And indeed, the entire vision seems to take place in a sort of nowhere, neither here nor there. In other works, such as *St Francis* (1639, National Gallery, London), the *allá* is not depicted, but implied

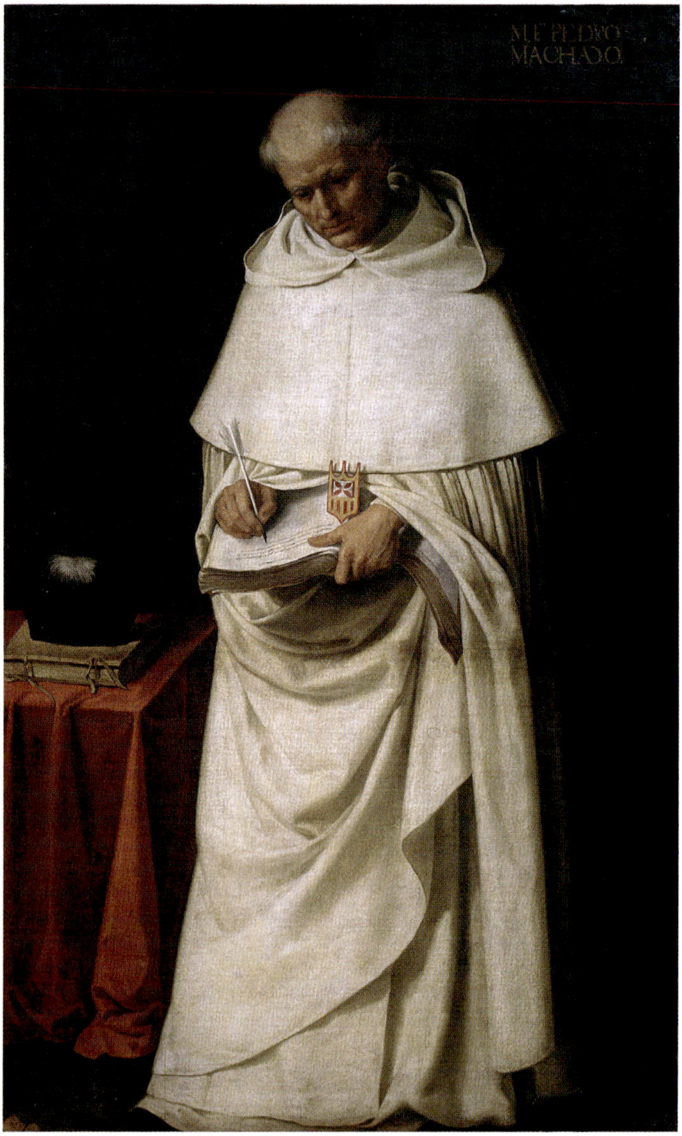

10 Francisco de Zurbarán, *Fray Pedro Machado*, *c.* 1630–32, oil on canvas.

through the diagonal that leads, as it were, in its direction. Of course, the diagonal is not always relational; it can simply be created through the lines and outlines of clothing. It remains, though, the characteristic way Zurbarán structures his compositions.

The second thing to highlight is Zurbarán's use of prints. Like many Andalusian artists he made extensive and lifelong use of these. The overall format of a composition may be based on one, as with the *Apotheosis of St Thomas Aquinas* (1631) on Cornelis Cort's 1576 engraving after Federico Zuccaro's *Coronation of the Virgin with Saints*, or a key figure, such as Gabriel in the *Annunciation* (c. 1638–9), which inverts an angel in Cort's 1571 engraving of Zuccaro's *Annunciation with Prophets*.[40] More often it is certain

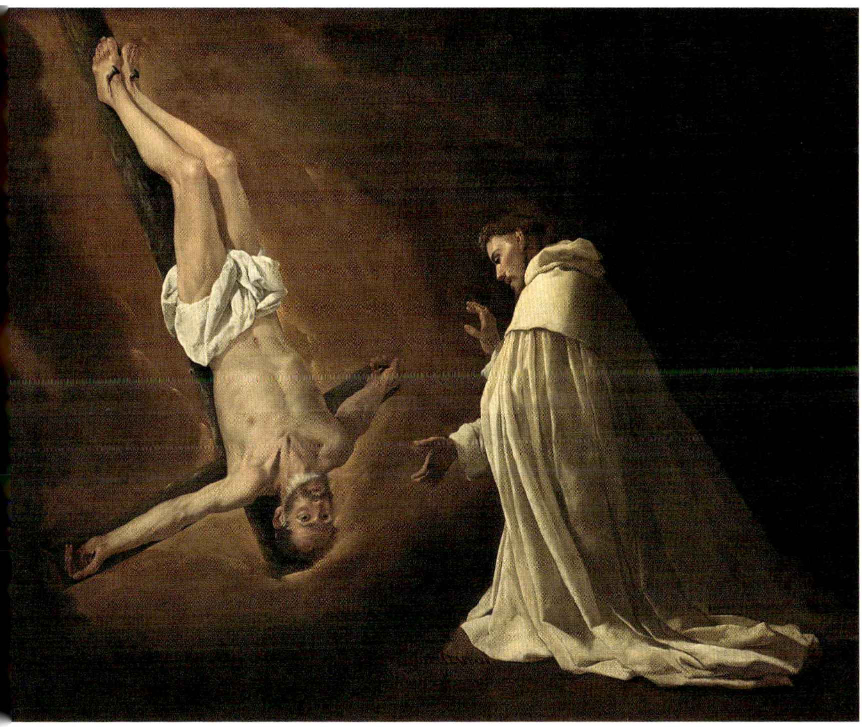

11 Francisco de Zurbarán, *St Peter Nolasco's Vision of St Peter*, 1629, oil on canvas.

details or aspects of a work that are based on elements in normally northern prints. These may provide background elements, sometimes architectural, as in the *Apotheosis of St Thomas Aquinas*, whose distant urban scene draws on engravings by Philip Galle after Hans Vredeman de Vries, and sometimes figural, as in the *Battle between Christians and Muslims at El Sotillo* (*c.* 1638–9), in which areas of the battle scene draw on a print by Antonio Tempesta, or the *Virgin of the Carthusians* (*c.* 1655), whose two cherubs holding open the Virgin's mantle are taken from Schelte à Bolswert's 1624 print of *St Augustine Protecting the Clergy*.[41] On occasion, even seemingly random and insignificant details appear drawn from a print, as with the stunted tree trunk in *St Anthony Abbot* (1636) after Jan Saenredam's 1604 engraving of Abraham Bloemaert's *Ahijah and Jeroboam*.[42] Even when a painting draws wholly on a print, as the *Burial of St Catherine* (*c.* 1636, Alte Pinakothek, Munich) for the Discalced Mercedarians does on a 1575 print by Cort after Pompeo dell'Aquila,[43] Zurbarán's touch is evident, here in the folds of the cloth used to lower the saint into her tomb that are made characteristically fuller and more gravid. Prints were also a means for his workshop swiftly and efficiently to produce paintings for the American market.[44]

For several paintings on Nolasco, Zurbarán drew on prints after drawings of the saint created in Rome by the Aragonese artist Jusepe Martínez as part of the canonization process. The creation of such works was a standard part of an order's attempt to establish the hagiographic imagery of a saint. Martínez's 25 drawings were engraved by Matthäus Greuter, Johann Friedrich Greuter and Luca Ciamberlano, and these in turn by Cornelius Cobrador, whose prints, given their inversion, were seemingly used by Zurbarán.[45] These may have been provided by the Mercedarians, prints functioning as a visual *memoria*.[46] In the case of *St Peter Nolasco's Vision of St Peter*, Zurbarán makes some small but telling changes to the print.[47] First, Martínez had represented architectural details to suggest the location, the altar, where the vision occurred as recounted in Remón's early seventeenth-century *Historia* as quoted above. Zurbarán suppresses these to create a non-space. Second, through the posture of Nolasco he forms a defined diagonal parallel to St Peter's, thereby creating a far greater sense of distance-yet-connection between the two saints. It is in such usage, and such changes, that we see his hand as a great artist.

FRANCISCANS (1629)

In 1603 the Observant Franciscans of the Casa Grande de San Francisco in Seville founded a college to train their friars, the College of St Bonaventure – the College's church was constructed 1622–6.[48] Francisco de Herrera the Elder, a leading artist who had decorated other areas of the church, was commissioned in 1627 to paint six works on the life of Bonaventure for its nave. Overcommitted elsewhere and possibly understaffed in his workshop, he only produced four.[49] Zurbarán was therefore brought in to paint another four in 1629. The joint cycle of works has been described as a 'model of naturalism', the style that had replaced late-Mannerism in Seville.[50]

Herrera's four works are varied and accomplished as can be seen in his *Healing of St Bonaventure by St Francis of Assisi* (illus. 13), but they pale in comparison with the chromatic impact of Zurbarán's. The *Visit of St Thomas Aquinas to St Bonaventure*, the only one of the four that Zurbarán signed and dated (1629), was destroyed in 1945 (see illus. 53). It showed Bonaventure disclosing to Aquinas the source of his knowledge by pointing to an image of Christ on the cross over his desk. (In terms of the discussions in Seville at the time, Zurbarán interestingly depicted Christ here with one nail through both feet.) In *St Bonaventure on His Bier*, the bier diagonally divides the composition. The saint's face is as grey as the habits of his fellow friars around him, and the brocade on the

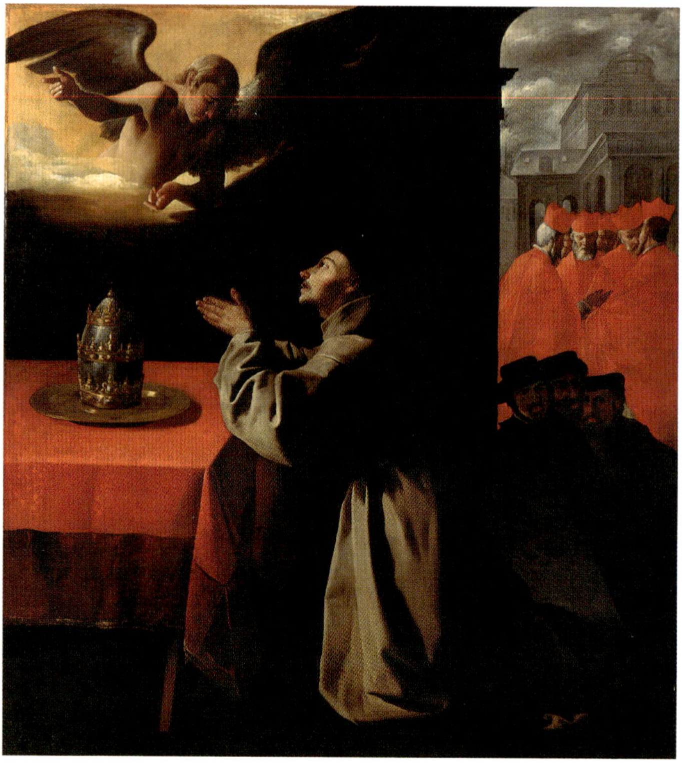

bier is rendered in all its heaviness, its descending folds flecked with white where light catches them. Zurbarán often struggled to pose figures so they appear to inhabit space collectively, and here he sidesteps this problem by crowding the figures together. In *St Bonaventure at the Council of Lyon*, there is an awkwardness to the spatial configuration, not unlike what we see in Herrera's *St Bonaventure Receiving the Habit from St Francis*, also for the nave, but this is offset by the greyish-blues and reds that dominate the composition. This use of almost solid chromatic planes is most arresting in *St Bonaventure Praying* (illus. 12). Showing Bonaventure seeking divine guidance to end the impasse at the

12 Francisco de Zurbarán, *St Bonaventure Praying*, *c.* 1629, oil on canvas.

papal conclave after the death of Clement IV, this is Zurbarán at his most severely tenebrist, the painting in effect a juxtaposition of black and startling reds that largely define the space, the saint and the gesturing angel above being linked through their mutual gazes and through the diagonal of Bonaventure's kneeling form. Each of these works is also striking for Zurbarán's sharp delineation of hands, the elegant gestures of which convey much of the meaning and emotion.

St Bonaventure Praying has been described as Zurbarán's most Caravaggesque work.[51] A link between Zurbarán and Caravaggio

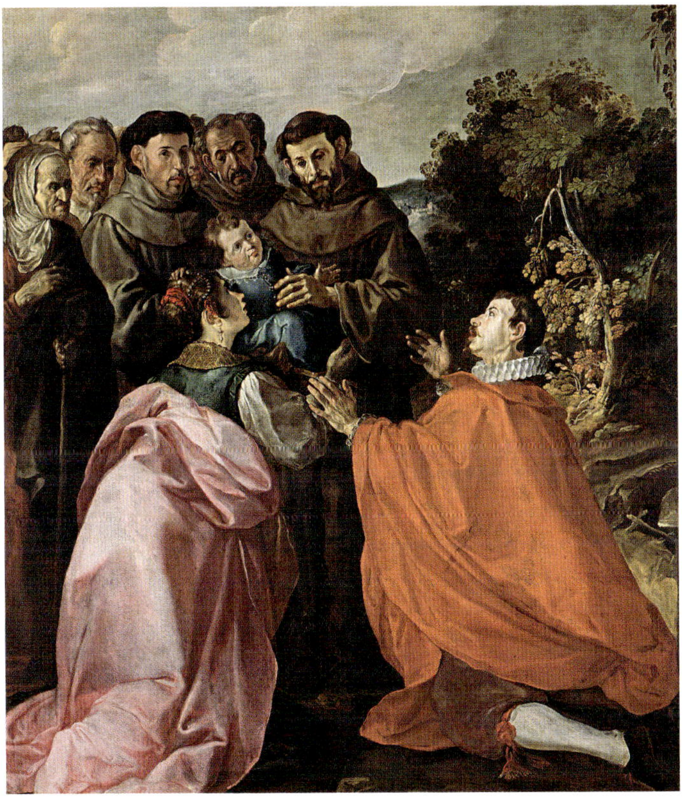

13 Francisco de Herrera, *Healing of St Bonaventure by St Francis of Assisi*, 1628, oil on canvas.

is made by Palomino when, after his claim that the Spanish artist depicted the body 'from life', he concludes that Zurbarán 'thus followed the school of Caravaggio, who he was so enthusiastic about that someone seeing his work and not knowing whose it was wouldn't hesitate to attribute it to Caravaggio'.[52]

Caravaggio's depiction of figures from life, his dramatic use of tenebrism and his creation of volume through sharp chiaroscuro impacted the development of Sevillian art in the opening decades of the century and accelerated its embrace of naturalism. This influence came primarily through copies and the work of followers, including Ribera.[53] Both Velázquez and Zurbarán were part of a decisive shift to a less idealized depiction of the human figure, thereby making a religious subject more immediately connectable to the reality of the contemporary viewer. One can also see such non-idealization in Herrera's works for the Franciscans, and a comparison with Zurbarán reveals that for all the 'individuality' and variation in the latter's faces they are noticeably less 'homely', more poised, than Herrera's. Against the naturalism of the figures, though, is what one might almost call the idealism of Zurbarán's rich, coloured fabrics rendered in all their specificity and seen most characteristically here in the clothing in *Bonaventure on His Bier* of King Jaime I of Aragon, present at the Council of Lyon where Bonaventure died.

Tenebrism is a defining feature of Zurbarán's style, and it is this that most connects him with Caravaggism. While he deploys dark backgrounds across his career, they are at their most pronounced and dramatic in its first half, whether in narrative works such as *Bonaventure Praying* or in single-figure works such as his 1627 *Crucifixion* or his images of St Francis. However, Zurbarán does not make light an active protagonist, as it is, for example, with Georges de La Tour. Light exists less to dramatize itself, more to focus the meditative mind, or indeed to reveal through chiaroscuro a saint in contemplation. If there is drama, it is more often than not the drama of colour.

On 27 June 1629, the year of the only dated work for the College of St Bonaventure, the City Council (Cabildo) of Seville agreed to a proposal from a councillor (*veinticuatro*), Rodrigo Suárez, that Zurbarán be invited to reside permanently in Seville. The minutes record Suárez mentioning the Calced Mercedarians bringing the artist from Llerena to create works for their cloister, and that 'from those that are finished and from the painting of Christ which is in the sacristy of San Pablo [el Real]' he can be judged an 'accomplished craftsman [*artífice*]'. The singling out of one specific work, the *Crucifixion* of 1627 for the Dominicans, speaks to its immediate impact on the city. A broader justification for the invitation is set out; namely, that 'painting is not the least ornament of a republic, rather among the greatest, both of its churches and its private dwellings.' In receiving the Council's invitation, Zurbarán was to be assured that they would take care to favour and help him.[54]

Zurbarán is mentioned in a 26 September 1629 contract for a new *retablo* for the monastery of the Calced Trinitarians, another order founded to redeem captives. In the contract he is referred to as 'maestro pintor de esta ciudad de Sevilla' (master painter of the city of Seville).[55] This wording seems to indicate that he had now settled in the city following the Council's invitation. But it is the reference to him as a 'master painter' that perhaps led to the Council's assurance to help him being almost immediately tested. This was, of course, because Zurbarán had not undertaken the final examination to qualify as a master painter at the end of his apprenticeship. The artist and sculptor Alonso Cano petitioned the Council to have Zurbarán take the required examination and from Zurbarán's submission to the Council considered alongside this on 29 May 1630, it seems that officials from the painters' guild, presumably seeking to protect its status and,

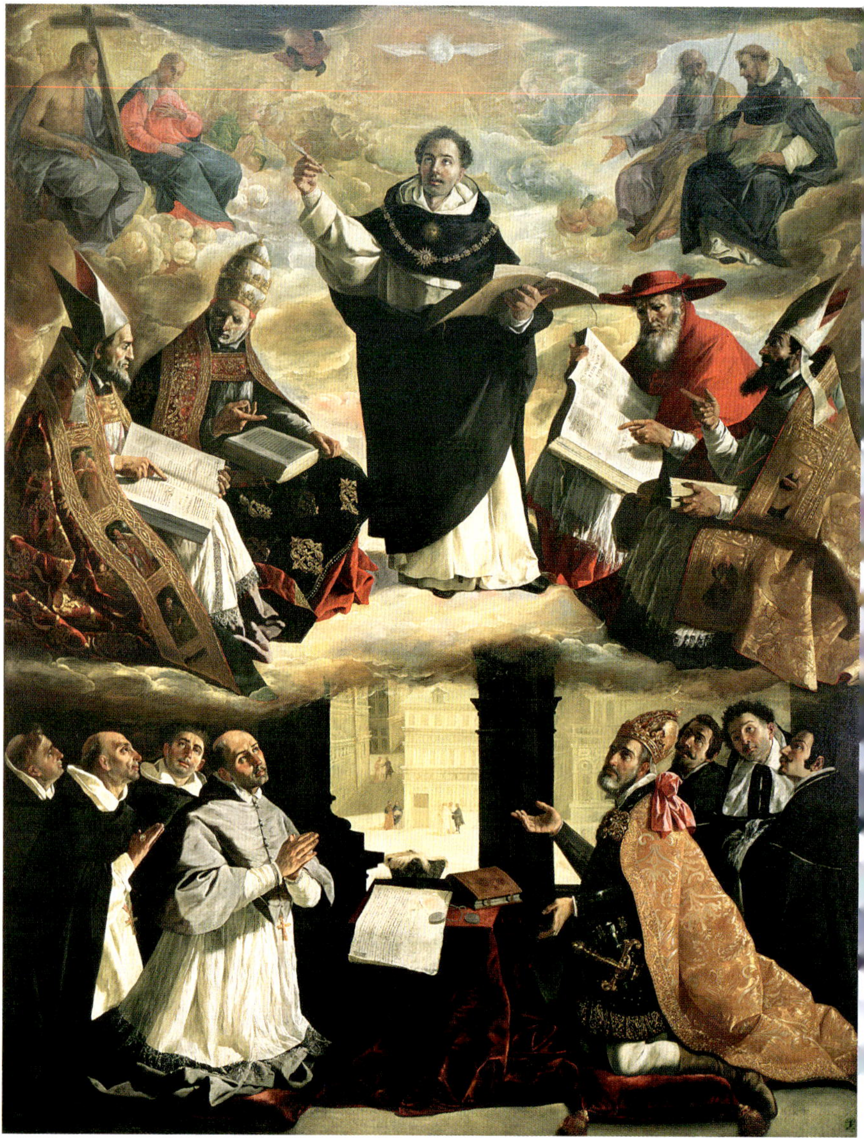

14 Francisco de Zurbarán, *Apotheosis of St Thomas Aquinas*, 1631, oil on canvas.

one assumes, concerned about the official favour shown to a rival whose work was making such an impact, had visited him on 23 May to tell him that he would be examined within three days. (Writing in the late 1650s, Díaz del Valle claimed that Cano was offered the Calced Mercedarian commission but had declined on the grounds he still lacked the necessary knowledge of perspective, valuing his reputation more than the advantages it would bring.[56]) Zurbarán's submission reveals him to be a subtle operator. He reminds the Council that they had invited him to take up residence in the city as an 'eminent individual', and says that other painters, envious of such favour, sought now to force him to undergo an examination whose purpose was to ensure that those ignorant in art did not practise as painters, but that, the Council having declared him an 'eminent individual', it was not right that the guild set itself up as superior to the Councillors in deciding who was or wasn't worthy to practise. He asks the Council in effect to stand by its own approval of him.[57] This they appear to have done, and on 10 June commissioned from him an Immaculate Conception for the town hall.[58] Zurbarán's position in the city was incontestable. He had arrived.

This Sevillian period comes to an artistic climax with the *Apotheosis of St Thomas Aquinas* (illus. 14). This was commissioned in January 1631 by the Dominicans for the high altar of the church of their College of Santo Tomás, the *retablo* itself to be constructed by Jerónimo Velázquez.[59] The *Apotheosis* is Zurbarán's largest painting (486 × 385 centimetres (191 5/16 × 151 9/16 in.)). The canvas is divided into a heavenly and a terrestrial zone separated by heavy cloud, a traditional horizontal division that he had recently employed in his only work for the Jesuits, the *Vision of St Alonso Rodríguez* of 1630 (see illus. 57).[60] The seventeen figures in the foreground, arranged symmetrically both above and below, make it one of Zurbarán's most populated works. The Dominican Aquinas stands in the centre of the heavens, book open and quill brandished, his eyes raised to the Holy Spirit overhead. At top left sit Christ and the Virgin; top right, saints Paul and Dominic; below them and either side of Aquinas sit the four Doctors of the Church debating with one another. Below this heavenly display are kneeling figures, most prominent among them Diego de Deza, the Dominican archbishop of Seville who, following papal bulls in 1515–16, founded the College in 1517, and Charles V, emperor and king of Spain, who had supported the College through gifts of rent and land, both archbishop and emperor looking at Aquinas.[61] Between these two is a velvet-covered table on which a document sits, presumably the foundation document of the College, though actually signed by Zurbarán and dated 1631. Behind the kneeling archbishop and emperor is an obtrusive column, a device found in many of Zurbarán's compositions to separate foreground and background; visible beyond this, a cityscape that looks, again typically, like a theatrical backdrop. The fabrics, colours and chromatic harmonies bring the canvas to life. Small details dazzle, not least the white rochet worn by Deza, whose myriad vertical creases seem like tiny shivers passing through the fabric. What is depicted is neither a miracle nor a recorded vision, but an almost quotidian 'awareness of the celestial by the terrestrial'.[62] It conveys a view of reality in which these two are ever separate yet ever enmeshed, the view of reality of both Church and monarchy at the time.

THREE

'Pintor de Su Majestad': Zurbarán in Madrid

Zurbarán's output consists overwhelmingly of religious and devotional subjects, and it is as a painter of cycles for religious orders that he made his name in Seville in the 1620s. But in 1634 he was called to Madrid to paint works of contemporary history and of mythology for the king. Given the final payment for his work is dated 13 November 1634, it is likely that he returned to Seville the same year.

In 1630 the Count-Duke of Olivares, Philip IV's favourite, started to construct the Buen Retiro, a new palace for the king on the eastern edge of Madrid. Initially intended as an extension of existing royal apartments attached to the monastery of San Jerónimo, plans expanded piecemeal. The palace was built round two large courtyards, themselves to be used for court festivities, and had a permanent theatre for court spectacles with their elaborate sets and stage effects and extensive grounds that included an artificial lake and numerous hermitages. The whole complex ended up covering a site 'almost half as large as the entire town of Madrid'.[1]

Modern historians have interpreted the motive behind the Buen Retiro's construction as the Count-Duke wishing not simply to please the king, who was known for his love of theatre and his growing love of the visual arts, but to distract him through these at a time when he was beginning to show signs of wishing to take the lead in political and military affairs.[2] Given this aim, speed of construction was important, and although new parts continued to be added across the decade, the keys were handed to Philip in December 1633. The focus then fell on the palace's decoration.

A centrepiece of the palace was what came to be known as the Hall of Realms after the arms of the 24 realms that made up the Spanish monarchy that decorated its upper level. It was intended for celebrations, performances and ceremonies. While the decoration of the new palace led to an increase in collecting and commissioning works from artists in Italy, works for the Hall of Realms, which was decorated in 1634–5, were all commissioned from artists in Spain, perhaps not surprisingly given its celebration of Spain's military prowess. The artists were all based at court with the exception of Zurbarán, who was called from Seville, possibly on Velázquez's recommendation or that of the Count-Duke, who had lived there. He was commissioned to paint more works than any other artist for the Hall, although Velázquez's contribution, encompassing five royal portraits as well as a battle scene, surpassed his in prestige. Quite why an artist who was based in Seville and known for his religious works, not works of mythology or multi-figure works of contemporary history, was given more than artists already based at court is unclear, though clearly his impact in Seville was known and the addition of an artist with a successful practice would speed up completion. On the room's two short walls hung the five equestrian portraits by Velázquez: Philip IV; the queen, Isabel of Bourbon; their son, Baltasar Carlos; and Philip's parents, Philip III and Margarita of Austria. Along its two long walls were ten deeds of Hercules by Zurbarán, five on each side and each hung above a large window, and twelve canvases, six on each wall hanging either side of the five windows.[3] These large canvases depicted Spanish military successes against the Dutch, French, Swedes, German Protestants and English between 1622 and 1633: Vicente Carducho's *Battle of Fleurus*, *Taking of Rheinfelden* and *Relief of Constance*; Jusepe Leonardo's *Surrender of Jülich* and *Relief of Breisach*; Antonio Pereda's *Relief of Genoa*; Juan Bautista Maíno's *Recovery of Bahía*; Eugenio Cajés's *Recapture of San Juan, Puerto Rico* and *Recapture of St Martín* (now lost); Velázquez's *Surrender of Breda*; Félix Castello's *Recapture of the Island of St Kitts*; and Zurbarán's *Defence of Cadiz*.[4] A document of 13 November 1634 makes clear that Zurbarán was in fact paid for 'ten paintings of the Feats of Hercules [*Las fuerzas de Hércules*] and two large canvases of the *Relief of Cadiz*, all for the large hall of the Buen Retiro', but the precise subject and whereabouts of the second of these Cadiz canvases are unknown.[5] Although it has been suggested that Zurbarán painted two versions and one was not used 'for unknown reasons',[6] it remains the case that 'the apparent existence of two paintings by Zurbarán . . . is a problem that remains unsolved.'[7] While celebratory, the range of adversaries and locations across the twelve history paintings and the fact that the actions celebrated largely concern not conquests but defences, reliefs and reconquests are an indication how under siege the Spanish empire was during the Thirty Years' War (1618–48), a war that would shortly extend to a prolonged conflict between Spain and France (1635–59) for European hegemony.

The programme for the hall has been attributed to another Sevillian in the employment of the Count-Duke, his librarian, the poet Francisco de Rioja, a friend and advisor to Pacheco. It has been interpreted as a 'Hall of Princely Virtue', intended among other things to highlight a core policy of the Count-Duke that was widely criticized, the Union of Arms, whereby constituent territories of the Spanish monarchy would contribute more fully to its overall defence;[8] and more broadly as a Hall of Heroic or Noble Virtue; that is, celebrating not simply the king, but the military leaders shown in the paintings.[9] Given the critical perception of the palace as a pleasure palace to distract the king, the Hall of Realms also tacitly answered this by celebrating Spanish

Habsburg strength: the king's leisure does not preclude military success.[10] Of course, its response to such criticism is aimed primarily at the king, whose favour Olivares needed in order to maintain his own powerful position. But that said, anyone entering the Hall would encounter an impressive array of very recent Spanish victories, and even when not permanent – Breda, for example, surrendered to the Spanish in 1625 as depicted, but was retaken in 1637 – the lesson was still that Spain's military reach was extensive and not exhausted. As one panegyrist of the palace declared to Philip, 'proud of being cowardly, the world trembles on seeing your Catholic standards flying.'[11]

The two most discussed works in the series are Velázquez's *Surrender of Breda* and Maíno's *Recovery of Bahía*. The former depicts the magnanimity of Ambrogio Spinola who has dismounted to greet the defeated Justin of Nassau as he hands over the keys to the city and emphasizes Spanish military power subtly but firmly through the upright pikes of Spain's feared infantry, the *tercios*. In the latter, Maíno found a way to incorporate into the scene not only Philip but also, more surprisingly, the Count-Duke, by having the defeated Dutch in Brazil kneel before a tapestry shown to them by the victorious commander in which the king is being crowned by Minerva and the Count-Duke.

While Zurbarán's *Defence of Cadiz* (*c*. 1634; illus. 15) is less compositionally original, its format is the same as most of the paintings for the Hall, with the military engagement shown in the background and key protagonists – essentially, the victorious commanders – in the foreground, albeit that it exhibits his singular compositional trait, for the majority of the figures, here arrayed frieze-like, seem isolated and detached from each other and from their surroundings, 'as if turned to stone'.[12] Its subject is an attack on Cadiz on 1 November 1625 by the English, when, under Sir Edward Cecil, Viscount Wimbledon, they entered the port and took the fort of Puntal but, prevented from further advance by

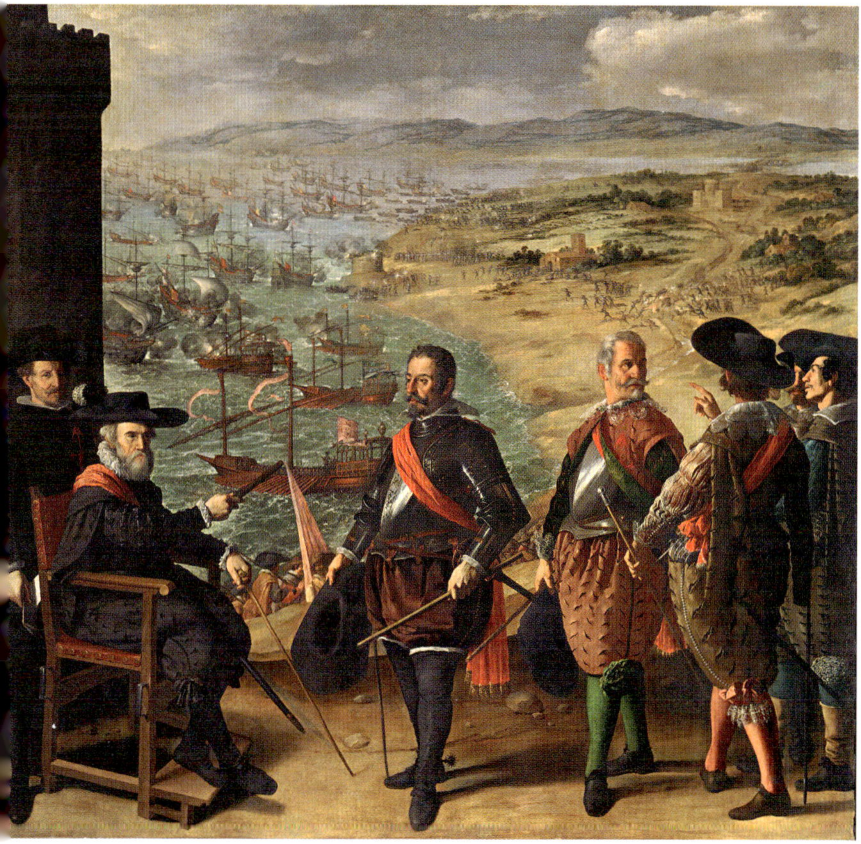

the Spanish, abandoned the city on 8 November.[13] (The occasion celebrated highlights the prime reason against transatlantic trade being sited in Cadiz rather than Seville for, despite its deep port, its exposed position made it extremely vulnerable to attack.) A contemporary account mentions the Spanish leader, Fernando Girón y Ponce de León, as Zurbarán depicts him: 'in spite of his poor health and advanced age, don Fernando Girón's stout heart made him go out each day on campaign. Seated on his chair he ran great risks, giving orders which were courageously carried

15 Francisco de Zurbarán, *The Defence of Cadiz*, c. 1634, oil on canvas.

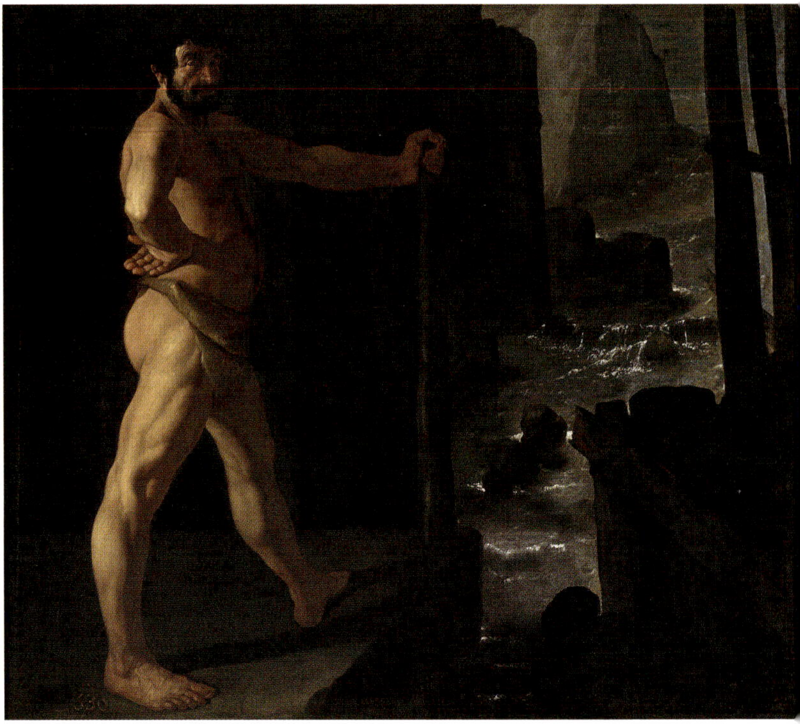

out by that brave and experienced soldier Diego Ruiz, the deputy commander.'[14] The armoured figure standing in front of the seated Girón is thought to be Ruiz, and the isolated detachment of these two from each other is particularly conspicuous. In relation to the foreground, the background looks like a theatrical backdrop, but if this suggests a dramatic staging of the event, the fact that the 'actors' stand statically in front of it undercuts any notion of action or drama or urgency.[15] What strikes one, as in virtually any work by Zurbarán, is the elegance of each figure's pose and, especially, their costume. One immediately appreciates the engineers of the defence, not the action itself; what matters is that Spain possesses such military leaders, and that these are

16 Francisco de Zurbarán, *Hercules Diverting the River Alpheus*, c. 1634, oil on canvas.

shown as embodiments of courtly values. To this extent Zurbarán's work is one with Velázquez's.

The ten Hercules canvases hung above the Hall's ten windows, and the fact that Zurbarán had initially been commissioned to paint twelve indicates the room's hang had not been finalized from the outset. One payment document refers to the works specifically as the Labours (*trabajos*) of Hercules, but not all the deeds shown are among the traditional twelve labours. These mythological works have received a muted and largely negative critical response, although the king apparently praised the artist while he was painting them. There are touches of painterly beauty in several of the works, like the silvery waters flowing into the Augean stables in *Hercules Diverting the River Alpheus* (*c.* 1634; illus. 16), and in all, the strongly lit, all-but naked body of the uglily robust Hercules dominates the foreground and stands out against the dark background, Zurbarán's standard compositional format working well by enabling the key figure to be seen when the works hung above the windows. These are images of Hercules, not extensive narratives of each feat, though the latter are discernible as is clear from the brief lines written about the works by Manuel de Gallegos in 1637.[16]

Hercules was a figure used to glorify many rulers, but this was particularly so in Spain. One of the labours depicted had taken place in the Iberian peninsula (*Hercules Defeats King Geryon*), and indeed Seville claimed him as one of its legendary founders along with Julius Caesar; another feat (*Hercules Separates Mounts Calpe and Abyla*) was connected with Charles V's device found across Habsburg Spain, the Pillars of Hercules either side of the Strait of Gibraltar; and a direct line of descent was drawn from the mythical hero to the Habsburg monarchs.[17] The hero's deeds were readily relatable to any number of situations and countries and, taken as a whole, signalled virtue, strength and a willingness and ability to overcome adversaries. Philip IV, by inference, is the equal of his 'ancestor' as the battle paintings demonstrate, and he too will be rewarded by being taken to heaven as Hercules was after his agonizing end, depicted in one of the series' most striking works, *The Death of Hercules* (*c.* 1634; illus. 17), where the hero pulls at the poisoned shirt unwittingly handed to him by his wife that so burns his flesh he kills himself on a flaming pyre.

The subjects of both the Hercules series and *The Defence of Cadíz* singularly fail to allow Zurbarán to play to his strengths. In the *Defence*, where one might expect dynamism and action, we have instead static figures lacking any real sense of interaction or mutual engagement, the work's striking quality resting – as usual in his works – in the figures' dress, whose fabrics and colours arrest the eye. And it is perhaps precisely the lack of such costuming in the nude Hercules series that is most missed.

This leads to the question of whether Zurbarán's sojourn at court was a success. On the one hand, his very invitation

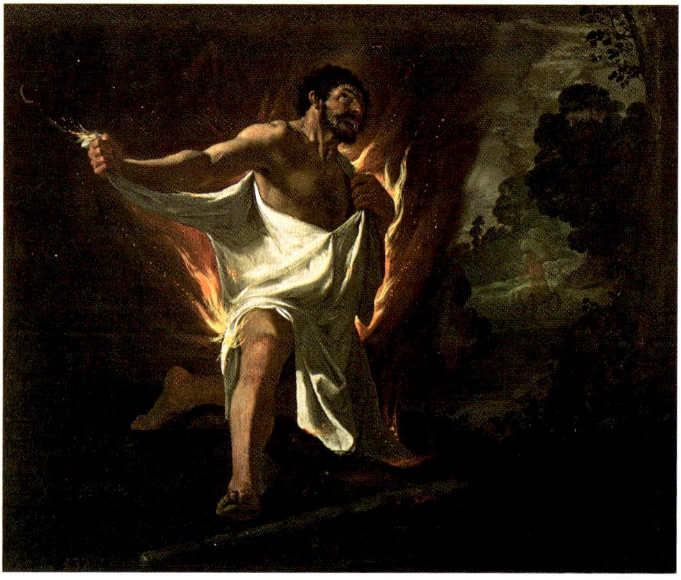

17 Francisco de Zurbarán, *The Death of Hercules*, *c.* 1634, oil on canvas.

speaks to his reputation and Palomino indicates he was highly regarded by the king, who, on one of his visits to watch Zurbarán paint, supposedly placed his hand on the artist's shoulder and declared 'Painter to the King and king of painters!'[18] He was given the honorary title 'Painter to the King' following his work for the Buen Retiro and used it in Latin on the illusionistic *cartellino* 'stuck' on the *Adoration of the Shepherds* (1638), part of a major commission for the Charterhouse in Jerez de la Frontera and, incidentally, one of his works where he does successfully integrate multiple figures into a composition, and he is called 'pintor de su majestad', painter to his Majesty, in several documents, including contracts for paintings for the monastery of the Encarnación in Arcos de la Frontera in 1637 and for the Hieronymite monastery of Guadalupe in 1639. The invitation and honorary title would certainly have further enhanced his standing in Seville. On the other hand, he returned to Seville with no further commissions from the king. But to consider the trip a failure or disappointment would depend on knowing that Zurbarán wanted to move to Madrid and work for the court, and there is no reason to suppose that he did – or indeed that he didn't. His practice was flourishing in Seville, and it is tempting to suggest that the artist, whatever his thoughts prior to the trip, might as a result of it have more firmly realized where his artistic strengths lay and where they might therefore be best expressed and employed: on religious commissions in a major city where he was now pre-eminent.

The time at court enabled Zurbarán to study the work of his contemporaries and the extensive royal collections that were rapidly expanding due to the king's love of art and the need to furnish the new palace. This raises the question of whether or how his work was impacted, and this is most often discussed in terms of the relationship between his small number of portraits and the court work of Velázquez.

The proposed date of Zurbarán's full-length portrait of an unknown *Doctor of Law* (illus. 18) varies greatly, suggestions ranging from 1633 to circa 1658–60. Odile Delenda's proposal of circa 1635–40 is based on its similarities with Velázquez's royal portraits of the 1620s, which Zurbarán would have seen in Madrid.[19] In the portrait the unknown figure stands in his robes, his body slightly turned to the right. Space is delineated simply by the join of floor and wall, the warm, dark browns of these are lighter than the darker, blackish backgrounds of his full-length images of Mercedarians, and their earthy tones play against the reds and reddish-browns of the figure's academic costume. The only piece of furniture is a chair on whose back the figure rests the wrist of his un-gloved, left hand. Such minimal furnishing recalls Velázquez's portrait of *Philip IV* (1623; illus. 19) that contains a table on which the king has placed his hat, but it also recalls the *mise en scènes* of the Mercedarian images. Unlike those, and indeed Velázquez's portrait, there is a dark, drawn-back curtain at upper left. The figure's gloved, right hand nonchalantly holds his other glove, a pose that directly recalls Velázquez's *Infante don Carlos* (1626–7). Jonathan Brown in fact sees in the ungloved hand's 'fingertips that almost melt into the air' evidence of Zurbarán's imitation of Velázquez's late technique and so dates the work to circa 1658–60.[20] Pose, minimal delineation of space, and that space being less dark and thus less stark than in the Mercedarian images, all resonate with Velázquez's royal portraits. The pose of Zurbarán's *Doctor Juan Martínez Serrano* (*c.* 1635) has similarly been linked with a Velázquez court portrait.[21] Martínez Serrano was holder of a chair of theology at Sigüenza university and his pose – standing, his right hand resting on the edge of a table at left – recalls that of the Count-Duke of Olivares in Velázquez's 1624 portrait (Museu de Arte São Paulo).[22] His sheer bulk is certainly a match for Olivares, and his academic robes are again harmonized with the warmer background tones that contrast with the sombre

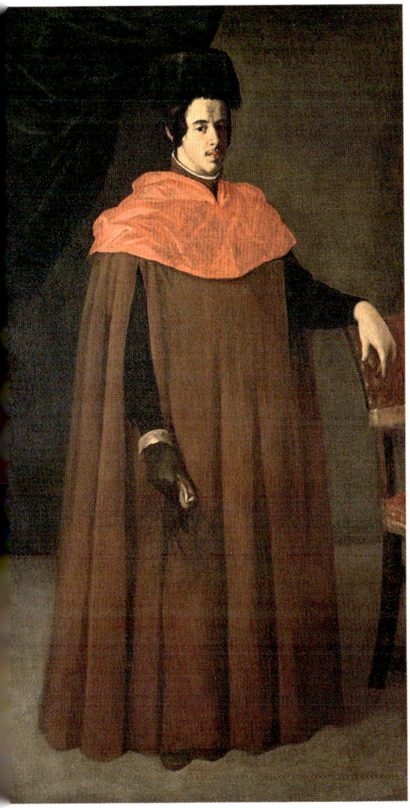

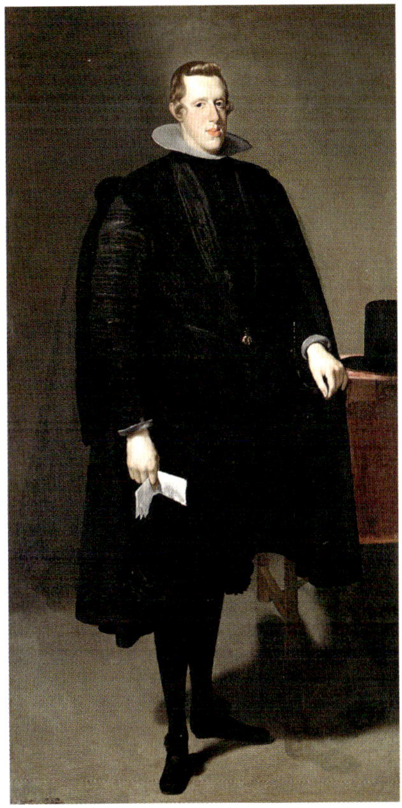

greys of Velázquez's backgrounds that offset the black of Habsburg court dress.

But Zurbarán continued to employ the very dark backgrounds familiar from his earlier images of Mercedarians that throw the figure portrayed into stark relief, as can be seen in his portrait of the twelve-year-old *Don Alonso Verdugo de Albornoz* (1635), who is shown dressed in military costume, having been made captain of his uncle's guards, and standing elegantly just like the figures in *The Defence of Cadiz*, some of whose attire echoes his. And the minimal delineation of space continues in his *Don Juan Bazo de Moreda*

18 Francisco de Zurbarán, *Doctor of Law*, *c.* 1635–40, oil on canvas.
19 Diego Velázquez, *Philip IV*, 1623, oil on canvas.

(*c.* 1655). Depicting an infantry captain from Logroño who served in the Spanish army in Flanders, as noted in the cartouche at the bottom left of the portrait, the work is striking precisely because it is not of a robed or a religious figure, his russet breeches and white-and-mustard-yellow stockings lending an elegant note to the be-spurred captain who proudly wears the shell of Santiago to indicate his membership of the elite order. The isolation of figures in contemporary portraiture was absolutely standard, but as we shall see, it is at one with Zurbarán's whole aesthetic.

The dating of several of these portraits depends on their perceived relationship to the portraits painted by Velázquez at court. That influence seems highly likely, but it is neither decisive nor absolute. For some critics the stylistic impact on him of his time at court was 'minimal', whereas for others it led Zurbarán to 'abandon the tenebrism of his early work'.[23] Rather than abandoning tenebrism, it is more accurate to suggest that it becomes less harsh, less crisply absolute. Zurbarán's seeing directly how Velázquez had evolved artistically from his own initial tenebrism was a likely factor in this.[24] With *The Defence of Cadíz*, Zurbarán undertook a work the likes of which he had not attempted before: a large-format portrayal of contemporary events with a setting that, because the painting depicted a naval assault and land engagement, also included a sweeping, daylight sea-and-landscape, marking a sharp contrast with his standard dark settings used not only with stand-alone figures but in multi-figure works such as *St Peter Nolasco Leaving for Barcelona*, *The Discovery of the Virgin of Puig* or *The Surrender of Seville* for the Calced Mercedarians in the late 1620s with their very dark foregrounds and mere glimpses of landscape or cityscape in the distance. Post-Madrid, landscape settings become immediately and increasingly a favoured option in works showing a single saint or figure, such as *St Lawrence* and *St Anthony Abbot*, both for the church of San José of the Discalced Mercedarian monastery in Seville (1636), *St Bruno in Ecstasy* and

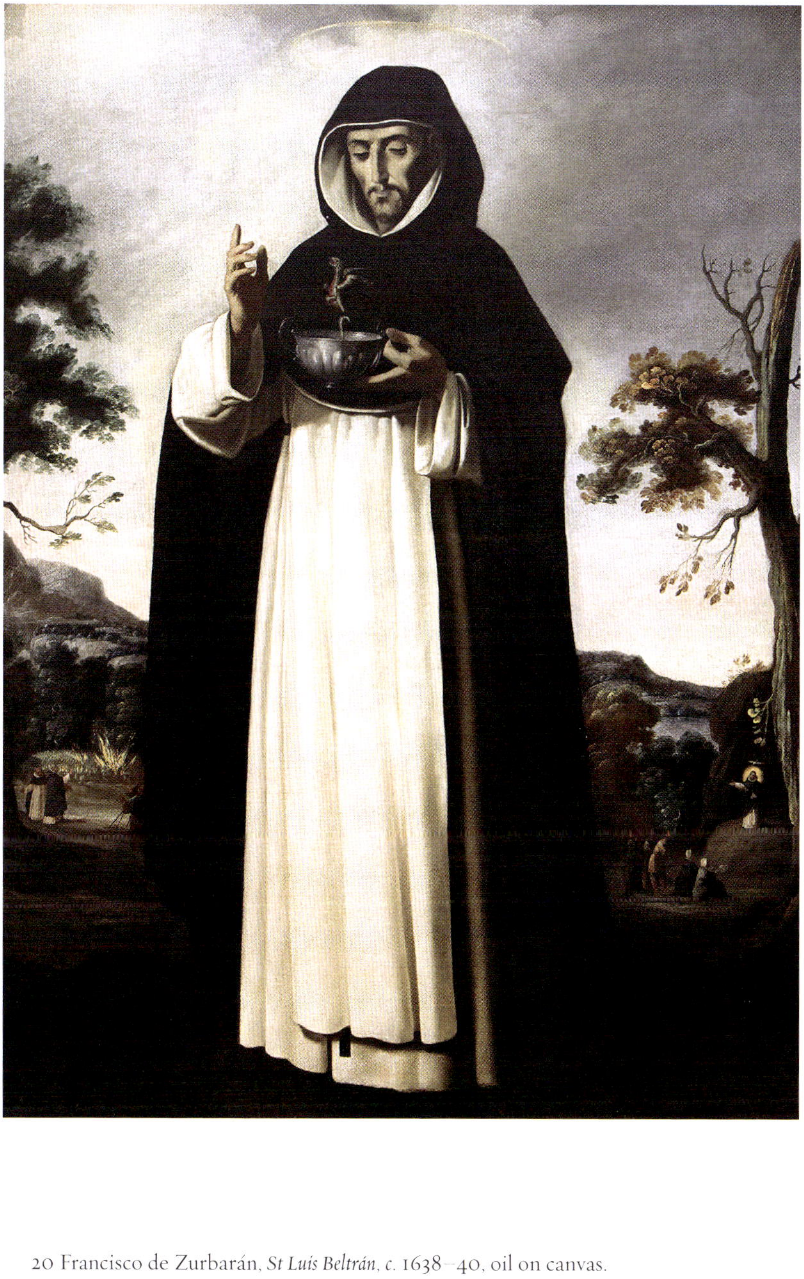

20 Francisco de Zurbarán, *St Luis Beltrán*, *c.* 1638–40, oil on canvas.

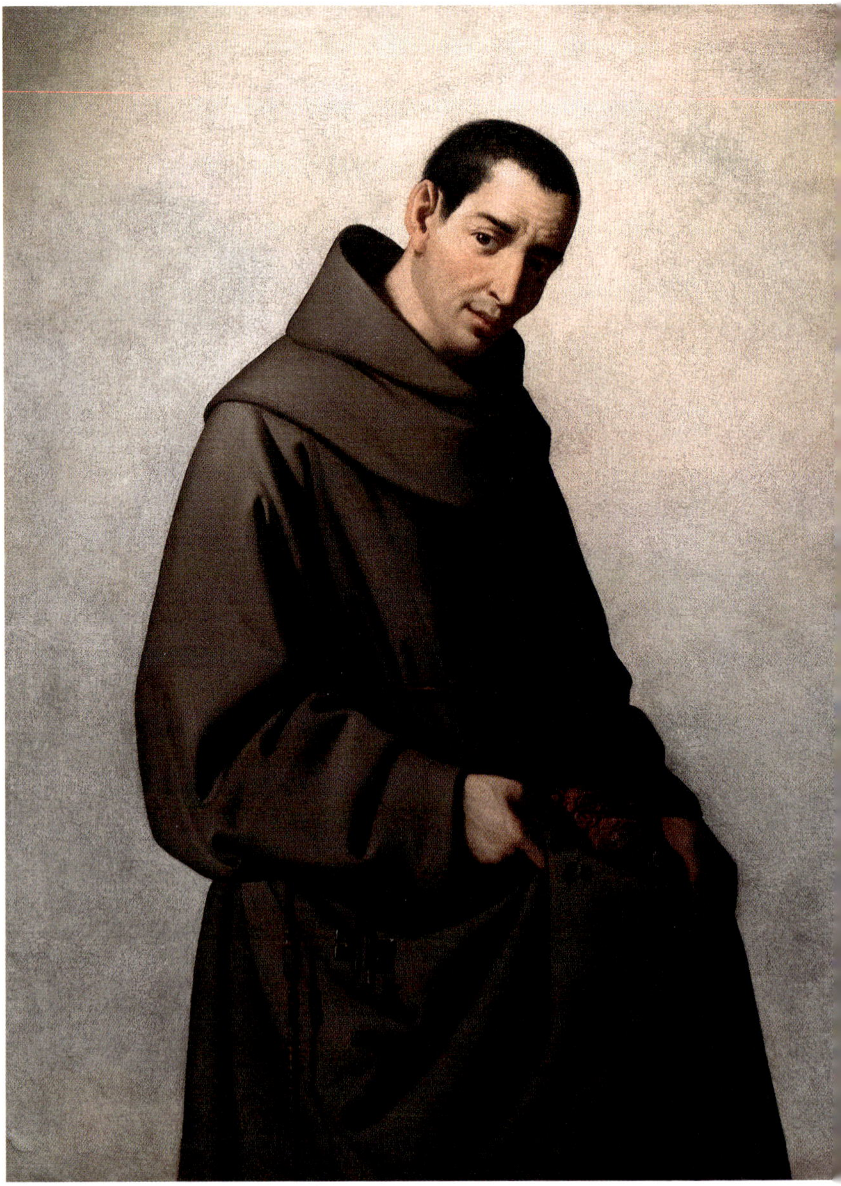

21 Francisco de Zurbarán, *St Diego of Alcalá*, *c.* 1658–60, oil on canvas.

St Lawrence for the Charterhouse of Nuestra Señora de la Defensión in Jerez de la Frontera (*c.* 1638–9), *Blessed Henry Suso* and *St Luís Beltrán* (illus. 20), the sixteenth-century Valencian missionary, for the church of the monastery of St Dominic of Porta Coeli in Seville (*c.* 1638–40), or indeed the series of individual figures making up *Jacob and His Twelve Sons* (*c.* 1640–45). The effect is a less stark presentation of the subject. In *St John the Baptist in a Landscape* (*c.* 1659), the Patinir-influenced landscape and the figure are evenly balanced, neither subordinated to the other, while in *St Diego of Alcalá* (*c.* 1658–60; illus. 21) the daylight landscape disappears and the three-quarter length figure is simply set against a clotted-cream background with tints of palest blue.[25] But at the same time, and as noted in terms of secular portraits, he continued to employ to dramatic effect dark, empty settings, albeit now very subtly chromatically modelled, as with his single figure female saints of the 1640s. What we see in the wake of his time in Madrid, then, is his artistic range expand, with a lightening of his palette and a diversification of settings now within his repertoire.

Zurbarán's work for the Buen Retiro had a curious coda. In 1638 Seville gifted Philip IV a miniature galley, complete with artillery, for the artificial lake constructed in the Buen Retiro. The galley was named *El Santo Rey Don Fernando* after Ferdinand III who had conquered Seville in 1248, and Zurbarán was paid for unspecified 'paintings' for the vessel as part of its fitting out in Seville.[26] Had he wanted further work for the court, this is probably not what he envisaged, but for a final time his brush was called upon to embellish the palace complex.

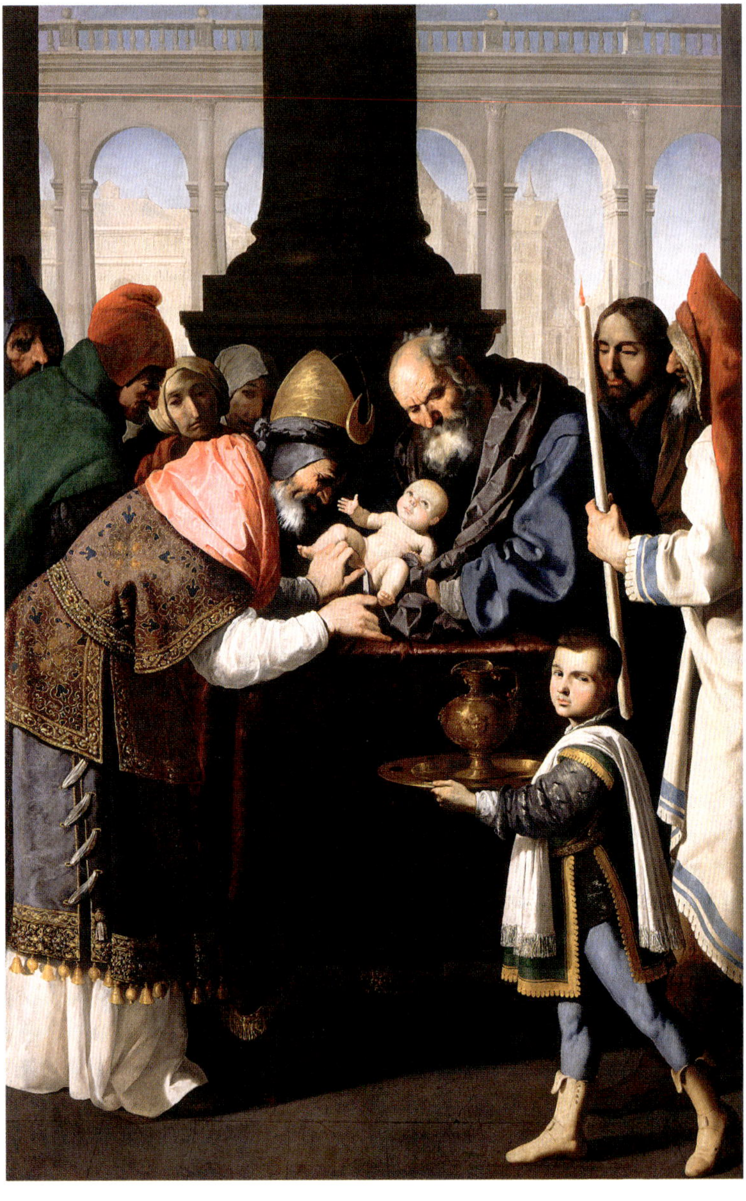

FOUR

Stilled Life and Mysticism

The decoration of the Hall of Realms celebrated Spanish victories and in so doing sought to justify the Count-Duke's national and international policies in the face of growing domestic criticism, but from the moment France declared war on Spain in 1635, Spain moved quickly to a position of almost total war. In 1640 war broke out on two fronts in the peninsula itself. First Catalonia and then Portugal rejected rule from Madrid and sought independence. The Catalans would seek help from the French, who saw an opportunity to further their conflict with Spain, and their revolt would last until 1652 when Barcelona surrendered to Madrid, but the Portuguese war would continue into the reign of Philip IV's son and end with independence in 1668. The human cost and the drain on resources of this military overreach was significant, as was the impact on the country's self-perception as it failed to reach victory quickly, or at all in the case of France and Portugal. Andalusia itself could have become a third front in 1641 with the conspiracy of the Duke of Medina Sidonia and the Marquis of Ayamonte. Medina Sidonia was the leading Castilian nobleman who controlled a significant part of the Spanish coast north and south of Cadiz and whose seigneurial lands included the port of Sanlúcar de Barrameda, vital for European and transatlantic trade and a perennial rival to Seville. His sister had married the Duke of Braganza, who, following the Portuguese revolt of 1640,

22 Francisco de Zurbarán, *Circumcision of Jesus*, 1639, oil on canvas.

was declared king of Portugal. Together with Ayamonte, Medina Sidonia attempted to turn Andalusia into a republic under his protection but failed through lack of support. He was stripped of his major seigneurial possession, Sanlúcar de Barrameda, and internally exiled and the Marquis was executed in 1648.[1]

If the 1640s were a decade of crisis for Spain – with the revolts of 1640 being followed by the dismissal of Olivares as the king's favourite (1643), the deaths of the queen (1644) and the crown prince (1646) and the revolt of both Naples and Palermo (1647) – that crisis left no trace in Zurbarán's work. Nonetheless the decade did mark a turning point in his career. Around 1638–9 he delivered a major commission for the Charterhouse in Jerez de la Frontera, and in 1639, the year in which his second wife Beatriz de Morales died, he also signed a contract to decorate the new sacristy for the Hieronymite monastery in Guadalupe. Given their scale and quality, these two cycles mark the high point of his career; after them Zurbarán received no further large-scale commissions as religious orders themselves were affected by the economic and social crises, the country's ruinous situation further compounded in Seville by the devastation caused by the plague at the end of the decade. (The establishing of new religious foundations that had characterized the first third of the century in Seville had already all-but ceased by this point.[2]) As tastes changed, commissions then began to go to emerging artists, Murillo being engaged by the Franciscans in 1645–6, Juan de Valdés Leal by the Hieronymites in 1656–7.

Although the work for the Carthusians at Jerez de la Frontera did not have the recorded impact that his work for the Calced Mercedarians in Seville did, it is a commission unsurpassed in Zurbarán's oeuvre in range and quality, consisting of twelve works for the enormous *retablo* and eight full-length images of individual Carthusian saints and martyrs, including the serene *Blessed John Houghton* (*c.* 1638–9; see illus. 40), along with two images of incense-wielding angels, that hung both sides of the passageway leading from the *retablo* to the *sagrario* (tabernacle). Zurbarán also painted a *Virgin of the Rosary with Two Carthusians* for the charterhouse and, in all probability, the *Immaculate Conception with Joachim and Anne*.

The Charterhouse of Nuestra Señora de la Defensión (protection) was built on the site of a battle in the Middle Ages between Christians and Muslims, part of the lengthy process of 'reconquest' of Muslim Spain by the Christians, a process still celebrated in the early modern period.[3] The Virgin miraculously intervened to enable the routing of the Muslims, hence the monastery's name, and this is depicted in the *Battle between Christians and Muslims at El Sotillo* for the *retablo*.

The *retablo* was 15 metres (49 ft) high and 10 metres (33 ft) wide, its wooden structure with Solomonic columns by Alejandro de Saavedra, its polychromed sculptures by José de Arce.[4] With its three channels and three tiers the placement of a number of paintings within it is not certain, but the likely arrangement was, on the bottom tier and from left to right, the *Annunciation* (*c.* 1638–9), the *Battle at El Sotillo* (*c.* 1638–9) and the *Adoration of the Shepherds* (1638); on the second tier, the *Adoration of the Magi* (*c.* 1638–9), *St Bruno in Ecstasy* (*c.* 1638–9), depicting the Carthusians' founder canonized in 1623, and the *Circumcision of Jesus* (1639). At the centre of the top tier was a sculpted crucifix. Among the large canvases were six smaller ones: the four evangelists, by Zurbarán's workshop, one above each of the Biblical scenes, and *St John the Baptist* and *St Lawrence* (both *c.* 1638–9), beneath the *Battle at El Sotillo* and immediately above the altar.[5]

The four Biblical scenes are a stunning symphony in colour. In the *Circumcision* (illus. 22), cool blues and indigos arch round the baby Jesus at its centre, and earthy tones dominate the crowded *Adoration of the Shepherds* (illus. 23). The latter's heaven-earth structure of harp-playing angel in fiery-red-and-white and cherub singers above the nativity, and several angels in green amid the

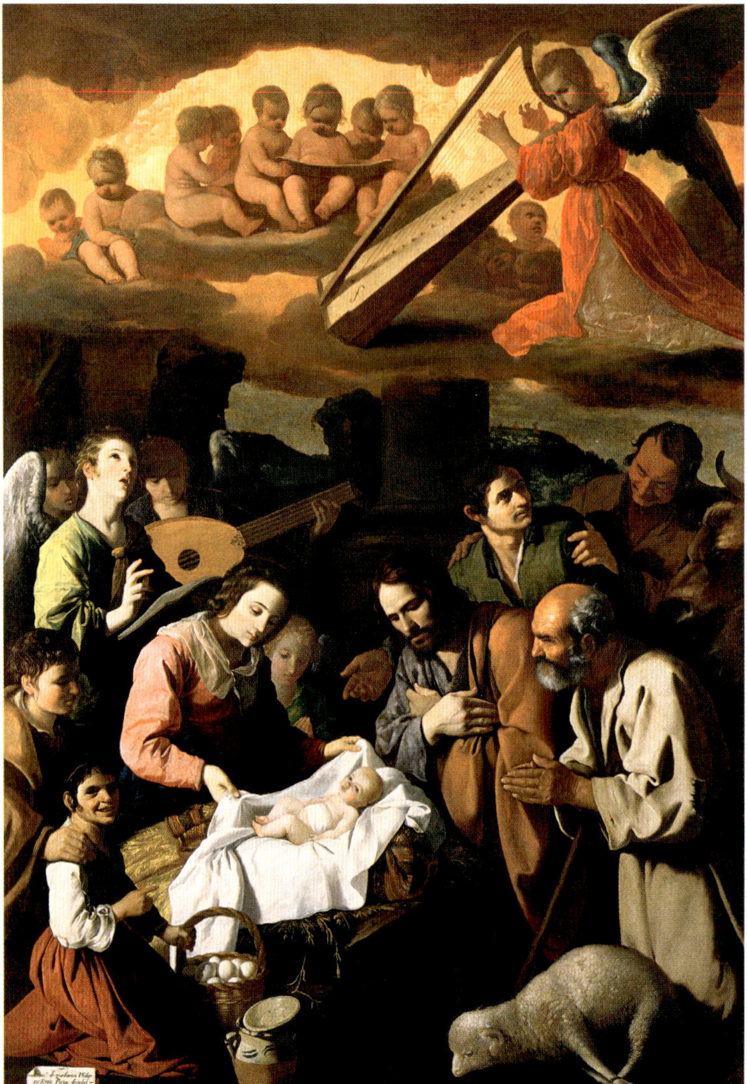

23 Francisco de Zurbarán, *Adoration of the Shepherds*, 1638, oil on canvas.

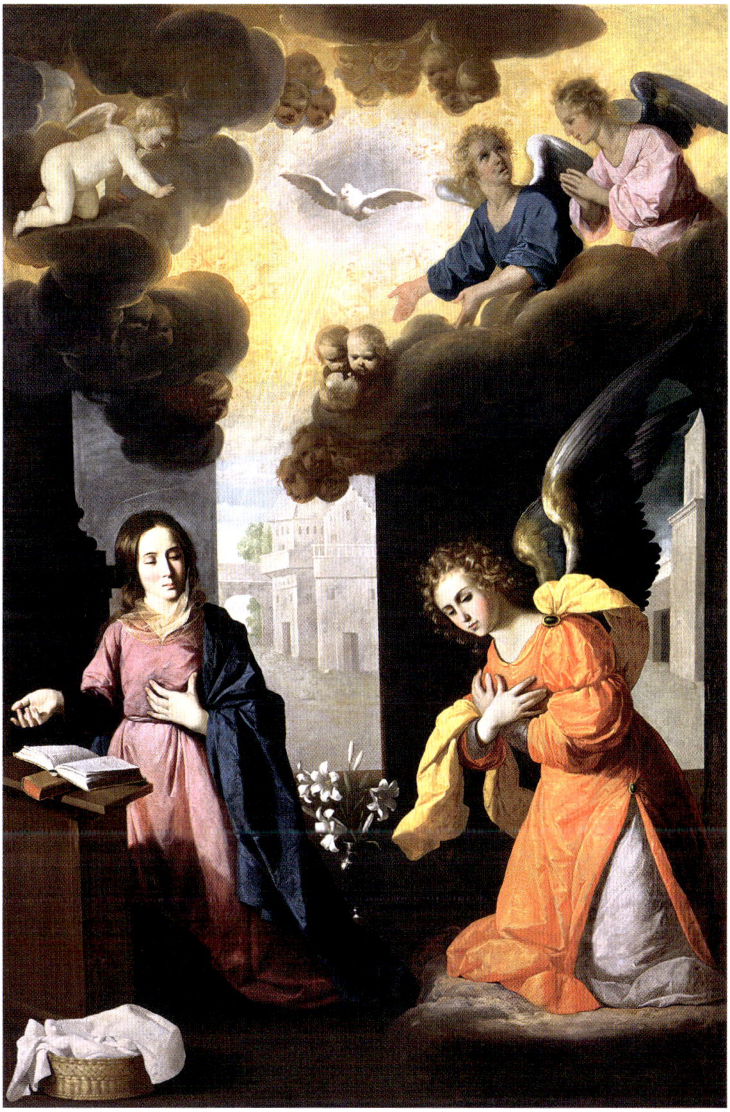

24 Francisco de Zurbarán, *Annunciation*, *c.* 1638–9, oil on canvas.

shepherds, is matched by that of the *Annunciation* (illus. 24). Here, angels in heaven watch in declarative astonishment as Gabriel, clothed in the colours of Zurbarán's celestial visions with fiery-orange tunic, yellow-flecked where folds catch the light, yolk-yellow sash unfurled over shoulder and arm, kneels before Mary, whose blue and mauvish pink are palely echoed in the clothing of the two angels diagonally above her. In the *Adoration of the Magi* (illus. 25), one of Zurbarán's most spectacular depictions of fabric, the front plane is dominated by the gravid folds of the gold-and-red brocade of the kneeling wise man. Behind him stand the other two magi, one turbaned and enfolded in gently creased, palest pink, the other, in the centre, helmeted and in blue with gold-brocaded, military-like costume – all three contrasting with the simple clothing of Mary and Joseph placed at extreme right, Joseph in a dun-coloured cloak, Mary's pink and blue again picking up the tones of the standing magi.

Coinciding with the Carthusian commission was one from the Hieronymites for the decoration of the sacristy of the Royal Monastery of Santa María de Guadalupe in Guadalupe (illus. 26), the only major cycle by the artist still in its original location. The contract for this was signed in March 1639, probably following approval of a test piece, *The Mass of Fray Pedro de las Cabañuelas* (signed and dated 1638), which subsequently formed part of the cycle.[6] The Hieronymites had established themselves at Guadalupe in 1389, the monastery having been begun in 1340 under Alfonso XI. It was a major Marian shrine housing the sculpted image of the Virgin of Guadalupe whose discovery led to the building of the monastery.[7] The order had close links with the Spanish monarchy, Philip II having entrusted to it the royal monastery of San Lorenzo de El Escorial whose foundation stone was laid in 1563. While a signal mark of honour for the order, the link with the Escorial, a single building that symbolically intertwined dynasty and God by combining monastery, basilica, palace and Habsburg pantheon,

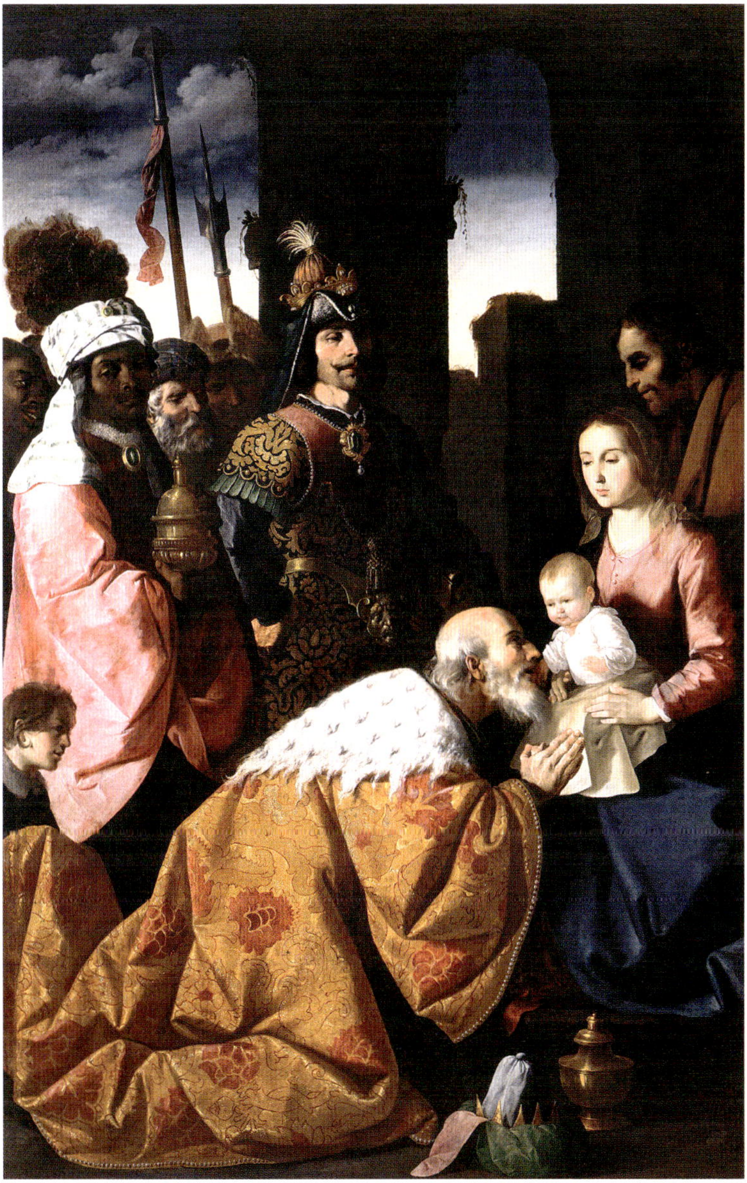

25 Francisco de Zurbarán, *Adoration of the Magi*, c. 1638–9, oil on canvas.

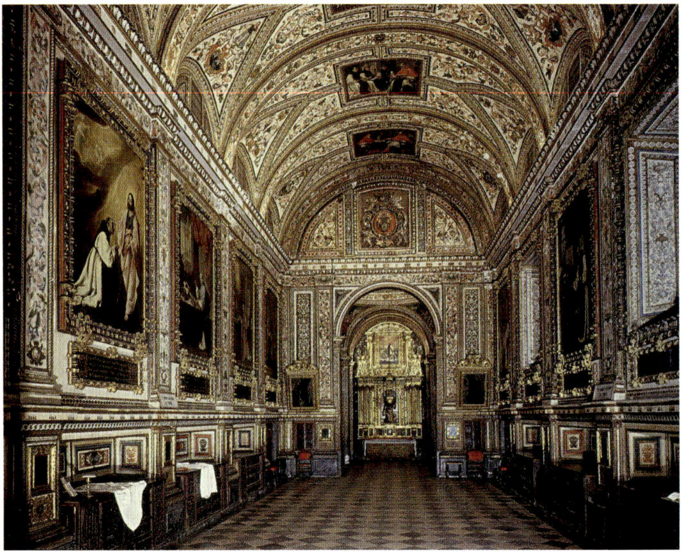

meant that Guadalupe lost its position of prestige. The decision to commission images of significant members of an order was not unusual. But the brief was such that all eight monks portrayed were from this one monastery and all from the fifteenth century, the period of its maximum influence, such that what was celebrated was not the order, as with the Carthusians painted for Jerez de la Frontera, but the monastery.[8] As Guadalupe's pre-eminence faded, so the monastery, through Zurbarán, celebrated its own illustrious history.[9] The monks embody such things as charity (*Fray Martín de Vizcaya Distributing Bread*),[10] mystical experience (*The Vision of Fray Andrés de Salmerón* (1639); see illus. 35),[11] miraculous visions (*The Mass of Fray Pedro de las Cabañuelas*),[12] humility (*Fray Fernando Yáñez Rejecting the Archbishopric of Toledo*, which Enrique III had wanted Yáñez, the prior when the Hieronymites took charge of Guadalupe, to accept),[13] or a grounded connection with power (*Fray Gonzalo de Illescas*, councillor and confessor to Juan II).[14] Unlike the earlier portrait-like images of Mercedarians, the Hieronymites

26 Sacristy, Royal Monastery of Santa María de Guadalupe, 1638–47.

are mostly depicted in defined architectural spaces, albeit that the need to create a convincing spatial recession is often obviated by architectural features placed mid-scene to cut foreground from background, as in the outstanding work of the series, *Fray Gonzalo de Illescas*. There Zurbarán also offers two still lifes, one of books, writing materials, hourglass and skull on the monk's table, and the apple-on-a-book placed on the colonnade that partially screens the background.

The initial commission then extended to the sacristy's chapel for which Zurbarán painted three works celebrating St Jerome, the figure after whom the Hieronymites were named.[15] The two works hanging on the walls perpendicular to the altar depict events described by Jerome in a letter to Eustochium.[16] *The Flagellation of St Jerome* shows him being whipped by angels after he had been taken before Christ and accused of lying when he answered 'yes' to the question of whether he was a Christian since, such was

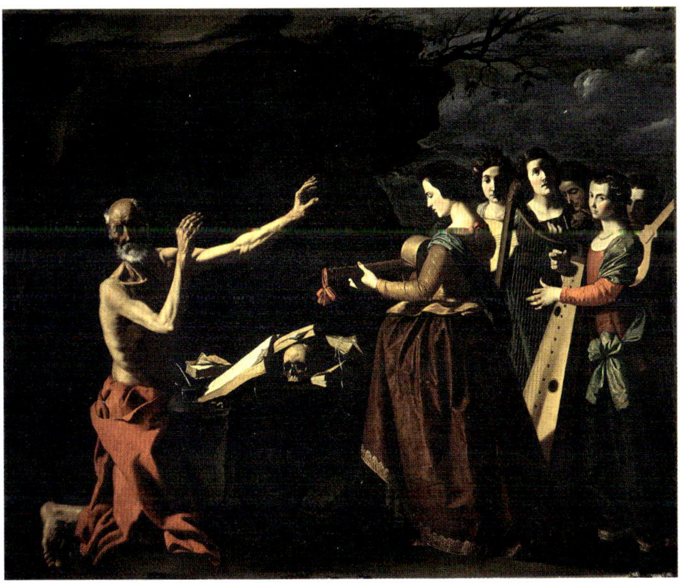

27 Francisco de Zurbarán, *The Temptation of St Jerome*, c. 1640–43, oil on canvas.

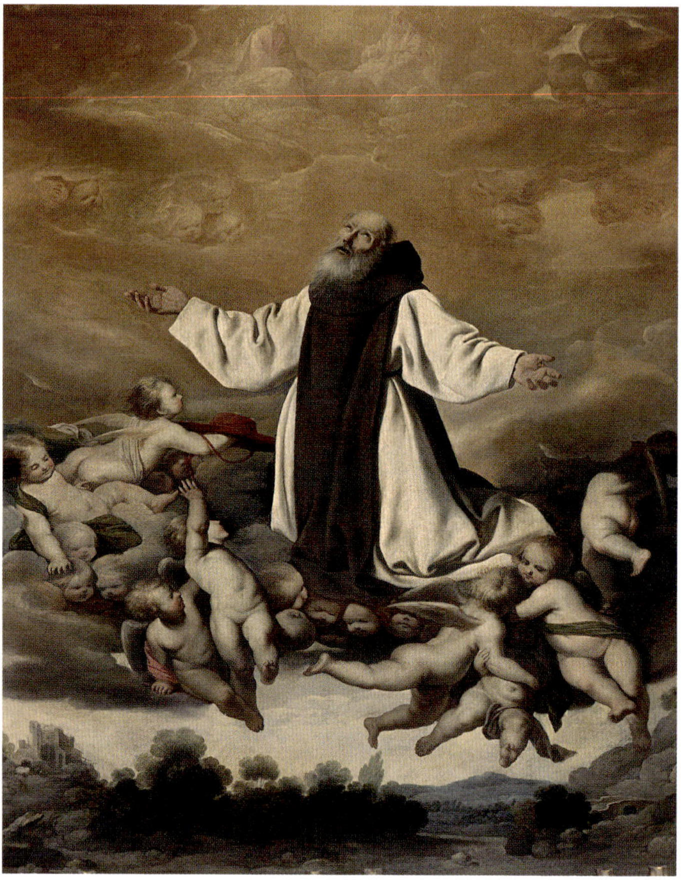

his devotion to Classical Latin culture, he was rather a 'Ciceronian'. While in *The Temptation of St Jerome* (*c.* 1640–43; illus. 27), Zurbarán shows the emaciated saint kneeling, at the left, one arm outstretched, the other raised, and head turned away, all to ward off the six 'temptresses' at the right, who, rather than dancing as in Jerome's account, play instruments and look like Zurbarán's chaste and demure female saints. The orangey-gold tones of the *Flagellation*, typical of Zurbarán when depicting divine visions,

28 Francisco de Zurbarán, *The Apotheosis of St Jerome*, *c.* 1640–43, oil on canvas.

contrast sharply with the blackness of the night-time temptation in which the bravura use of chiaroscuro dramatically contrasts the aged flesh of the saint with the youthful skin of the musicians and makes his outstretched arm a lightning bolt aimed at them. Finally, over the altar is *The Apotheosis of St Jerome* (*c*. 1640–43; illus. 28) where the saint is carried upwards by a cloud of twisting cherubs towards the barely visible Trinity in the orangey heavens. On the altar's predella were ten small, workshop images of stand-alone Hieronymites, some of whose poses directly reproduce those of certain of the Carthusian figures for Jerez de la Frontera, including that of the *Blessed John Houghton*, an indication of efficient workshop practice.[17] Lastly, and in the late 1650s, Zurbarán painted for the monastery *St Nicholas* and *St Ildephonsus Receiving the Chasuble*.[18]

STILL LIFE, STILLED LIFE

In the absence of large-scale commissions like those for Guadalupe and Jerez de la Frontera that had typified the first phase of his career in Seville, Zurbarán began to turn more fully to devotional subjects, whether for churches or private individuals. While in some respects he is therefore no longer the 'painter of monastic life', to use Paul Guinard's expression, he remains a creator and purveyor of religious and devotional expression. This is perhaps the point to explore a broader question: how did his art, subject matter aside, express contemporary spirituality?

Part of his attraction lay in the clarity and precision of his compositions 'meeting' post-Tridentine and post-Mannerist expectations as to the function and thus the desired nature of religious art: to convey accurately and in a focused way the prime subject, and to do so in a way that immediately captures the viewer's attention. This explains the obvious and recorded impact in Seville of his early tenebristic works and their sculptural forms,

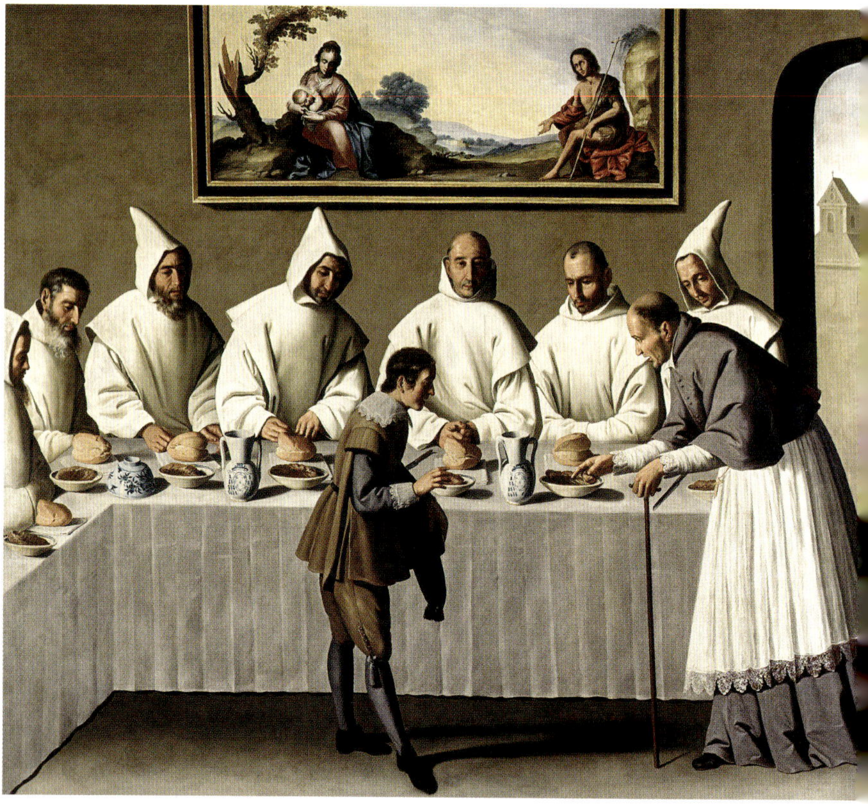

for their immediacy places the viewer in the 'real' presence of the sacred. But a consideration of one of his smaller-scale commissions, his second from the Carthusians, helps pinpoint a further and profound attraction of his style, its absolute quietude. Threading its way through my consideration of these works as examples of his style will be his still lifes to establish a common still-life aesthetic across his oeuvre. This will lead us to one of the defining and most dangerous aspects of Golden Age culture: mysticism.

29 Francisco de Zurbarán, *St Hugh in the Refectory*, c. 1655, oil on canvas.

The work for the sacristy of the Charterhouse of Santa María de las Cuevas in Seville consisted of just three canvases.[19] More than many of his works, these have been assigned strongly divergent dates, with much resting on the perceived nature of the artist's early and later styles, and on how one views such things as the obvious maladroit elements in one of the works, *St Bruno and Pope Urban II*, in that context. The dates suggested range from mid-1620s, early to mid-1630s to mid-1650s. The last – circa 1655 - is accepted here, Odile Delenda's argument for it resting partly on the costume of the page in another of the works, *St Hugh in the Refectory*, which is typical of the 1640s/50s.[20] The three are arresting works and, in terms of my argument here, show arrested movement.

St Hugh in the Refectory (illus. 29) depicts the miracle that confirmed Carthusian abstinence from meat: St Hugh, bishop of Grenoble, has sent meat to the first Carthusians for Shrovetide; at table, St Bruno and his fellow monks discuss whether they should eat it but fall asleep; Hugh visits them, having first sent his servant ahead who returns aghast, telling him the monks seem to be about to eat meat during Lent and in Holy Week; the monks awaken, Hugh asks Bruno what day it is, and they realize they have miraculously been asleep since before Lent started; the meat turns to ash when Hugh touches it.[21] The seven Carthusians are motionless at table, Bruno looking directly at us. Above them hangs a painting of the Virgin and Child and St John the Baptist who are seated apart but in the same landscape, the Virgin and John not simply patrons of the order but deemed to have been Carthusians themselves, the order tracing its heritage back to Elijah.[22] Their placement in a landscape is one of the many ways that these works embody Carthusian practices and values, here the order's withdrawal from society and the construction of its monasteries in isolated locations. In front of the table stand a page and the elderly bishop, whose mouth is open in astonishment

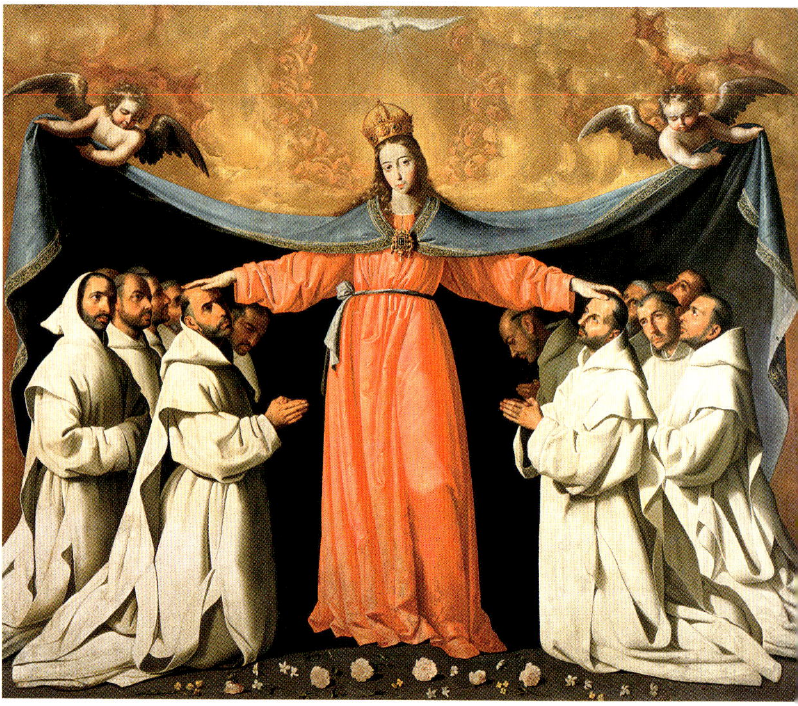

and who appears either to point at or more likely touch the meat, though his finger is incorrectly positioned to do either. On the table are bread rolls on napkins, knives, bowls with meat, an upturned bowl of Chinese porcelain and two blue-and-white pottery jugs with the arms of Gonzalo de Mena, the archbishop of Seville who gave the site of the Santa María de las Cuevas monastery to the Carthusians in 1400 (illus. 31).[23]

In *St Bruno and Pope Urban II* (see illus. 4), we see a moment from Bruno's obedient but reluctant sojourn in Rome as advisor to the pope.[24] Urban II sits under a baldachin, hands resting over the arms of his chair and looking out at the viewer; Bruno on a stool opposite, literally and figuratively withdrawn, each hand tucked entirely within the opposite sleeve of his habit, eyes focused

30 Francisco de Zurbarán, *Virgin of the Carthusians*, c. 1655, oil on canvas.

on nothing external, effective portraits of the active and the contemplative lives respectively. A still life of books and writing material lies silently between them. The third work, the majestic *Virgin of the Carthusians* (illus. 30), hung on the end wall of the sacristy, the two other works on walls either side of it. In a symmetrical composition typical of his work, the Virgin stands crowned at the centre, her hands resting on the heads of two Carthusians either side of her who kneel with others, all in their distinctive habits, their protection by the Virgin symbolized by their sheltering underneath her mantle held out over them by two cherubs. Apart from the sharp white folds of their habits and the Virgin's imposing deep coral robe, the flowers that lie before the Virgin across the front of the composition – roses, jasmine and primroses[25] – are the work's most striking feature. Each looks as though it has been placed with minute precision – these are not flowers thrown or scattered; none touches or visually overlaps with another, each is in isolation.

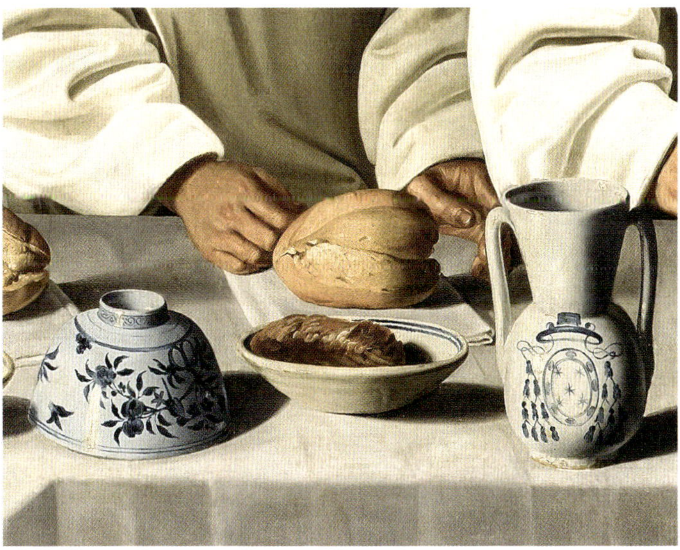

31 Francisco de Zurbarán, *St Hugh in the Refectory*, detail.

The singular placing of flowers is found in a number of works by Zurbarán – *The Miracle of the Portiuncula* (*c.* 1630–31), *The Virgin of the Rosary with Two Carthusians* (*c.* 1638–9), *The Young Virgin* (*c.* 1640–45; see illus. 50), *The Apparition of Virgin and Child to St Francis in the Portiuncula* (1661) – and *The Presentation of the Virgin* (*c.* 1630), possibly part of a *retablo* commission from the Calced Trinitarians in Seville, painted by the member of his workshop who has been called the 'Master of Besançon'.[26] Most show flowers on steps, and this has been linked to Philip Galle's engraving of a work by Maarten van Heemskerck.[27] The bowls, jugs, knives and rolls on the refectory table in *St Hugh in the Refectory* are similarly placed, so that our view of each is entirely unimpeded, and given each thing's tangibility, their quiddity, the effect is to create a profound impression of the isolation and withdrawal of one thing from another, of all things from everything. (Where the full view of several items is slightly blocked, it is a result rather of Hugh and his page who stand in front of the table.) There are precedents for this discrete placing of objects. One is Pablo de Céspedes's *Christ Served by Angels* (*c.* 1600), which originally hung in the refectory of the Jesuit Casa Professa in Seville. Long thought lost, it has recently been identified with a painting in the Palacio Real, Madrid, and it is significant to note in connection with the stylistic feature of Zurbarán I am foregrounding that it had previously been attributed to someone in his sphere of influence or to his master, Pedro Díaz de Villanueva.[28] This painting was seemingly the prototype for those Andalusian artists, including Pacheco, who praised it, who depicted its unusual subject – Christ served food by angels following his temptation by the Devil.[29] Céspedes places the objects on the table so that there is virtually no visual overlap between them; in Pacheco's 1616 version, there is none; and in both, single flowers lie on the table in similar isolation. Zurbarán's precise and discrete placing of objects thus builds on early Sevillian naturalism, but in him it creates a profound sense of detached isolation absent, for example, in Velázquez's early *bodegones* despite their similar placement of objects. It typifies not simply Zurbarán's still lifes, but his entire oeuvre. A unique and defining characteristic of his style, it is this sense of detached isolation, of what one critic calls 'collective disconnection' and 'dissociation', that I want to explore.[30]

Zurbarán's work requires the viewer to ask what constituted an 'object' for him. The obvious answer is the inanimate things that are found across it, miniature still lifes within his figure paintings. He also painted a small number of stand-alone still lifes. In both, his ability to paint an object such that its materiality becomes tangible, and the object present, means that his still lifes convey each object's 'inscape', to use the term coined by Gerard Manley Hopkins; that is, its haecceity, its 'thisness'. This is the case with his two mesmerizing still lifes that are masterpieces of the genre: the *Still Life with Citrons, Oranges and a Rose* (1633; illus. 32) and the *Still Life with Vessels* (*c.* 1650–55), this last in two autograph versions, my comments here being to that in the Prado (illus. 33). In his *Still Life with Quinces* (*c.* 1635), which is cut down,[31] we can see the effect when objects are set back from the front plane, as in the previous two still lifes, as opposed to when they are seen, as in this, in cropped close-up, for with the latter there is far less a sense of the object's detachment. The double sense of singularity – that is, of objects' haecceity and of their standardly being placed in isolation one from another in the same space – is heightened by Zurbarán's use of intensely dark backgrounds that, in *Still Life with Citrons, Oranges and a Rose* and *Still Life with Vessels*, further throw the objects into dramatic relief. And, as critics have observed, the objects in the latter are painted as if encountered individually, the shadow cast by the second vessel, for example, oddly seeming to basically bypass the third slightly behind it.[32]

Certain still-life motifs recur. One such is a wicker basket, as in works for Jerez de la Frontera (*Annunciation*, *Adoration of the*

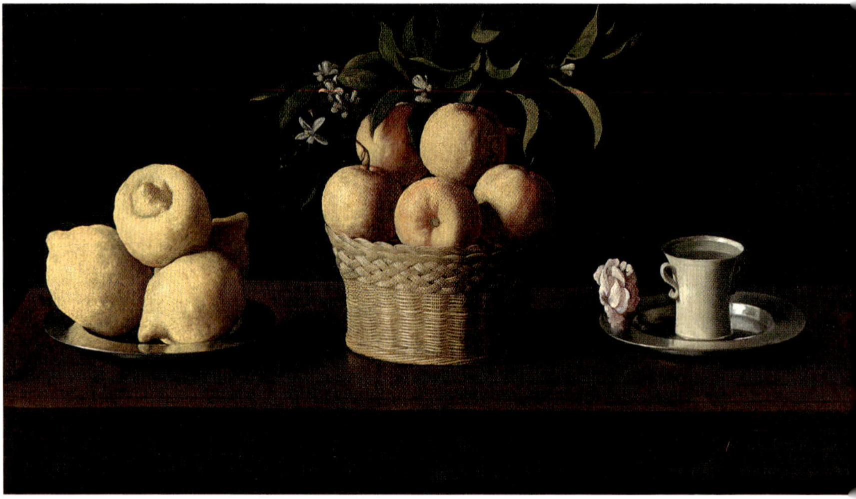

Shepherds) and Guadalupe (*Fray Martín de Vizcaya Distributing Bread*), which might contain bread, flowers, sewing or fruit in the case of *Still Life with Apples and Peaches* (*c.* 1630). Another, more striking, the white ceramic cup placed on a silver or pewter plate alongside a rose that occur together not only in the *Still Life with Citrons, Oranges and a Rose* but in the *Miraculous Cure of the Blessed Reginald of Orléans* (*c.* 1626–7; see illus. 6), the *Family of the Virgin* (*c.* 1630–35) and, on their own, in a *Cup of Water and a Rose* (*c.* 1630; see illus. 1), trimmed on three sides and therefore possibly part of a larger work.[33] These raise the question of whether potential symbolic meanings (the cup of water symbolizing the Virgin's purity; the rose, the most Marian flower, devotion through the rosary) remain when the motif is (part of) a stand-alone still life.[34] I will return to the contemporary viewer's interpretative engagement below.

Zurbarán's still lifes are austere in content as well as form with none of the varied presentation of accumulated objects on stepped ledges and the abundance of sweet delicacies typical of Juan van

32 Francisco de Zurbarán, *Still Life with Citrons, Oranges and a Rose*, 1633, oil on canvas.

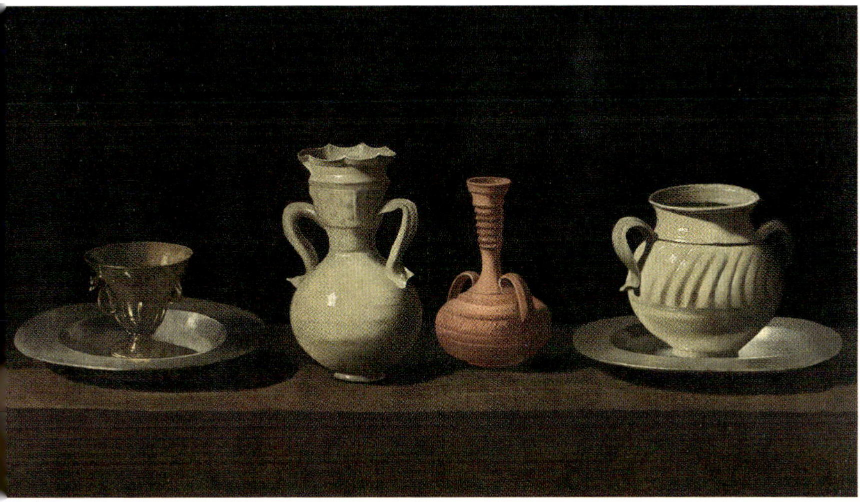

der Hamen y León, his own *Still Life with Sweetmeats* (*c.* 1630–32) presenting just the one plate of these, but they are not devoid of luxury, far less of grace. (This still life seems a study for the similar plate of sweetmeats that X-rays reveal he first painted where the citrons and basket approximately now are in *Still Life with Citrons, Oranges and a Rose*.[35]) And the reticent objects of *Still Life with Vessels* are evidence both of Seville's status as a major port and commercial centre and of its industry. The vessels approximately aligned on a wooden surface against a black background are varied in shape as well as material: a wide-mouthed cup (a *bernegal*) of gilded silver on a pewter plate; a white Triana jug, Triana pottery being made from clay extracted from the Guadalquivir, including near the Charterhouse of Santa María de las Cuevas, and named after the location of the potteries in Seville; a red-clay vase (a *búcaro*) from Guadalajara, Mexico; and a squat, white Triana pot with curved striations on another pewter plate.[36] As Norman Bryson has observed, 'every vessel records and dramatises the history of its manufacture' so that, for example,

33 Francisco de Zurbarán, *Still Life with Vessels*, *c.* 1650–55, oil on canvas.

> in the earthenware vessels there is a strong sense of the potter's wheel turning and, as it turns, of the hands cutting notches and rims in the soft clay. It is the softness, even the slipperiness, of the clay that is registered in the loose, flopping curves of the handles . . . And the eye also registers the textures of things as part of their being, inseparable from their weight: the relative roughness of earthenware, the feel of a glaze, the hardness and coolness of metal; here the sensing instruments are the fingertips.[37]

Yet, as he also comments, with Zurbarán's still lifes the viewer is not invited to touch, such is what we might call the aura of compositional inviolability typical of the artist.[38]

It was once suggested that the Barcelona version of *Still Life with Vessels* might be a copy by Zurbarán's son of the Prado version.[39] Juan de Zurbarán trained under his father and was a still-life artist, but his oeuvre is still not firmly established. His *Still Life with Lemons in a Wicker Basket* (*c*. 1643–9; illus. 34) marks out similarities and differences between his work and his father's.[40] On a stone surface, against an extremely dark background, sits a large wicker basket filled with lemons and flowers (orange lilies, red carnations, a red-and-white flamed tulip, blue delphiniums, white roses and lemon blossom). To the left of the basket, and on a footed silver or pewter salver, is a china bowl filled with water, an orange lily resting in it and a goldfinch on its edge; to the right, two lemons still on their branch. What differentiates this work from Zurbarán's is precisely its noisiness, the more 'disordered' presentation of objects in the basket, the closer placing of things, resulting in little sense of their 'self-presentation' or withdrawn presence as in his father's work.

An artist often viewed as an important precursor of Zurbarán is Juan Sánchez Cotán, who painted still lifes in Toledo at the very start of the seventeenth century as the genre emerged independently in Spain, Italy and the Netherlands.[41] The similarities between Zurbarán's still lifes and Sánchez Cotán's are clear. In Sánchez Cotán's *Still Life with Quince, Cabbage, Melon and Cucumber* (*c.* 1602), for example, the objects are shown on or hanging above a stone opening, each separate from the other and against a black void, their almost hyperrealism striking. But whereas the composition and the style, the marked *rílievo*, of Zurbarán's still lifes remain in the still-life elements of his religious works, in Sánchez Cotán's they do not, and the inanimate is thus less heightened there, less present to the viewer. The latter's *Apparition of the Virgin of the Rosary to the Carthusians* (1618), painted for the Charterhouse in Granada that he entered as a lay brother in 1604, lacks the essential intensity, clarity and singular focus of Zurbarán's *Virgin of the Carthusians* or his *Virgin of the Rosary with Two Carthusians*, for all the elements in common. So, in Sánchez Cotán there are roses and petals scattered on the steps and platform on which the Virgin's throne stands, but they lack the sense of focus, of being seen, of Zurbarán's, and though discretely scattered, also that of having been carefully, individually placed.

It is hardly surprising that certain of Zurbarán's figures have been likened to still lifes, for the effect of his style is to render all life stilled.[42] This can be seen in the three Santa María de las Cuevas works, in which stillness, isolation and introversion are a feature of the human figures as much as of the objects depicted. It is inadvertently emphasized by Palomino when he recorded that individuals encountering Zurbarán's 1627 *Crucifixion* in its chapel mistook it for a sculpture; that is, a three-dimensional object.[43] In depicting the animate and the inanimate, then, 'objects, so carefully and austerely depicted, have the presence of living characters, even if it may be argued that Zurbarán's characters have the presence of earthen pots.'[44] The effect of this double transference – people as inert as objects, objects as vividly present, real, alive as people – is that all matter is rendered equally.[45]

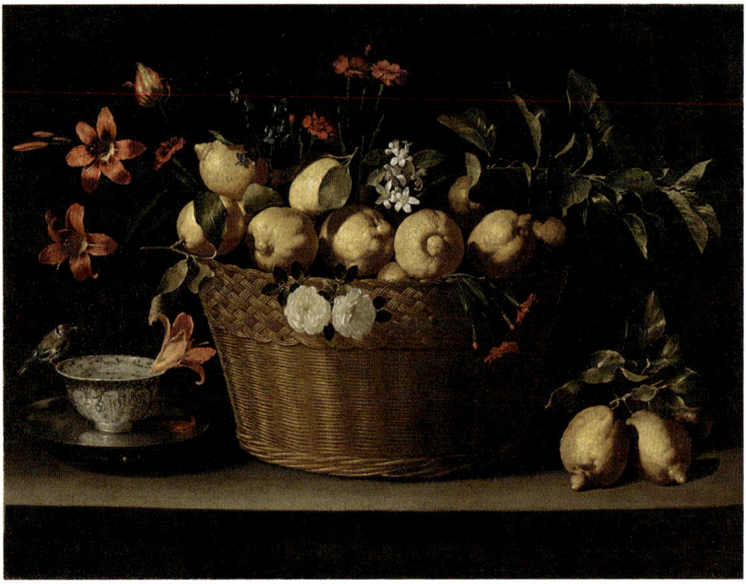

The three Carthusian works have been linked to core aspects of Carthusian life: abstinence in *St Hugh in the Refectory*; silence in *St Bruno and Pope Urban II*; Marian devotion in the *Virgin of the Carthusians*;[46] and the singular importance of silence and solitude to the order to the 'static forms' of all three.[47] But did Zurbarán mould his style to convey these particular Carthusian qualities? There are two responses to this question: one artistic concerning Zurbarán, the other spiritual concerning the Golden Age.

First, and as noted, isolation and stillness, solitude and silence, are characteristic of Zurbarán's style per se. Significantly, they occur in both religious and secular works, as we have seen with his *Defence of Cadiz* where his compositional maladroitness in placing figures to convey either action or realistic interaction results in many looking isolated and self-absorbed within their shared space. Regardless of subject, with Zurbarán all things are typically secluded within the shared space they occupy. When

34 Juan de Zurbarán, *Still Life with Lemons in a Wicker Basket*, c. 1643–9, oil on canvas.

these stylistic traits meet certain religious or devotional subjects, they contribute inestimably to the conveying of those subjects, and he obviously explored and exploited such traits to do so. Second, while the qualities mentioned in terms of the Carthusian works are a feature of the Carthusian life, particularly silence, they are not simply qualities distinct to one order, but spiritual qualities per se. To state this more strongly, the highly distinctive qualities that result from Zurbarán's style – withdrawal, introversion, stillness, self-containment, detachment – are all states and/or necessary conditions of contemporary spirituality and mysticism that would have been familiar to religious and many lay viewers.

MYSTICAL RESONANCES

Many of Zurbarán's subjects connect with meditation and contemplation, whether depicting major writers on these or showing individuals in the act of meditation or undergoing a mystical experience. Meditation and contemplation, and the progression from one to the other, were a major part of spirituality. The medieval *lectio divina* had systematized this into connected stages: *lectio*, *meditatio*, *oratio* and *contemplatio*. As the twelfth-century Carthusian Guigo II explained,

> Reading is the careful study of the Scriptures, concentrating all one's powers on it. Meditation is the busy application of the mind to seek with the help of one's own reason for knowledge of hidden truth. Prayer is the heart's devoted turning to God to drive away evil and obtain what is good. Contemplation is when the mind is in some sort lifted up to God and held above itself, so that it tastes the joys of everlasting sweetness.[48]

Or as the Discalced Carmelite Juan de la Cruz says, 'Seek in reading, and you will find in meditation; knock in prayer, and it will open to you in contemplation.'[49] Monserrate Geli, a Carthusian writing in the seventeenth century, has the good monastic alone in his cell engaged in these four activities.[50] More broadly, meditation involves discursive reasoning, often starting with reflection on a text or indeed an image; in contemplation, reasoning, sensory images and the like are left behind and the individual waits passively on God, ultimately enjoying, with God's grace and in different degrees or forms, union with the divine.[51] In the Franciscan Pedro de Alcántara's analogy, meditation actively strikes the flint to get a spark, contemplation silently and peacefully enjoys this, that is, God's presence.[52] (In images of saints, Zurbarán often shows a book closed or not being read to indicate that the individual has moved to a state of contemplation.) The soul experiences union without understanding it, the Carmelite reformer Teresa de Jesús writing of 'perfect contemplation' that 'the divine Master suspends the soul's faculties . . . it is aflame in love and doesn't understand how it loves; it knows it enjoys what it loves, but doesn't know how it enjoys it.'[53]

In the early modern period, Spain played a significant role in the expansion of interest in contemplation for religious and laity alike through the writings of the Spanish mystics Teresa de Jesús (1515–1582) and Juan de la Cruz (1542–1591), Teresa's works in particular being avidly read across Europe. Following their deaths there was an intensification of interest in mysticism across Europe, and in Spain mysticism, 'at least among the urban middle and upper classes', 'took on the character of almost a mass movement'.[54] And it is at this time that the term 'mystic' began to replace 'contemplative', though both covered substantially the same experiential field, the nature of the experience of the divine and the steps towards achieving this.[55]

In terms of Spain there is something of a paradox. Religious figures like Teresa and Juan de la Cruz had inadvertently driven the renewal of mysticism, yet many, not least the Spanish Inquisition, remained intensely suspicious of this. The mystical tradition had always emphasized that union with God through contemplation was open to everyone with God's grace, but in Spain there was sharp disagreement over whether such 'monastic' spirituality was appropriate for the laity.[56] Moreover, the Inquisition was sceptical of and concerned with claims to mystical experience precisely because an intense, interior and personal experience of God seemed to bypass the external guidance of the Church, and it believed this could lead to or indeed indicate what it termed 'Lutheranism', and thus heresy.[57] The dangers were real: Teresa's *Life*, written in 1554–65 and circulating in manuscript before posthumous publication in 1588, was denounced to the Inquisition, as was she by a novice in the convent that she had founded in Seville, though she was ultimately cleared.[58] Despite these risks the attraction of mysticism was intense: Spaniards strove to encounter the divine, and artists and spiritual writers struggled to express what could not by definition be expressed; namely, the ineffable.[59] This is the context in which Zurbarán's works were commissioned and, perhaps more importantly, viewed. In looking at this, I am not focusing on how his works showing saints or Biblical figures and scenes might have been a vehicle for meditation, which will be considered in Chapter Seven, or indeed on those that depict a mystical experience. I want rather to sketch the spiritual horizon of expectations of contemporary viewers – not simply those in religious orders, though certainly not least those – as they encountered his work.

Contemporary viewers familiar with mystical and meditative literature would be familiar with notions such as solitude, passivity, darkness and absorption, brought together, for example, in a poem by Juan de la Cruz to describe a moment of contemplative ecstasy, an apophatic experience 'transcending all knowledge', and they are precisely among the stylistic qualities and effects characteristic of Zurbarán and variously exemplified in his Santa María de las Cuevas works and still lifes.[60] In briefly considering this literature I am not offering an exhaustive account of contemplation/mysticism, but contextualizing concepts within this that suggestively resonate with Zurbarán's style.

Silence and withdrawal were more than ideal preconditions for meditation and contemplation. In Carthusian practice, for example, the solitude they occasioned was the foundation of monastic life. Such solitude was praised by Monserrate Geli as 'the fiery furnace where faults are refined and purified, souls cleansed . . . the place where man and angels cohabit . . . the wedding bed where the soul's spiritual nuptials [with God] are consummated'.[61] 'Silence' signified a withdrawal into the self from external and internal distractions, a total disengagement of the senses and our discursive understanding so that one was focused entirely on God.[62] Silence thus became eloquent.[63]

Such introversion through the silencing of the senses and mind is at the heart of one of the most important but controversial spiritual terms of early modern Spain, *recogimiento* (recollection). This was a key term in sixteenth-century Franciscan contemplation and is central to the influential *Tercer abecedario espiritual* (Third Spiritual Alphabet) of 1527 by the Franciscan Francisco de Osuna. There he writes that

> the Lord will come and enter your soul if the doors of your senses are tightly shut . . . The no of recollection ['no del recogimiento'] rejects everything created that pushes through the portals of the senses, and it opens our hearts to God, for the no does not renounce God but rather rejects everything else so that we are with him alone.[64]

A stilling of the senses and of the mind, a withdrawing of them, Teresa teaches this is a 'turning of the eyes of the soul on the Lord'.[65]

Recogimiento was acceptable as a practice but was problematic because of similarities with *dejamiento* (abandonment [to God]), which was entirely unacceptable. In Kevin Ingram's useful comparison,

> Through *recogimiento* (gathering of the senses), Franciscan friars learnt how to distance themselves from all ideas, even the most saintly, silence the intellect, and obliterate all desire, so that they could fill themselves with the presence of God. *Dejamiento* (freeing of the senses) was similar to *recogimiento* in its goals. What most differentiated it from the orthodox practice was its adherents' belief that no particular method or ritual was required to achieve mystical union with God, only a sincere wish to open oneself to His love.[66]

More damning was the belief expressed by the *dejados*, that is those deemed to be practising *dejamiento*, as stated in a tenet set out and condemned by the Inquisition in 1525 that 'the love of God in man is God, and that they should surrender themselves to this love of God, which orders people in such a way that they cannot commit sins.'[67] These unacceptable practices and beliefs were associated with Alumbradismo (Illuminism).[68] This involved an intense inner spirituality and the direct engagement of the individual with God, often unmediated by the Church. This struck the Inquisition as 'Lutheran' and so it vigorously attempted to uproot the Alumbrados (Illuminists) as heretics.

In the late sixteenth and early seventeenth centuries, Extremadura and Andalusia, including Fuente de Cantos, Llerena and Seville, were investigated as 'centres' of Alumbradismo. In the case of Extremadura, Alonso de la Fuente, a Dominican friar trained in the College of Santo Tomás in Seville, led the campaign, identifying the core element of Alumbradismo as an undue emphasis on contemplation and union with God.[69] His obsession led to the Inquisition arresting individuals from 1573 and culminated in an *auto-da-fé* in Llerena in 1579.[70] This has been seen as 'part of a campaign to discredit mysticism of any kind'.[71] As for Seville, it became the focus of a major Inquisitorial investigation in the 1620s, with *autos-da-fé* in 1624 and 1627. Among Alumbrado beliefs identified as erroneous were a disparagement of vocal prayer, the rosary and religious images and an unacceptable emphasis on the importance of mental prayer for salvation.[72] Juan de la Cruz's mystical treatises were discovered among the Alumbrados, and the Dominican Domingo Farfán asserted that they contained condemned illuminist ideas.[73] Although this was rejected after formal scrutiny, the Sevillian inquisitors still 'emphasised the dangers of mystical works read without the necessary theological knowledge and without fulfilling the basic conditions stipulated by the writers'.[74] Parallels between the 'spirit' of Zurbarán's art, the Alumbrados and specifically the Quietism of the Spaniard Miguel de Molinos (1628–1696), condemned by the papacy in 1687, have occasionally been mooted.[75] Absence of evidence aside, what this ignores is that the few Molinist quotations adduced to support this largely present features of contemplation and mysticism in general, as do the Alumbrado ideas held unacceptable because unduly emphasized. This is why mysticism was such a fraught arena.

To return to *recogimiento*, Osuna equates this with mystical theology and union with God.[76] At its most perfect, it is an exclusive concentration on God.[77] Conditions for achieving this include solitude ('recogimiento corporal'), a dark place where the senses 'will not flit about but become more united and absorbed' in what one is contemplating, and guarding the eyes from distractions by closing them or, if in company and to avoid engagement, gazing at the ground as if 'lost to the world in thought'.[78] In this way, 'intent only on God and his love', you 'can be deeply recollected even in a crowd'.[79] The aim is to try 'always to be recollected', 'heart stilled', 'like . . . a turtle withdrawing beneath his shell'.[80] Zurbarán's world as portrayed is precisely this world of *recogimiento*, a world in which each person, each thing, is withdrawn even in a crowd.

The impossibility of putting into language the experience of God means that mystics necessarily resort to rhetorical figures such as oxymoron, antithesis and paradox. One such is the darkness that nevertheless illuminates. This notion traces its way from the late fifth-century theologian Pseudo-Dionysius through mystical writers such as Bonaventure and into the early modern period. As Pseudo-Dionysius writes, 'for a sight of the mysterious things' you need

> to leave behind you everything perceived and understood, everything perceptible and understandable, all that is not and all that is, and, with your understanding laid aside, to strive upward as much as you can toward union with him who is beyond all being and knowledge. By an undivided and absolute abandonment of yourself and everything, shedding all and freed from all, you will be uplifted to the ray of the divine shadow which is above everything that is.[81]

Darkness is one of the essential metaphors of the mystical writings and poetry of Juan de la Cruz. When discussing the 'passive night of the spirit', in which the soul is purged and illuminated by God through what is called 'infused contemplation or mystical theology' to prepare it for union with him, Juan explains that this is described as a 'dark night' even though 'divine light' is illuminating the soul because just as 'the brighter the light, the more the owl is blinded, and the more the sun is looked at directly, the more our sight is darkened and stunned,' so 'the divine light of contemplation . . . causes spiritual darkness, for it not only far outstrips the soul, but stuns it and darkens its natural understanding,' which is why Dionysius refers to such contemplation as a 'ray of darkness'.[82] We will return to the mystical connotations of darkness in Chapter Five, since darkness plays an important role in the impact of Zurbarán's work and in 'activating' a devotional and reverential response to its subjects.

Another paradox is expressed in the notion of stillness. Initially, such stillness contrasts with the restlessness that drives our sensory engagement with the world. In the words of the Dominican Henry Suso,

> Letting one's senses wander about far and wide removes a person from inwardness. See to it that you take up no business that carries you outward. When such business is looking for you, do not let it find you. Turn quickly inward to yourself. Natural life manifests itself in movement and the activity of the senses. For anyone forsaking himself and losing himself, supernatural life begins in stillness.[83]

As Juan de la Cruz once more explains, with the move from meditation to contemplation comes a passivity because the soul now 'cannot work or reason on the things of God', God alone now being active. This 'doing nothing' is difficult and counter-intuitive, but the soul must rest in calmness and stillness, 'content simply with a loving and calm attentiveness to God'. Instead of acting, it must wait entirely on God.[84] Teresa describes the effect on the individual of the 'prayer of union', 'the soul almost faints away, breathing and all bodily forces fail so that you can't even

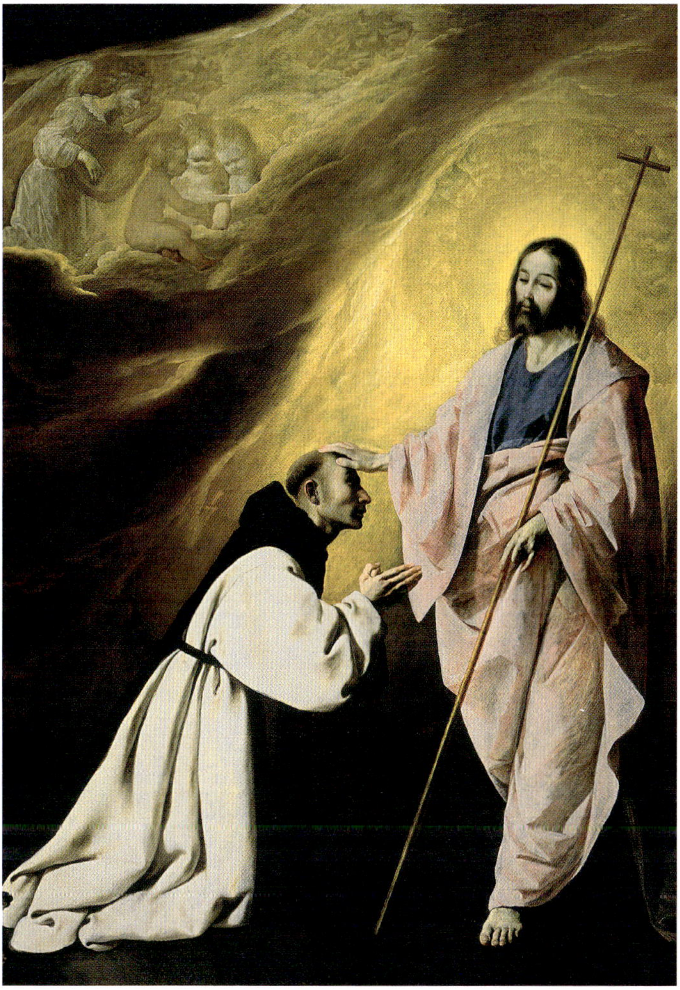

move your hands without great difficulty; your eyes close without you wanting them to, or if they are open, you see hardly anything . . . All external force is lost and the soul's increases to better enjoy its glory.'[85] Stillness may become absolute stasis as the individual reaches mystical union. This state is described by Sigüenza

35 Francisco de Zurbarán, *The Vision of Fray Andrés de Salmerón*, 1639, oil on canvas.

when he treats the mystical experiences of Andrés de Salmerón, whose intimate vision of Christ was depicted by Zurbarán for the sacristy at Guadalupe (illus. 35). Sigüenza discusses his fellow Hieronymite praying for some five hours during which his heart was taken up within God and describes him as 'remaining so fixed and immobile that he seemed like marble' – that is, as essentially an object dead to the world.[86] Such stillnesses Zurbarán makes his own. (Elsewhere, Sigüenza describes Salmerón's enraptured state by saying that he was surrounded by celestial light, his face dazzling with supernatural clarity.[87] This is the light with which Zurbarán consistently surrounds manifestations of the divine.)

In *Christ and the Virgin in the House at Nazareth* (*c.* 1644–5; illus. 36), we can see in play some of the resonances between contemplative states and qualities, and Zurbarán's distinctive style. This was one of the artist's most popular subjects, with three versions by him and numerous copies.[88] Jesus and Mary occupy the same space, but they and everything in it seem alone, literally and figuratively withdrawn into themselves, into the 'inner room of the spirit'.[89] This is more than a world of introversion; it is a world entirely introverted. Silence reigns. Even the two doves, close together as they are, do not engage with each other. The young Jesus contemplates a drop of blood caused by a prick from the crown of thorns that he is making, the *Spinario* a Classical parallel here; the Virgin, head resting pensively on one hand, looks obliquely towards him, lost in tearful premonition; both are aware of what this prefigures: his crucifixion. They are intensely present in the present moment, both emotionally (the Virgin) and corporeally (Jesus's painful finger), but also, obviously, elsewhere in thinking of the future. So, too, is the viewer.

The introspection of the Virgin and Jesus rests upon the duality of present-future. A further duality, temporal-eternal, is occasioned by light, the ordinary Galilean sky visible through the window at right contrasting with the pale golden-orange light infused with cherubs' heads that shines down behind Jesus at left. The scene is thus caught in time while collapsing it; it is not a mystical vision, but as in one, it cojoins antithetical states and realities.

The sense of intense presence comes also from the objects. Whether objects in Zurbarán's still lifes carry symbolic meaning is a critically divisive issue, and suggestions can seem forced. Here, each object has been read symbolically: the white cloth being worked by the Virgin symbolizes work or Christ's shroud; the open book, the word of God; the two closed books, the Old Testament prophecies; the fruit and the open drawer, eternal life; the earthenware bowl, the clay from which humans were created and thus the flesh, its water, purification, baptism or the Virgin's immaculacy; lilies, the Virgin's immaculacy; roses, love, the rosary; and the doves, divine love, the Holy Spirit or the Purification of the Virgin.[90] Whether all these are convincing is less important than that here the work's meditative emphasis prompts such speculation.

The overall effect of Zurbarán's style and composition is, as here, to make all things intensely present, rooted in the here-and-now, and yet to imbue them with a sense of transcendence, in the case of objects, an otherness, in the case of people, an elsewhere.

In discussing Zurbarán's depictions of mystical visions and ecstasy, José María Carrascal Muñoz has suggested, as I cited in Chapter One, that his style 'creates in the viewer an unease, an intellectual tension and . . . a feeling of passivity similar to the psychological effects produced in the person experiencing the vision, albeit to a different degree' and the viewer thereby becomes a 'co-participant in the sensations shown'.[91] Be this as it may, I would certainly suggest that a core factor in his appeal, particularly to religious orders, was the fact that there were affinities between

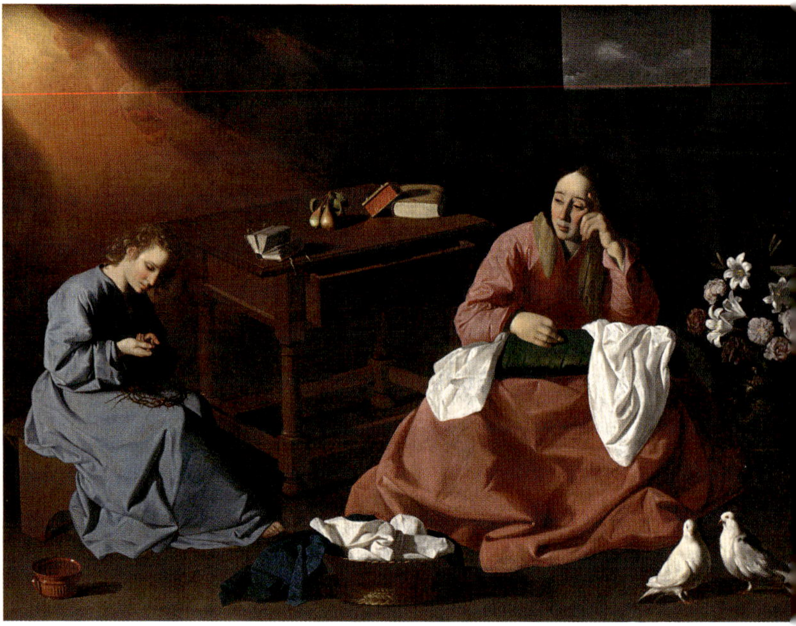

defining aspects of his style and the mystical literature so widely read at the time. His unique stylistic characteristics and quirks, and even, paradoxically, his relative inability to convey figures interacting or inhabiting space collectively, mean that his style was singularly able to convey the mystical yearnings that defined Spanish culture, not least, though by no means only, in his works addressed to religious orders. While contemporaries knew that the ineffable could not be depicted, what they found in Zurbarán was that the qualities and the conditions of its experience could be, and often sublimely so.

IF THE 1640S WERE a challenging decade for Spain, for Seville they closed with an outbreak of the plague in April 1649 that spelt the definitive end of a century-and-a-half of glory.

36 Francisco de Zurbarán, *Christ and the Virgin in the House at Nazareth*, *c.* 1644–5, oil on canvas.

Immediately following major flooding, it killed 46 per cent of the population, some 60,000 people.[92] A contemporary chronicler notes the human means that were diligently employed to deal with the plague, but says people preferred divine ones 'to beg for mercy and appease divine justice': prayer, penance, 'processions of candles and blood', all entreating God, the Virgin and the saints.[93] But the plague relentlessly laid waste whole districts and desolated communities; the prestigious Dominican monastery of San Pablo el Real, for example, for which Zurbarán had painted one of the works that made his name, his *Crucifixion*, had two hundred friars at the start of the century and saw 95 die in the plague.[94] And Zurbarán's family was affected too, his artist son, Juan de Zurbarán, dying in June, almost certainly of the plague.

We know virtually nothing about Zurbarán's own religious life; however, one of the few things we do know is that in the wake of the devastating social, economic and psychological impact of the plague, he joined one of the city's charitable brotherhoods. The Hermandad de la Santa Caridad (Brotherhood of Holy Charity) was a religious organization devoted to helping the poor, and Zurbarán was enrolled in his absence in January 1652 at a time when it was undergoing an initial expansion following the 1649 plague. The brotherhood would dramatically expand further after Miguel de Mañara became head in 1663.[95] Under him, the brotherhood's newly built church was lavishly decorated and is now one of the iconic monuments to the Sevillian Baroque. Its decorative programme included paintings by Murillo that illustrated the acts of charity to which the brotherhood was committed; striking works by Juan de Valdés Leal that forcibly remind the viewer in macabre detail of the omnipresence of death and of the bodily dissolution and eternal judgement that will follow; and a gilded *retablo* with sculptures by Pedro Roldán, polychromed by Valdés Leal, that depicts the burial of Christ, burying the destitute being the brotherhood's foundational act of charity.[96]

There is no reason to doubt charitable and religious motives for Zurbarán joining the brotherhood, and he presumably engaged in its charitable deeds. Indeed, shortly after joining, he is recorded as forming part of its Palm Sunday procession on 24 March 1652. But being a member was increasingly a marker of social prestige. It was also a useful form of social networking at a time when Seville's art market had been hit by the plague and large, multi-work commissions had dried up for him. As his clientele changed to include more lay patrons so works of more intimate and affecting subjects – such as the Virgin as a Child, the Virgin and the Infant Jesus, the Holy Family – came to the fore, and with this a more affecting style, a slightly softer tone as spiritual needs and thus expressions also changed. The world of personal piety increasingly became the focus of his art, as of a plague-devastated Seville.

FIVE

Saints and Martyrs

Feted since Zurbarán's rediscovery in the nineteenth century, his stand-alone figures of friars, monks and saints constitute his most distinctive contribution to European art. The figures that are the focus of this chapter – female saints and Francis of Assisi – were also among his most popular in the seventeenth century. Through a consideration of these I want to examine three distinct aspects of Zurbarán's art and career. I will start by considering his marked preference for very dark backgrounds, which has a clear compositional function. But darkness also has important contemplative meaning lost to modern viewers. While dark, sometimes almost black settings define Zurbarán's oeuvre, so does his incredible and distinctive use of colour, seen not least in the elaborate fabrics in which he clothes his female saints. The chromatic contrasts within his clothing are unusual and striking, but always harmoniously balanced. Zurbarán is not simply an artist remarkable for his portrayals of white fabric as Palomino had noted at the start of the eighteenth century, rich in its variations of cream, alabaster and ivory, lily or porcelain white, but an artist with an incredible eye for colour and for colour combinations. Living as we do in a world saturated with colour, a work such as *St Dominic in Soriano* (*c.* 1626–7) inadvertently reminds us of the more achromatic world of Zurbarán's patrons and viewers with its contrast between the black and white Dominican habits and the elegant

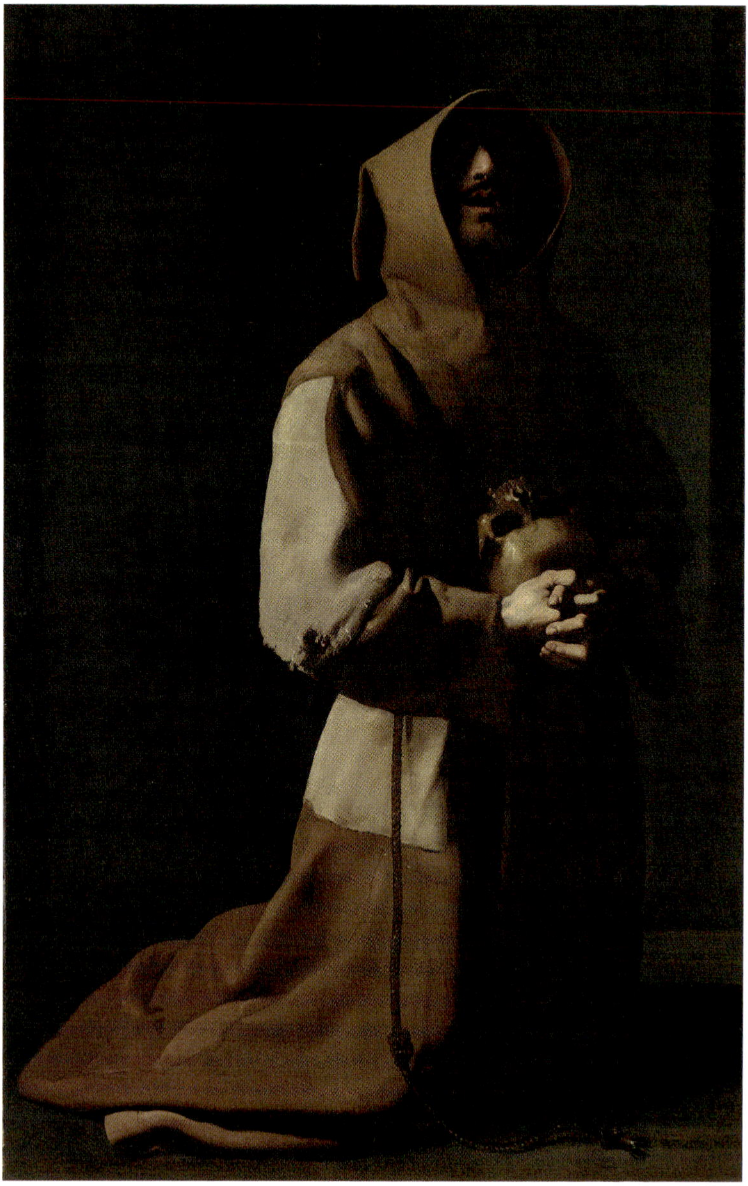

37 Francisco de Zurbarán, *St Francis*, *c.* 1640–45, oil on canvas.

colours worn by the Virgin, the Magdalene and St Catherine. Such colours, vestments aside, would not form the basis of clothing for any other than the elite, and even among them, men's clothing was overwhelmingly an intense 'Habsburg black'. Zurbarán's painting of fabric is the second major focus of the chapter, both its appearance and its spiritual eloquence, for, as can be seen in accounts of court events that describe in precise detail the clothing worn by royal and noble participants, clothing, like darkness, communicates. Zurbarán's female saints were popular subjects in the New World, and Zurbarán's engagement with such trade is my third focus. The role of his workshop was vital here as he sought through participation in transatlantic trade to diversify sources of income at an increasingly challenging time for him in the 1640s. But, as we shall see, this market was not without its own risks and uncertainties.

EFFECTS OF DARKNESS

Until the dispersal of art following the French invasion of Spain during the Peninsular War that saw Napoleon's commander, Marshall Soult, plunder paintings from Sevillian churches and monasteries and send them to Paris, and, subsequently, the Spanish government's closure of many monasteries in 1835 and its appropriation and sale of their land and contents, little was known of Spanish painting outside Spain itself. Zurbarán was one of the greatest discoveries, and the display of his work in Louis-Philippe's Galerie Espagnole in the Louvre between 1838 and 1849 had a tremendous impact, especially the work now in the National Gallery, London, and called there *St Francis in Meditation* (*c.* 1640–45; illus. 37), which seemed a summation of 'Spanishness'.[1] Zurbarán shows the saint kneeling in an empty, darkened space, his clasped hands holding a skull against his body, his face deeply shadowed by the cowl over his head, but his mouth open and eyes raised heavenwards. Writing at the time, Théophile Gautier highlighted the painting's 'sinister poetry of renouncement, mortification, and nothingness, which no one had understood to a greater degree than [had Zurbarán]',[2] and twenty years after the Galerie's own closure and dispersal, an art historian commented that on seeing it in the Louvre 'there was among the masses a reaction of stupefaction and almost terror . . . Not only the Spanish School, but one might say all of Spain, was summarized in this passionate painting, at once devout and somber, mystical and brutal.'[3]

St Francis was one of the most popular saints, and it is therefore unsurprising that he was one of Zurbarán's most frequent subjects, one that he painted throughout his career. The 'iconic' images are those like the work that astonished the nineteenth-century French public. That is to say, the saint alone, against a very dark background, standardly in meditation or contemplation.

A variant subject is the miracle witnessed in 1449 by Pope Nicholas V when he apparently saw Francis's body in his tomb, standing perfectly upright, uncorrupted, eyes open, 'as if he were alive'.[4] This was a popular subject in seventeenth-century Spain.[5] There are several paintings by Zurbarán that depict just the upright body in the dark tomb, the one now in Lyon being illustrated here (illus. 38).[6] The niche in which the dead saint stands is just discernible and his body casts a slight shadow, placing the viewer thereby in the position of the pope and his party with their torch as they discover the body.[7] Across all the numerous depictions of Francis by Zurbarán, the saint's rough and standardly patched habit is tangibly present, its form varying according to the Franciscans that it was created for (for example, Observants, Capuchins, Descalzos/Alcantarinos).

Although in the 1650s Zurbarán painted a couple of works in which St Francis is shown alone in a lighter setting or against a daylight landscape, what I want to consider here are the effects of dark backgrounds as used in the most dramatically impactful images of Francis, some representing the location where Pope Nicholas saw him, others an entirely empty interior (the National Gallery work already described) or a cave (the National Gallery's 1639 *St Francis* in which a minimally delineated cave opens onto a distant, dusky landscape). The extremely dark background is common to his depictions of female saints, where space may be minimally signalled by the barely visible join of floor to wall or by the vaguest suggestion of light indicated by the background being slightly less dark on one side of the composition than the other or by faint shadows, as well as to his images of Mercedarians from the start of his career and his still lifes, as we have seen. Although he begins in the late 1630s to lighten his backgrounds and depict figures in a landscape, as discussed in Chapter Three, even occasionally against a totally light but non-defined background (*St Diego of Alcalá*, *c*. 1658–60; see illus. 21), the dark, often non-spatially defined background is one that he will continue to use in devotional images until the end of his career.[8]

Extremely dark settings may be justified by the subject – St Francis in his tomb, the darkness that fell when Christ was on the cross – but whether setting or simple background, extreme darkness has a primary compositional function: it focuses the viewer's attention, brings the subject forward, almost throwing it into relief. Such backgrounds were used in classic *Andachtsbilder* (devotional images) such as the *Mater Dolorosa* and *Ecce Homo* by Titian or Luis de Morales, and the tenebrism of Caravaggio was a significant impetus behind their use in the seventeenth century. (Here, it is interesting to recall that Palomino asserts that Zurbarán initially trained with a 'disciple of Morales'.[9]) Darkness was often recommended for meditation, for similar reasons of focusing the mind by removing distractions. In the *Spiritual Exercises*, for example, Ignatius of Loyola writes that the exercitant should 'deprive themselves of all light, thus closing windows and doors . . . except while saying Divine Office, reading and eating'.[10] If we imagine

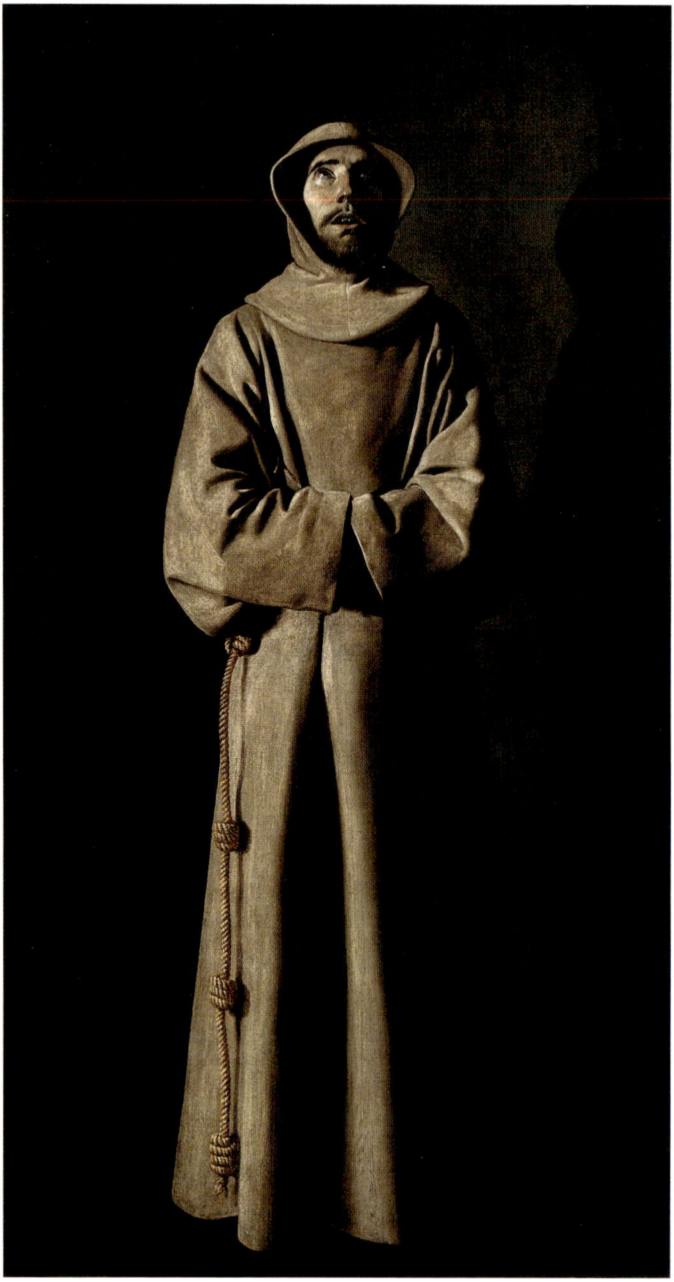

38 Francisco de Zurbarán, *St Francis According to the Vision of Pope Nicholas V*, *c*. 1640–45, oil on canvas.

that the space occupied by St Francis in the circa 1640–45 National Gallery painting is his cell, then the saint has done precisely this.

But tenebrous settings are more than negative space, for darkness was also pregnant with mystical meaning for contemporaries. This can be seen in the image that has come to define the mystical thought of Juan de la Cruz, the 'dark night of the soul'. Darkness had long played a part in Western mystical thought, from the 'ray of the divine shadow' of Pseudo-Dionysius to the anonymous fourteenth-century *Cloud of Unknowing* in which 'a darkness or a cloud' is used to represent the impossibility of understanding or apprehending God and thus to figure an 'absence of knowing', and where alongside the 'cloud of unknowing that is between you and your God' there must be a 'cloud of forgetting beneath you, between you and everything that was ever created'.[11] It is in the writings of the Spanish mystic, however, that night, and thus darkness, reaches its fullest expression.

Juan de la Cruz identifies four 'nights': the active night of the senses and the active night of the spirit, and the passive night of the senses and the passive night of spirit. The active nights are where the soul itself plays an active part, and the passive, where God alone works in the soul.[12] (We have briefly encountered already the passive night of the soul.) What is being described is in effect purgation, and in the passive phase that of the senses is described as 'bitter and terrible', but that of the spirit, that is of understanding, will and memory, is 'beyond compare, horrendous and frightful'.[13] (Wanting to move directly to the conclusion of the traditional three-fold way of purgation-illumination-union was an error of the Sevillian Alumbrados who thereby misread Juan de la Cruz, according to the Augustinian friar who assessed his work at the behest of the Inquisition in 1623.[14])

At one point Juan distinguishes between two phrases, 'noche oscura' (dark night) and 'a oscuras' (in darkness), used in his poem that he is spiritually explicating, the *Noche oscura*:

> The first stanza, talking of the senses, says the soul left on a 'dark night', and here, talking about the spirit, it says it left 'in darkness', for the obscurity of the spirit is greater just as darkness is greater than the night, for however dark the night is, one can still see something, but in darkness, nothing can be seen. So, in the night of the senses there remains some light, because understanding and reason still remain and are not blinded, but this night of the spirit, which is faith, takes away everything, both from the understanding and the senses.[15]

It is only through such darkness that the soul can be illuminated, and the soul can reach union with God, who is described also as a 'dark night to the soul in this life', only through darkness.[16] In making spiritual distinctions between forms of darkness, Juan also reveals that he has an acutely observant eye, writing of gradations of darkness across the night, from very early night, 'when things have just lost their form', to the total darkness in the middle of the night, and then the moment just before actual dawn.[17]

Zurbarán's dark backgrounds exhibit similar gradations, but I am not suggesting these are linked to the four dark nights of the soul. They can, however, convey a core aspect of these. In her discussion of one form of 'supernatural' prayer, so-called since it cannot be reached by one's own efforts, Teresa de Jesús describes this as an 'interior recollection [*recogimiento*] felt in the soul . . . that makes the soul want to close the eyes and not to hear, see, understand anything other than what it's focused on, which is to treat with God all alone'.[18] How to depict such withdrawal? Zurbarán uses darkness to suggest this in the National Gallery *St Francis* (*c.* 1640–45; illus. 37). So, Francis is internally withdrawn and is shown in darkness, which stands in for his non-sensory and non-intellectual engagement with the world, for his having purged his appetite and desire for all things, precisely by making that world momentarily absent, all but a void.[19] There is nothing there, but that nothing is everything because it signals union. Moreover, God's presence in such union casts a shadow over the soul according to Juan de la Cruz, and this has been related to the dark shadow in which Francis's face is so often cast.[20] The work thus shows Francis not in meditation, which he has passed beyond, but in perfect contemplation, Zurbarán depicting figures in contemplation with slightly opened mouth and eyes raised. (As an aside, it says much about Spanish devotional interest and focus that a significant majority of the artist's depictions of Francis, some three-quarters of them, show him simply in meditation or contemplation.)

In his still lifes, whose black backgrounds it is difficult not to see as indebted to those of Sánchez Cotán, the darkness shapes, intentionally or not, the viewer's engagement by subliminally evoking the dark backgrounds used in many small devotional works such as those by Morales.[21] Along with the singular focus on a limited number of objects, this is a part of raising the status of the objects, indeed potentially of 'sacralizing' them, their very arrayment suggesting to some placement on an altar.[22] With all his dark backgrounds the effect is as a sudden vision, Juan de la Cruz saying spiritual visions, that is those not seen with the eyes, are 'seen' not in natural but supernatural light, 'as on a dark night when a flash of lightning suddenly illuminates things and makes them clear and distinct, leaving them subsequently in darkness, though their forms and shapes remain in the mind'.[23] This could almost be a description of the way that Zurbarán's images impress themselves on the mind. As for the female saints, their detachment from the material world is again signalled by their standing in dark, empty space, the world reduced to nothingness, since their withdrawal from it and its values is absolute, for despite the very tangibility of their presence they belong in the purely spiritual

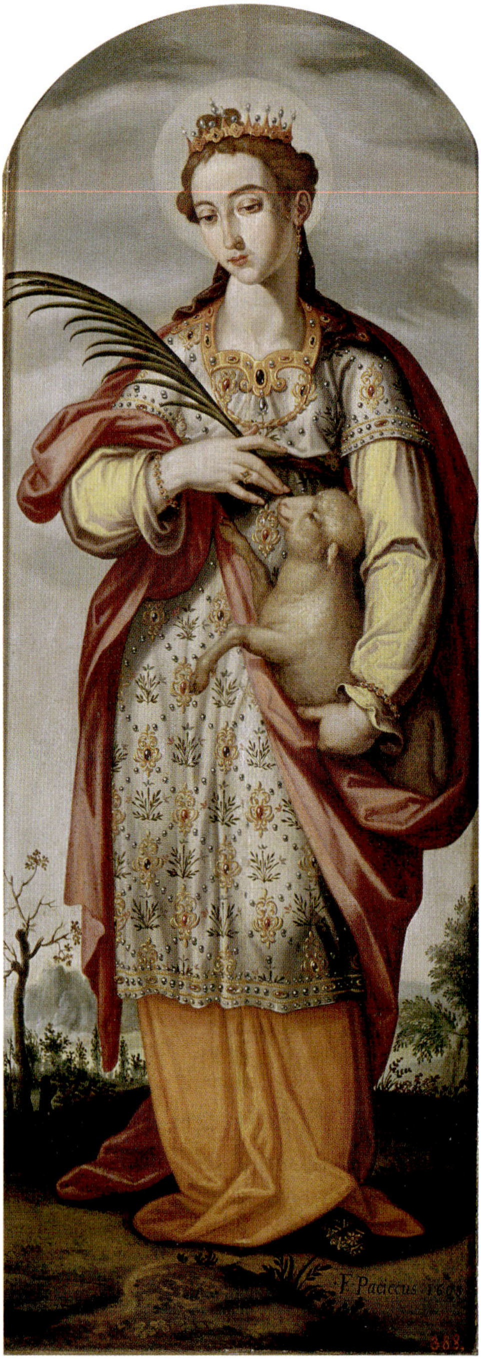
·F· Paciecus

realm of heaven. It is to the seeming tension between the material and the spiritual in these works that I now turn.

THE FABRIC OF FAITH AND THE FABRIC OF THE WORLD

Zurbarán's stand-alone female saints, mainly painted in the 1640s, are shown calm and graceful in dark and empty or undefined space. Most are full length, placed close to the picture plane, face left or right in three-quarter view and look heavenwards or, with a nonchalant and indifferent expression, at the viewer. Their pain and torture are never displayed, but some do hold the instrument of their torture and/or the body part associated with this: a tooth held in pliers (St Apollonia), eyes on a salver (St Lucy), a sword (St Catherine of Alexandria). Francisco Pacheco's *St Agnes* (1608; illus. 39) and *St Catherine* (*c.* 1608), standing frontally in daylight landscapes, offer a local precedent for these stand-alone saints, while a comparison with Guido Reni's *Martyrdom of St Apollonia* (*c.* 1600–603) highlights the distinctiveness of Zurbarán's format. Reni's Apollonia stands, dressed, against a very dark background, liquid eyes raised heavenwards, visible signs of pain eschewed, but her clothing is far less extravagantly lavish than that of Zurbarán's female saints and the composition includes one torturer holding pliers with a tooth, and a second holding pliers near her mouth ready to remove another. Most of the female saints depicted by Zurbarán were deemed virgin martyrs. For the laity these were often popular intercessors, their virginity less 'an example to be followed' than 'the source of their special intercessory relationship with Christ', a 'symbol of sacred power, a concrete realization within this world of the divine spirit'.[24]

In Spanish art the non-representation for reasons of pictorial decorum of the torture of female martyrs, or its visual down-playing, was standard and is in marked contrast to the way that

39 Francisco Pacheco, *St Agnes*, 1608, oil on wood.

male martyrs were usually depicted. José de Ribera, for example, spares nothing in his graphic images of torture, his *Martyrdom of St Bartholomew* (1644) showing the saint, who was flayed alive, being tied up while the skin is stripped from his arm. But even in his depictions of male martyrs, Zurbarán avoids any sign of bodily torment. The Carthusian John Houghton, for example, who was hanged, drawn and quartered in the reign of Henry VIII, is simply shown by Zurbarán in his immaculate white habit, rope round his neck and holding his heart that was removed while he was alive (illus. 40).[25] Instead of agonized suffering, what we see are the clothed bodies of the saints. In the case of his female martyrs, they are attired in astonishingly elaborate clothes whose beautiful and carefully rendered materials and interplays of colours create images of absolute harmony. These stand in stark contrast to the plain habits worn by male martyrs such as Houghton or the Mercedarian Serapion (see illus. 9) that identify them as members of specific orders.

St Agatha (*c*. 1635–40; illus. 41), *St Rufina* (*c*. 1645–50; illus. 42) and *St Margaret of Antioch* (*c*. 1645–50; illus. 43) are perfect examples of Zurbarán's art. In presenting each I want to highlight particularly their clothing, the import of which I will then consider across the series. I will also highlight the gulf between the saints as depicted and the martyrdoms as described. That gulf would be meditatively bridged by a viewer who, recognizing the saint, would be as aware of what is not depicted as of what is, for each painting is an interplay between horrific absences and harmonious presences.

Agatha was a third-century Christian from Sicily, martyred for refusing to renounce her faith and accept the advances of a Roman magistrate. She was stripped, hung by her arms, her body 'wounded with iron rods, torn with hooks and steel barbs' and her breasts cut off.[26] St Peter appeared in her cell and restored her breasts, so she was thrown on coals; returned to prison, she

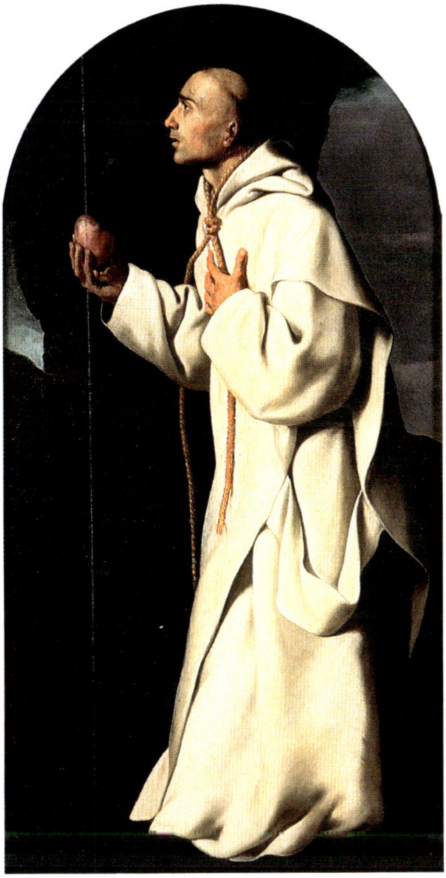

died.[27] In the Spanish hagiography I have quoted, her violent mastectomy is linked with what the Spouse says of his beloved in the Song of Songs, 'Our sister is little, and hath no breasts,'[28] while in another, her fortitude and welcoming of suffering is evident in her declaration, 'Torture, burn, tie up, crush, flay, break, wound, pull apart, drown, dislocate and kill my body, for the crueller you are, the greater good you will do me, the more I will be favoured by my sweet spouse, Jesus Christ.'[29] She is described

40 Francisco de Zurbarán, *Blessed John Houghton*, c. 1638–9, oil on wood.

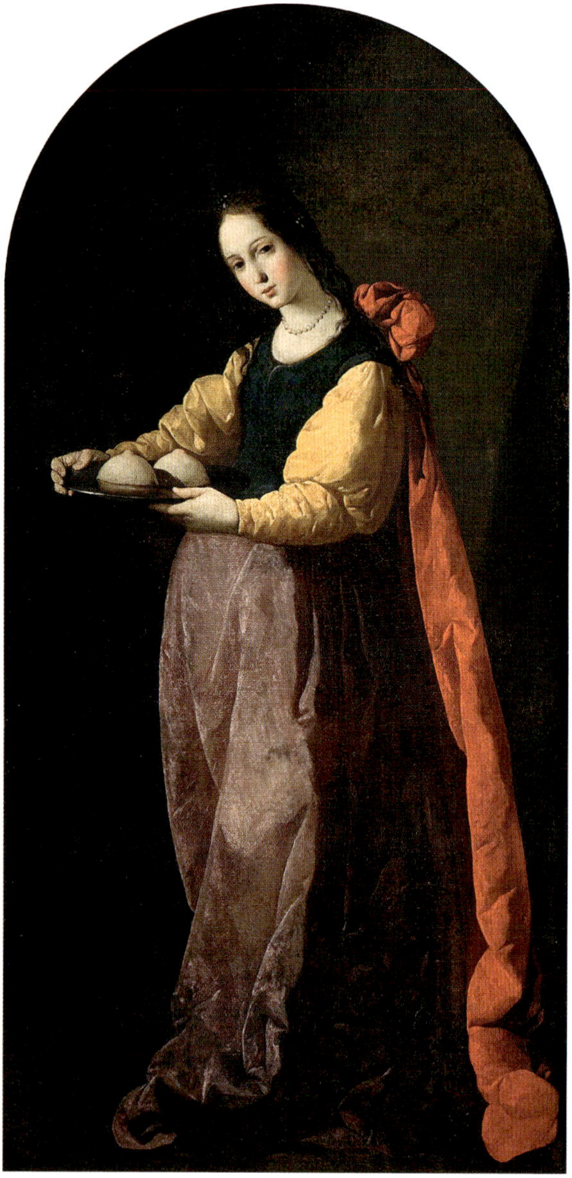

41 Francisco de Zurbarán, *St Agatha*, *c.* 1635–40, oil on canvas.

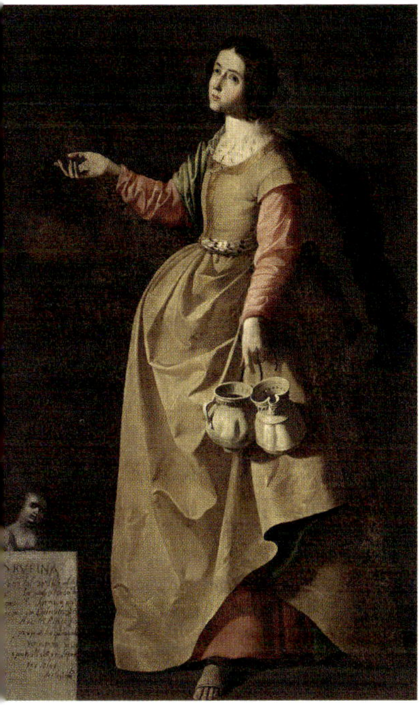

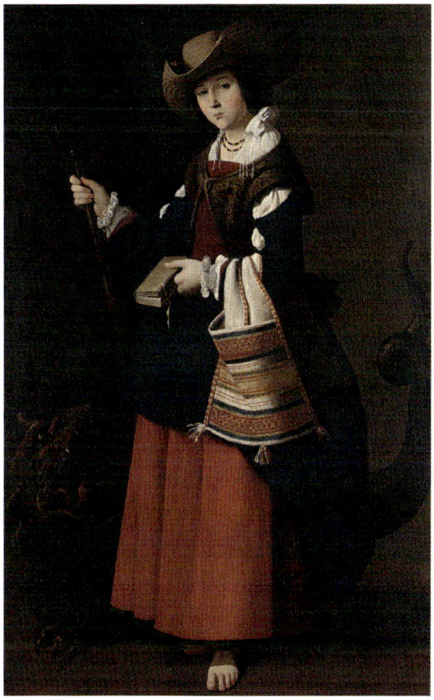

as 'endowed with four things that are greatly esteemed in women: she was extremely noble, rich, beautiful and virtuous,' and this is how Zurbarán depicts her.[30] She holds a silver dish on which her breasts are placed. Her clothes have that heaviness in their draping that typifies Zurbarán, here in the plum-coloured skirt that gathers on the floor and the chrome-red mantle that falls from its bunched knot at her back. She wears a deep blue bodice and yolk-yellow sleeves, the left especially with zig-zagging folds. Her head is tilted slightly downward but turned to look at the viewer with a calm, almost inquisitive expression that individualizes her.

Rufina was the object of more localized devotion. She and her sister Justa were from Seville and were martyred in the third century; the two were so closely linked that there must have

42 Francisco de Zurbarán, *St Rufina*, c. 1645–50, oil on canvas.
43 Francisco de Zurbarán, *St Margaret of Antioch*, c. 1645–50, oil on canvas.

been a companion piece depicting Justa. The sisters were patron saints of the city, interceding to save it from plague (1568), drought (1571) and floods (1626).[31] They were pottery sellers, and this further linked them with Seville whose potteries were a key industry. That the saint holds two earthenware pitchers identifies her as one of the sisters, the largely illegible inscription at bottom left specifying Rufina. (This inscribed panel is unique in the series of female saints.) The sisters are linked by one hagiographer to St Paul's comment that our souls are placed in 'earthen vessels', our fragile bodies, which then connects to their martyrdom.[32] They refused to give anything for a festival of Venus, so an enraged crowd smashed their pots; imprisoned for then destroying the goddess' image, their bodies were torn with iron hooks. Justa eventually died from hunger and the effects of torture, Rufina was thrown to a lion that refused to harm her, so her head was crushed.[33] Zurbarán shows Rufina gazing heavenwards, her right arm held out in an elegant gesture. She wears an ochre skirt and bodice and salmon-pink sleeves and petticoat. The skirt is hitched up beneath her hand holding the pitchers, revealing its pale-green lining and her petticoat, and a pale-green shawl winds round one shoulder to float out and downwards in the shadow behind her. Folds as ever bring the skirt to life, four ripple out in ever larger curves from below the waist, one descends in a curving zig-zag from the fabric hitched up behind her hand, and one leads in a straight diagonal from there to her open-toed shoe.

Zurbarán's painting of material reaches a high point with *St Margaret*. If Agatha was a noble, Rufina a working woman, Margaret, another third-century saint, was both. The daughter of a pagan priest, she became a shepherdess after her father disowned her for being a Christian.[34] Arrested by the Roman governor, she refused to sacrifice to the gods, and so was whipped, her limbs disjointed, her flesh torn open. She was returned to jail, where the Devil appeared as a dragon but disappeared when she made the sign of the cross. (Uniquely, Zurbarán shows her not alone but with the dragon crouched behind her.) She was then burnt and thrown into water to drown, but died only when her throat was cut.[35] Margaret is dressed in rustic clothing: a straw hat, sheepskin jerkin, a burgundy bodice, a white chemise, a woven saddlebag over her arm, deep blue sleeves and a deep blue skirt folded up at the front to reveal a red petticoat with dark green hem, these two not reaching the ground and lacking the volume of material making them atypical of Zurbarán's skirts. The elegance of her pristine clothes is matched by her cool, distanced look at the viewer. But as so often with Zurbarán, it is the small details that stand out and make the fabrics and materials sing: the narrow, white cords hanging from her chemise's collar, each with a tiny knot and frayed threads at its end; the coloured strands of red, white and yellow, tassel-like at the bottom of the saddlebag; the roughness of the woollen texture of the saddlebag's coloured patterns; the knots of wool on the fleece. This is Zurbarán at his very finest, reproducing the surface appearance of things in all their singularity.

The whole series of such paintings prompt various questions. One is whether some are 'portraits *a lo divino*'; that is, commissioned portraits of individuals posing as saints.[36] The Habsburgs certainly had themselves inserted into Biblical scenes not as donors but as participants, even on occasion as the central figures, as in Juan Pantoja de la Cruz's *Annunciation* (*c.* 1604) in which the Virgin has the appearance of Margarita of Austria, wife of Philip III, and Gabriel that of their daughter Ana, and a recent suggestion is that Zurbarán's *St Isabel of Portugal* (*c.* 1635) in the Prado might be an *a lo divino* portrait of Isabel of Bourbon, wife of Philip IV.[37] Other courts did likewise.[38] And the practice was not just the preserve of royalty and rulers, as evidenced in Michaelina Wautier's *Two Girls as St Agnes and St Dorothy*. This might be viewed as evidencing unacceptable spiritual pride, but it has recently been suggested that the meditative purpose of such images was to force the individual depicted 'to debase themselves when they saw themselves so clearly elevated: in sum, to *efface* themselves' in a process of 'meditative unmaking'.[39] In support of the argument that some of Zurbarán's female saints are *a lo divino* portraits is the fact that while the majority have somewhat idealized and generic faces, several seem more individualized, like the two three-quarter-length saints in Bilbao (both *c.* 1640), Catherine and, following the museum's identification, Elizabeth of Thuringia (illus. 44), who are also shown as girls rather than young women as standard. The issue rests on the perceived 'individuality' exhibited in the face. The majority of Zurbarán's saints, however, were likely painted to hang in a church, *St Apollonia* and *St Lucy* (both *c.* 1636–40), for example, almost definitely for the main *retablo* of the church of San José of the Discalced Mercedarian monastery in Seville.

Standing in front of these paintings one often feels less the presence of a person and more that of the fabrics clothing them. If evidence of *a lo divino* portraiture rests on the perceived individuality of appearance, the individuality of the saints' clothing raises a further question: are these saints dressed in seventeenth-century fashion? They are certainly dressed in ways not seen in contemporary portraiture. Consequently, one suggestion is the costumes are inspired by those worn in saint plays or Corpus Christi processions. (Some view the saints as walking or processing, though even in those that might be viewed as such no movement is shown and any processing seems halted, as in the Prado's *Isabel of Portugal* displaying the miraculous flowers in her gathered skirt.[40]) In terms of their clothing, fashion historians suggest this is made up of existing items of dress, but in styles that are part contemporary, part invented and part based on sixteenth-century fashion.[41] Pulling against the naturalism attributed to him, Zurbarán has thus fashioned imagined couture.[42] This imagined couture establishes a dissonance between the familiar and the unfamiliar,

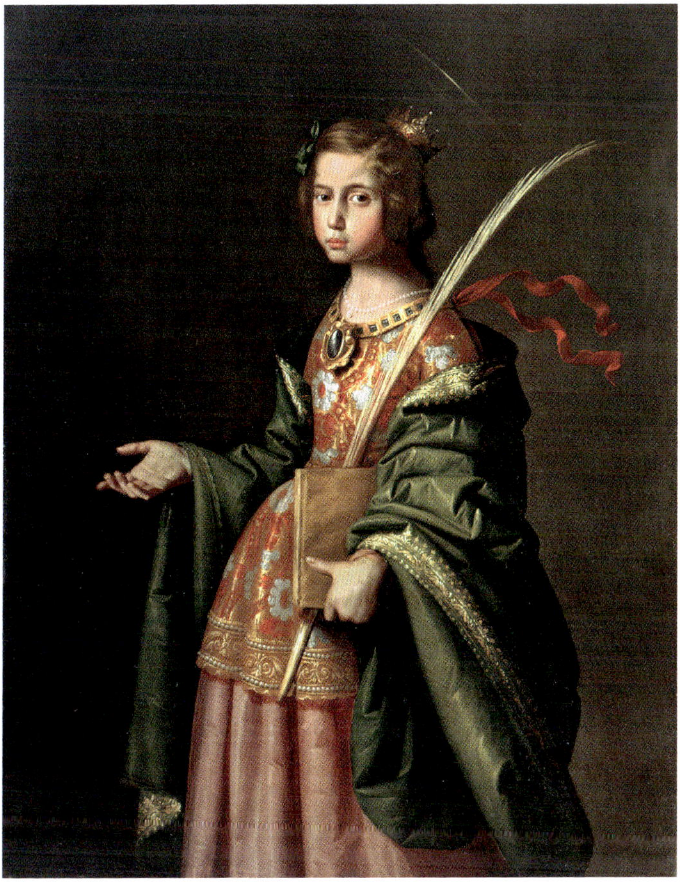

between closeness to the contemporary viewer and distance from them. The saints are like us, not the same as us.

What makes these saints compelling is their grace and quietude. Their clothing is eloquent here, its elegance and beauty, as Julián Gállego observes, a symbol of their inner elegance and beauty.[43] Further, and as I have noted elsewhere, these clothes 'are not the light, streaming and twisting drapery of so many airborne angels and saints in the seventeenth century, and their

44 Francisco de Zurbarán, *St Elizabeth of Thuringia*, *c.* 1640, oil on canvas.

folds are not the agitated folds of Bernini's marble. Their lack of such dynamism conveys serenity, their heaviness gravitas.' Zurbarán thus shows his female saints, and not least the virgin martyrs, 'not as they lived, or died, but rather as manifestations of their virtue'.[44]

The form of this eloquence went entirely against the prevailing conceptualization of reality, for one of the most distinctive aspects of early modern Spanish culture is that its moral, ascetic, religious and literary discourses were to an unusually pronounced degree structured around the play of appearance (*parecer*) and reality (*ser*). It is difficult to overstate the central importance of these terms to Spaniards' understanding of the world and to their epistemological, moral and salvational engagement with it. Appearance and reality encompassed and were further expressed through other binary opposites such as material/immaterial, falsehood/truth, transience/eternity, earth/heaven. The first term in each binary is the one we mistakenly hold closest according to moralists, but it is the second that we must learn to place first, for the world is nothing but deceptive appearances, its values inverted. For those thinkers inclined to Neostoicism, the majority, deciphering appearances to get at the reality or truth 'beneath' them, to use the spatial metaphor prevalent at the time, was an arduous, constant and urgent process because without this we will be misled by the lures of the world, valuing the transient over the eternal and thereby imperilling salvation. For the sceptically inclined it was impossible to decipher when appearances were deceptive and when they were not, since there was no way of knowing whether the information received through our senses was true or not. To all intents and purposes, we can never knowingly grasp reality, *ser*. The only way out of this sceptical impasse was fideism.[45]

The clothing that the saints wear is eye-catching. In the secular world such finery might be condemned by moralists as vanity, and there were those who strongly opposed attiring female saints in extravagant, worldly fashions and bedecking them in jewels and trinkets, arguing that to depict them so profanely was to martyr them twice.[46] But the fabrics' grace, beauty, heavy stillness and monumentality here express the qualities of the saints that they enfold. Zurbarán's fabrics thus effect a reversal of the dominant cultural norm: the outer perfectly expresses and conforms with the inner. Beauty, virtue and nobility were frequently linked in Golden Age fiction, but Zurbarán effects a more radical manoeuvre, for he mesmerizingly conjures up before us the tactility, vibrancy, colour and beauty of the fabrics; that is, the sheer materiality of the transient, to assert through them the opposite, the spiritual and the eternal. Appearance and reality are not pitted against one another here, but entirely collapsed into one another.

The fabrics and clothing return us to the distinctive presence of objects in Zurbarán. The suggestion that he sacralizes objects is appealing,[47] but I would suggest that what he primarily does is simply let them *be* in all their singularity. Things may be enticing, they may be deceiving, the moral value we attach to them wrong. Such was the stance of moral and ascetic thought at the time. But typically, in Zurbarán, they are simply present and, as we have seen, almost vibrate with the spiritual qualities that his society, not least his clients from religious orders, valued. Indeed, the inanimate and the man-made can be the most visually arresting, because most visually present things in his work, constituting after all a significant part of the visual field. That the man-made is included here, such things as vessels, books and, not least, actual fabric, is what distinguishes this from a purely Neoplatonic stance of seeing the traces of the divine in creation, of 'reading' God in the 'book of creation', a stance that might, of course, be part of a contemporary viewer's engagement with Zurbarán's works, co-existing as it did with the more prevalent idea of the vanity of earthly things.[48] But beautiful as the inanimate and the man-made might be, it is their presence that impresses, in all senses. What makes them so present is not simply their tangibility but the powerful sense that they have been *seen*.[49] Here it is not the artist's hand that we are aware of, as with Velázquez, whose visible facture evokes his brush conjuring up illusions in pigment, but rather the artist's eye.

There are many ways that one might describe the effect of Zurbarán's treatment of matter, of what I am describing as the 'fabric of the world'. One of these is Jane Bennett's concept of 'vibrant matter'. Looking at randomly accumulated objects in a street (a glove, pollen, a dead rat, a bottle cap and a stick), Bennett sees them as

> stuff that commanded attention in its own right, as existents in excess of their association with human meanings, habits, or projects . . . I caught a glimpse of an energetic vitality inside each of these things, things that I generally conceived as inert. In this assemblage, *objects* appeared as *things*, that is, as vivid entities not entirely reducible to the contexts in which (human) subjects set them, never entirely exhausted by their semiotics.[50]

Zurbarán gives us just such a glimpse of the inert. Each thing is of course an 'agent' in a composition; what distinguishes Zurbarán's things is that they are also emphatically and thereby magnetically existent in their own right. To put this in Golden Age terms, though nobody then would have done so, inanimate things in his work often seem as if ensouled.

ZURBARÁN AND TRANSATLANTIC TRADE

Depictions of such female saints were not simply popular in Seville, they were the most popular religious subject in the art trade between the city and the New World.[51] In a 1647 contract between Zurbarán and Juan de Valverde, a captain acting on behalf of the abbess of the Convento de la Encarnación in Lima, Zurbarán agreed to produce 36 works for the convent's church.[52] These included 24 full-length saints: Agatha, Agnes, Anastasia, Apollonia, Barbara, Basilia, Casilda, Catherine, Cecilia, Christina, Clare, Dorothy, Engracia, Eulalia, Gertrude, Helena, Leocadia, Lucy, Margaret, Marina, Martha, Prisca, Sabina and Victoria. A further saint, this time not depicted alone, was *St Ursula and the Eleven Thousand Virgins*. The remaining works were Marian in focus, Marian works being the fourth most popular religious subject in the transatlantic art trade after virgin saints, angels and Old Testament patriarchs (the sons of Jacob).[53]

Both painting and sculpture were exported. Two fleets a year sailed from Seville, one to Veracruz, the other to Nombre de Dios or Portobelo, the port from where Peruvian silver was sent to Spain and where a fair to sell goods was held when the fleet arrived.[54] Zurbarán's work for Spanish America included both commissions and paintings for sale on the open market. He is recorded as engaged in this market from the second half of the 1630s, giving canvases in April 1636 to Diego de Mirafuentes for sale in Portobelo, and he may have started earlier. His participation increased in the following decade, presumably in response to the contraction of commissions at home.

Transatlantic trade was obviously not risk free. Ships might be lost at sea or captured. Zurbarán's series *Jacob and His Twelve Sons* (*c.* 1640–45), twelve of which are in Auckland Castle and the thirteenth in Grimsthorpe Castle, were most likely intended for the Americas and may not have reached there due to one such maritime disaster.[55] If disaster struck on the return journey, money earned from sales would be lost, as it would be if the Crown, ever desperate for money, seized merchants' incoming silver.[56] Payment itself might be extremely delayed. Thus we find Zurbarán in September 1660 handing over authority to recover the proceeds of a consignment received in Buenos Aires in February 1649. This consignment is interesting for what it shows us of Zurbarán's activities as a trader, for alongside fifteen virgin martyrs, fifteen monarchs and illustrious men and twenty-four saints and patriarchs, Zurbarán had sent nine 'Flemish landscapes'. These are presumably not works by Zurbarán 'in the style of' Flemish landscapes, although his skill here is evident in his landscape settings, but rather evidence that he was trading others' work. Also of note is that the consignment included for sale large and small brushes and various pigments – *anílte* (likely *añil*, indigo), *azul* (azurite), *genolí* (lead-tin yellow), *azul verde* (synonym for *azul de costras*, copper blue) and *bermellón* (vermilion).[57]

The format and difficulties of such trade emerge from the lawsuit that Zurbarán brought in March 1640 against Mirafuentes, the captain to whom he had consigned works in 1636 for sale in Portobelo. Mirafuentes was to sell the works in Portobelo keeping in mind the prices set down for him in instructions by Zurbarán. If he could not sell for a fair price, he was to hand the works to Antonio de Velasco who would take them for sale in Lima. Clearly Mirafuentes could not sell them in Portobelo, but when Velasco returned to Seville he told Zurbarán that although he had asked for the paintings, Mirafuentes had entrusted them to another to take to Lima. The paintings reached Lima, but damaged, and Zurbarán sought to argue that this was due to the negligence of the person who took them to Lima, though Diego Muñoz Naranjo, one of the artists testifying for Zurbarán, said he had heard that damage was also caused by Mirafuentes hanging the paintings for a *fiesta* during the transatlantic crossing. Mirafuentes, in turn, said the crates reached Lima undamaged, but the paintings emerged damaged due to the sea climate affecting them during the journey from Portobelo. The pair eventually reached agreement to cease the process.[58]

Serial subjects for export were clearly popular, and to those already mentioned by Zurbarán can be added his 'twelve Roman Caesars on horseback'.[59] Among these subjects, the Patriarchs were uniquely popular in Spanish America. This was probably due to a widespread belief that the indigenous people of the continent were descendants of the Lost Tribes of Israel.[60] Some series were numerically defined (the twelve sons of Jacob, the twelve Caesars), others open-ended in number (the virgin martyrs), and an obvious question is how they were bought on the open market, individually, or as a set to 'instantly' decorate a church, monastery or dwelling.

Artists painting affordable works, often for the New World market, were called 'pintores de feria', and from Palomino's comments about Murillo's supposed engagement with this market at the start of his career, one can infer that they needed less training and ability to operate successfully within it.[61] Zurbarán does not fall into this category. His workshop would be central to his export work, painting to his designs and with his oversight, and several painters from it – namely, José Durán, Alonso de Flores, Muñoz Naranjo and Ignacio de Ríes – were among those who testified for him in his lawsuit against Mirafuentes.[62] This said, he certainly had a major part in the execution of *Jacob and His Twelve Sons*.[63] Whether this was a transatlantic commission is not known; if it was, it might suggest that he was more directly involved with work commissioned as opposed to that sent for sale. Regardless, Zurbarán's work for Spanish America made an impact, and a 'Zurbaranesque style' is discernible in Spanish colonial art, his female saints and his angels being especially influential.[64] Such influence was often thematic rather than stylistic, and due to his workshop rather than works by his hand;

Zurbarán was not the only source of the 'Zurbaranesque'.[65] His workshop, or followers, also produced series for Spanish clients, as with the female saints for the Hospital de las Cinco Llagas, eight of which are now in the Museo de Bellas Artes in Seville.[66] The quality varies, but a comparison of *St Marina* from this series with the comparably attired *St Margaret* from the National Gallery is revealing. Both carry a saddlebag, for example, but Marina's lacks the carefully textured tangibility of Margaret's, and its woven detail is only fully depicted in its middle section as this curves outwards and catches the light.[67]

When contemplating one of Zurbarán's intensely spiritual works it is easy to forget that his workshop was a commercial enterprise. The vicissitudes of New World trade, and indeed his very engagement with this market, are a sharp reminder that for all the focus of his art on the divine and the spiritual, he was an artist who need to sell in order to live.

SIX

The Immaculate Conception and Seville

On 29 June 1615 an enormous procession of more than 20,000 people took to the streets of Seville to demonstrate support for the Immaculate Conception. Made up of clergy, members of religious orders, titled nobles, the general population, adults and children, they sang a lyric that encapsulated the essence of the belief:

Todo el mundo en general
a voces, Reina escogida,
diga que sois concebida
sin pecado original.

Let the whole world
say aloud, chosen Queen,
that you are conceived
without original sin.

The poem was written by Miguel Cid and set to music by Bernardo de Toro, and Mateo Vázquez de Leca paid for 4,000 sheets to be printed; these were circulated in early 1615, especially among children.[1] The event was 'recorded' in a 1616 painting by Juan de Roelas (illus. 45), which was in the possession of Philip III shortly after its completion.[2] Roelas gives details of the event in a lengthy inscription, bottom left of the canvas. Several things

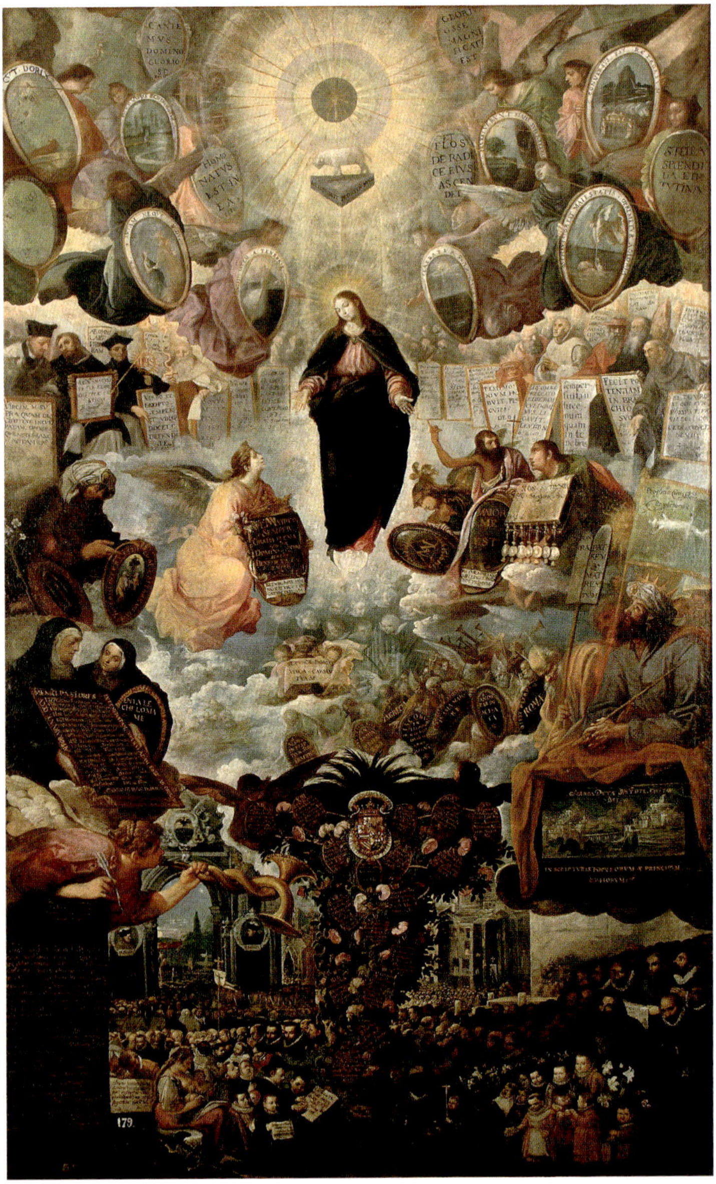

45 Juan de Roelas, *Allegory of the Immaculate Conception*, 1616, oil on canvas.

stand out in the painting. First, the crowded streets in which we see all segments of Golden Age society. Although portrayed as overwhelmingly white, there are several members of Seville's large black community, including a Mercedarian friar. On the sheet held by a kneeling boy are the opening words of Cid's Immaculist poem, and close by him is a nursing mother whose baby, rather than feed, gazes up at the Virgin as the Immaculate Conception in the heavens. Second, and most obviously, the crowded heavens full of saints and theologians who, over the centuries, had supported the idea of the Immaculate Conception and who here, along with angels, carry banners with inscriptions, quotations or emblems concerning the belief.[3] And third, at the top of the palm tree at centre that is intertwined with roses, one of the most Marian flowers, and that has at its base the emblem of the Franciscans, vociferous supporters of the immaculacy of the Virgin, is prominently displayed the coat of arms of Philip III, the reigning monarch. This in part recognizes Spanish Habsburg devotion to the Immaculate Conception. But it is also part of a broader act of persuasion to have Philip III petition Rome hard to have the belief declared a dogma, one of the painting's testamentary purposes to highlight the depth of popular devotion to the Immaculate Conception.[4] The breadth of that support is outlined in the printed version of a sermon preached in Seville in May 1615,

> [the Immaculate Conception] is the subject of innumerable sermons in churches, the common topic in public squares, the main study of the learned; I see it written in school children's notebooks, in ladies' needlework, in nuns' breviaries, and on the walls in the street; indeed, it's written in the very air because the faithful declare it out loud.[5]

Whether this devotion was driven top-down or bottom-up has been debated, but the strategy evident in sermon and painting is to suggest that it is not a question of either/or, but of both/and.[6]

Marian devotion was an integral part of the *pietas austriaca*; that is, of the self-belief and self-presentation of Spanish and Austrian Habsburgs that their piety was exemplary and that God had rewarded this with a global empire.[7] An increasing part of this in the seventeenth century was belief in and advocacy for the Immaculate Conception. Although most clergy and religious orders in Spain supported this belief, not all did, not least the Dominicans. Consequently, advocates actively sought royal support for the Immaculate Conception, which would also help in Rome since, for all the often-conflictive relationship between the monarchy and the papacy, Spain's military, financial and material support of the papal states meant its voice still needed to be listened to. This Marian aspect of the *pietas austriaca* is well illustrated in a Rubens oil sketch, the *Franciscan Allegory in Honour of the Immaculate Conception* (1631–2), in which we see the Spanish Habsburgs alongside the Franciscans, Philip IV standing with his two brothers and his young son and the previous Habsburg monarchs, Charles V, Philip II and Philip III, in an eagle-drawn chariot above them, though in fact Charles V and Philip II had not lent 'unequivocal support' to the Immaculist position.[8] Belief in the Immaculate Conception had gained ever wider support in the later middle ages in the Iberian peninsula. The rulers of the kingdom of Aragon were active defenders from the end of the thirteenth century, and royal support spread to Castile through María of Aragon, wife of Juan II of Castile, in the fifteenth and continued with the 'Catholic Monarchs', Isabella and Ferdinand, who unified in their persons the two kingdoms.[9] But it was in the seventeenth century that there was sustained royal support to have the belief declared a dogma, as it would eventually be in 1854.

The 1615 public procession was part of what has been called the 'Marian war' in Seville.[10] A key event in its intensification was a sermon delivered in September 1613 by the Dominican Domingo de Molina.[11] An anonymous letter written towards the end of 1615 when that year's 'storm' was said to be dying down quotes from one of Molina's sermons, without saying when he gave it, in which he had stated that 'the Virgin was conceived like you and me and like Martin Luther.'[12] The 1613 sermon galvanized already strong Immaculist support in the city, and the letter is a catalogue of incidents revealing the wide-spread hostility in Seville and Andalusia towards the Dominicans because of their open Maculist stance.

Immediately following the 1615 procession, Bernardo de Toro and Mateo Vázquez de Leca went to Madrid on behalf of the city to garner royal support and then subsequently to Rome to advocate for the Immaculist position.[13] Their involvement was itself seen as a result of the Virgin's interventions for, in 1609, a Franciscan friar, Francisco de Santiago, declared that she had told him now was the time to establish the Immaculate Conception as dogma; he prayed before the altar of the Immaculate Conception at the tomb of Hernando de Mata, former leader of the Congregation of the Pomegranate, and asked who was to pursue the issue. Fortuitously he then met Bernardo de Toro, current leader of the Congregation, and Toro, after praying in turn to the Virgin of the Kings, felt called to go to Rome with Vázquez de Leca to pursue their advocacy.[14] (The Congregation of the Pomegranate was a millenarist brotherhood that believed a prophecy that said that once the Immaculate Conception was declared a dogma, they would reform the whole church.[15] It was investigated by the Inquisition in Seville in the 1620s for Alumbradismo, a factor behind this possibly being Dominican revenge for the Congregation's Marian advocacy.[16]) As a result of Toro and Vázquez de Leca's Marian embassy, Philip III established a Real Junta (Royal Committee).[17] Its function, in effect, was to petition Rome in favour of the Immaculist position. While Rome did not declare the Immaculate Conception a dogma, various popes across the century did issue decretals and bulls in its favour by, for example, forbidding preaching the Maculist position.[18] There was on occasion annoyance at Spain's strident and public engagement with the matter: following Paul V's bull in August 1616, for example, the papal nuncio in Madrid

> wrote to Philip III, blaming both the Immaculist clergy and the Dominicans for the disputes that were an embarrassment to the church. He placed special blame on the archbishop of Seville for permitting a serious theological issue to be literally dragged through the streets.[19]

Zurbarán was a sixteen-year-old apprentice in Seville at the time of the 1615 procession memorialized by Roelas, and whether he took part in it or not he cannot but have been aware of it and of the intensity of feeling that the Immaculist cause evoked. We know nothing directly about the artist's beliefs as I have mentioned, but it is worth noting that the 1636 contract for the *retablo* of the church of Nuestra Señora de la Granada in Llerena says he offered to work without financial gain as 'a son of the city and being so devoted to the Virgin'.[20] The very public and emotionally intense expression of devotion that the procession typifies was a marked feature of religious life in Golden Age Spain and the antithesis of the still, isolated and introverted world of devotion that Zurbarán depicts. Nonetheless, he played a central role in the formation and fixing of the image of the Immaculate Conception that took place across the seventeenth century. In so doing he was helping give visual expression to an image whose status was, as one critic puts it, 'situated somewhere between an object of veneration or worship and, iconographically, one of propaganda and apologia'.[21] Aside from a focus of devotion, the Immaculate Conception was an object of political import, radical theological disagreement and church politics, and Zurbarán created more innovative propaganda with his Immaculate Conceptions than he did in his work for the Buen Retiro, in part because of his willingness to experiment. It is his contribution to establishing the image of the Immaculate Conception that I want to focus on, but in so doing I will also consider that of other Sevillian artists, for Sevillian artists played a central role in its establishment in Spain. I will then explore other Marian subjects that Zurbarán painted, his innovation here giving singular shape to the Marian devotion of his time.

DEPICTING THE IMMACULATE CONCEPTION

The tree of Jesse and the embrace at the Golden Gate of the Virgin's parents, Anne and Joachim, were favoured ways of conveying the idea of the abstract notion of the Immaculate Conception in the late fifteenth and early sixteenth centuries.[22] These gave way in the sixteenth century to the Virgin *tota pulchra*, 'all fair' (Song of Songs 4:7), with the Virgin surrounded by attributes linked to her.[23] This is the tradition that Pacheco draws upon when he sets down what he regarded as the correct way to depict the Virgin as the Immaculate Conception. His starting point is St John's vision of the Woman of the Apocalypse, 'a woman clothed with the sun, and the moon under her feet, and on her head a crown of twelve stars' (Revelation 12:1). He says that she should be depicted as a twelve- or thirteen-year-old girl, wearing a white tunic and blue mantle as she did when she appeared to Beatriz da Silva, the late fifteenth-century Portuguese noblewoman who founded the Order of the Immaculate Conception in Toledo, and argues after discussing variant images that she should be shown not holding the baby Jesus but with her hands clasped in prayer. She should be shown surrounded by the sun, with twelve stars around her head and wearing an Imperial crown, standing on a crescent moon. Ever wanting pictorial 'accuracy', Pacheco says that the crescent should be shown with its points downwards, following the reasoning of the Jesuit Luis de Alcázar that it would appear thus were the sun above it, as is the case here. Finally, he says that either God the Father or the Holy Spirit, or both, are usually shown above the Virgin, that her symbolic attributes should be placed, as relevant, in the landscape beneath her or among the clouds around her, and that seraphim surround her along with angels carrying some of her attributes. Pacheco is making a distinction here between angelic forces depicted as almost disembodied presences and those fully embodied.[24] Such attributes applied to her include *porta caeli* ('the gate of heaven', Genesis 28:17), *turris David* ('the tower of David', Song of Songs 4:4), *stella matutina* ('morning star', Ecclesiasticus 50:6), *fons signatus* ('a fountain sealed up', Song of Songs 4:12), *puteus aquarum viventium* ('the well of living waters', Song of Songs 4:15). All in all the image of the Virgin as the Immaculate Conception encapsulates the woman in the Song of Songs who 'cometh forth as the morning rising, fair as the moon, bright as the sun' (6:9).

In the early decades of the seventeenth century in Seville, various Immaculate Conceptions depict the Virgin with a contemporary figure, normally beneath her at left. Roelas, for example, includes Hernando de Mata (1612–13), while Pacheco portrays Miguel Cid (1619; illus. 46) and, in a second work, Vázquez de Leca (1621); all three figures closely associated with the Immaculist position in Seville as we have seen. Records of individual and civic advocacy, the paintings become advocates in turn for the image they contain. The Virgin in these three works does not conform in dress to Pacheco's later suggestions, wearing red and blue rather than white and blue. This is the case also with

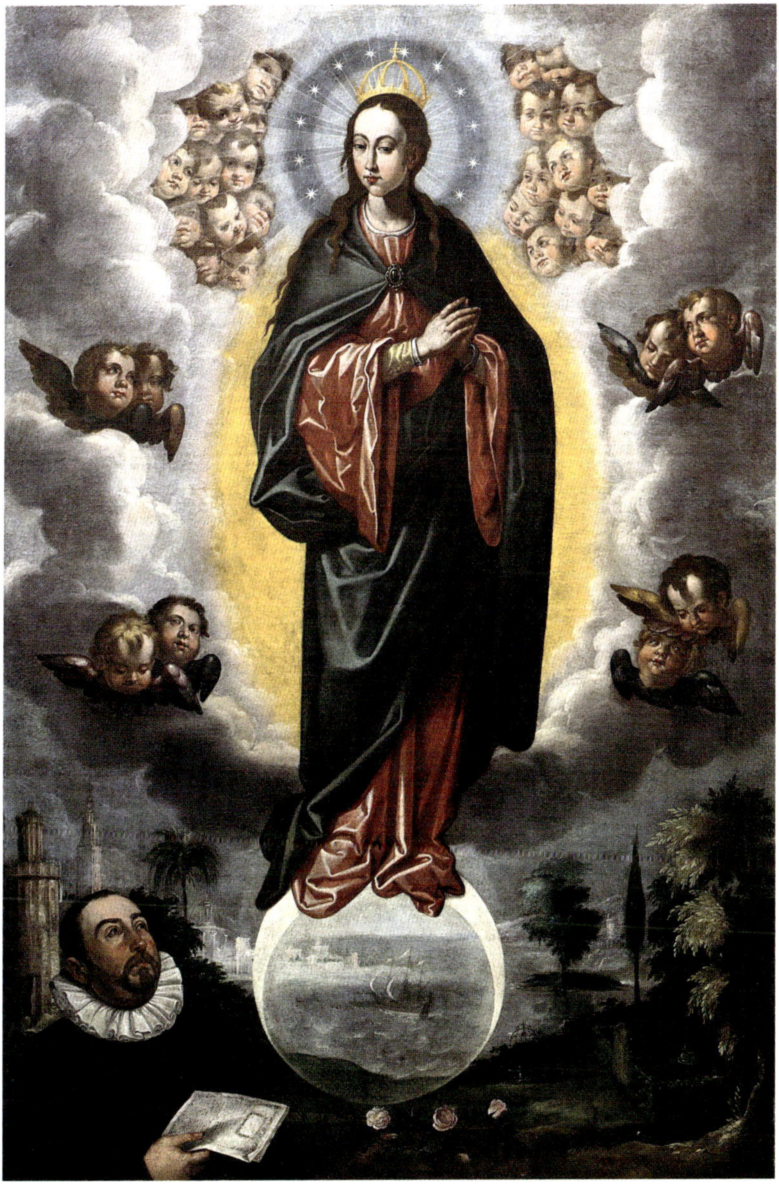

46 Francisco Pacheco, *Immaculate Conception with Miguel Cid*, 1619, oil on canvas.

Velázquez's version. This formed a pair with *St John the Evangelist on Patmos*, both paintings for the Calced Carmelites in Seville (1618–19). In *St John* we see John having the vision that will lead him to describe the Woman of the Apocalypse, the vision itself barely visible at the top left of the painting. In its companion piece that vision has now become the fully realized Immaculate Conception depicted alone and dominating the front plane against a cloudy, darkened sky, glimpses of golden light visible behind her between her blue mantle and the clouds that surround her. Both John and the Virgin are non-idealized, shown, in effect, as actual Sevillians. Zurbarán will continue this non-idealization.

In Zurbarán's numerous versions there are few constants other than the Virgin herself floating in the sky surrounded by golden light. She is usually shown as an adolescent, but in several late works as a young girl. (The perhaps inevitable suggestion is that his six-year-old daughter might be the model for the Virgin in the Prado's 1656 *Immaculate Conception as a Child*.[25]) She is mostly shown wearing blue and white, but in nearly as many works wears pink and blue, and is only occasionally depicted wearing an imperial crown. Normally shown looking upwards to God, in several works she looks out at the viewer or downwards. Symbolic attributes may be placed in the landscape over which she hovers, or both in the landscape and within the clouds around her, or they may be absent. (The appearance in the landscape beneath the *Immaculate Conception* (*c.* 1635, Museo Diocesano de Arte Antiguo, Sigüenza) of Seville's iconic Giralda, once a minaret then the cathedral belltower, may indicate that this is the painting commissioned by the city council for the town hall in June 1630 immediately following the unsuccessful demand by the painters' guild that Zurbarán undergo examination.[26]) While normally shown standing on a crescent moon that points downwards, the Virgin may be on one whose tips point upwards, on a full moon or on a terrestrial globe; in one version the crescent moon is above a heart and in another on a white globe beneath which is a large serpent, apple in mouth. She is standardly alone apart from cherubs, but in three works she is accompanied by other figures, as in Pacheco and Roelas. The cherubs that accompany her normally surround her, often as myriad, barely visible heads in the golden clouds, most strikingly in the *Immaculate Conception with Joachim and Anne* (*c.* 1638–9) where they seem to materialize and dematerialize before our eyes, but in one work they also stand along the bottom of the composition holding sheets of music and a cornett, and in another sit or stand holding Marian symbols either side of the terrestrial globe on which she stands. Some of these variations may have been specified in a commission, but they are also evidence both of Zurbarán's willingness to vary his many versions of the subject and of the image of the Immaculate Conception not yet being iconographically set, as it will be with Murillo who will build upon Zurbarán's refining and abstracting of earlier versions such as Roelas's and Pacheco's.

In the three *Inmaculadas* in which other figures appear – two boys in seventeenth-century dress kneeling in prayer either side of her (1632; illus. 47); her parents, Joachim and Anne; and two allegorical figures (*c.* 1658) – it is the last that is most difficult to interpret. One proposal is that the two figures, one with eyes completely covered by the Virgin's blue mantle, the other holding an anchor, represent Faith and Hope, the former occasionally depicted blindfolded, the latter typically with an anchor. On this reading the Virgin above them then embodies the third and greatest cardinal virtue, Charity. Another interpretation connects directly with the Immaculist campaign, the blindfolded figure representing 'the blindness of the Maculists to God's revelation of the Immaculate Conception', Hope expressing the Immaculists's endeavour to have their belief declared a dogma.[27] More recently, Rosilie Hernández has interpreted the two figures as sight and vision, that is, seeing with the 'eyes of the body' and seeing with

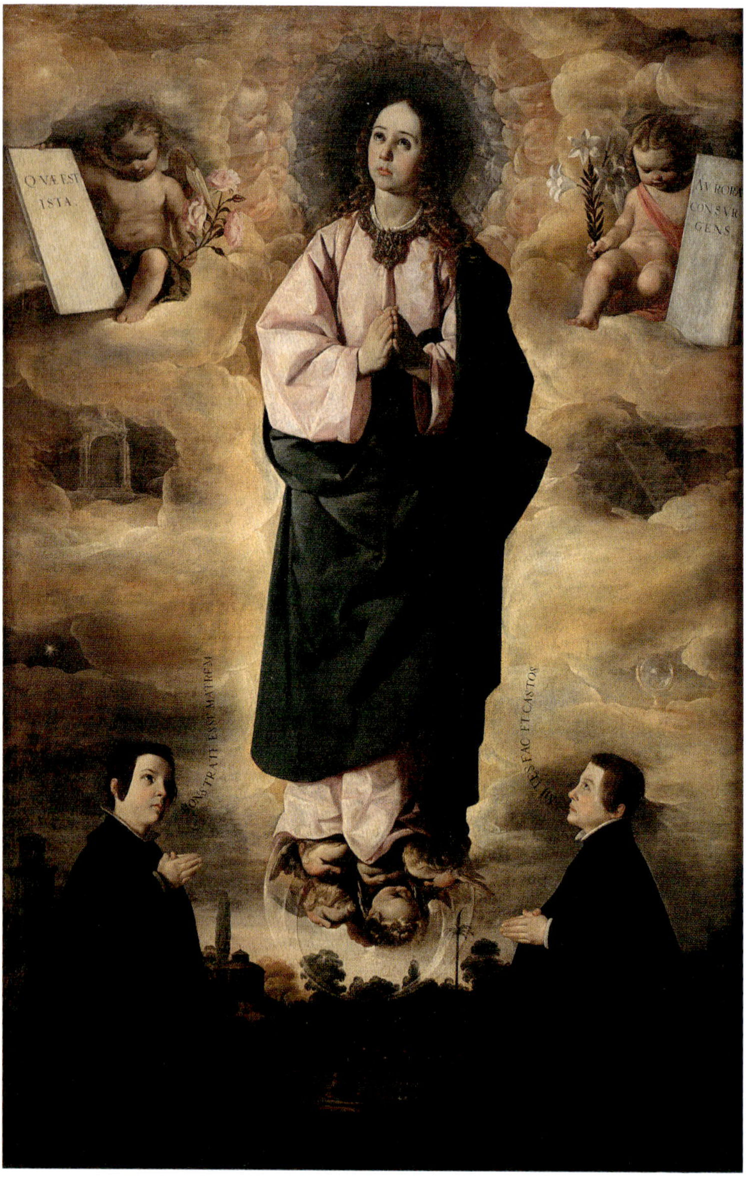

47 Francisco de Zurbarán, *Immaculate Conception with Two Boys Praying*, 1632, oil on canvas.

the 'eyes of the soul', for the contemporary viewer was 'invited to experience most Conceptionist paintings as a visionary continuum between this world and the sacred', and she links this 'doubling of seeing' to her reading of representations of the Immaculate Conception, not least by Zurbarán, as depicting both immanence and transcendence.[28] That is to say, the Virgin in these works is

> simultaneously accessible and otherworldly . . . mediating an encounter between the similar (she is a familiar child) and the extraordinary (she is a revelation) . . . In Zurbarán the vision is at once recognizable and strangely excessive, seen in this world but not of this world, contiguous with our experience, a saturated phenomenon both meaningful and yet ultimately inscrutable.[29]

This captures well the nature and impact of Zurbarán's Immaculate Conceptions. It is also, albeit achieved in different ways, a feature of the nature and impact of his art in general which makes the familiar unfamiliar, the fabric of the world, the expressive embodiment of the spiritual or the divine.

Zurbarán painted the Immaculate Conception throughout his career, with the earliest surviving version thought to be from circa 1628–30 (Prado), and six are signed and dated, the earliest 1632, the final two, among his very last works, 1661. Some evolution in Zurbarán's depictions is discernible. In the early *Immaculate Conception with Two Boys Praying* (1632; illus. 47) not only are Marian attributes prominent in the landscape below the Virgin and in the clouds around her, but banderols from each kneeling boy's mouth (MONSTRA TE ESSE MATREM (Show yourself a mother) and MITES FAC ET CASTOS (Make us gentle and chaste) from the ninth-century prayer Ave Maris Stella) and inscriptions on tablets held by cherubs either side of the Virgin (QUÆ EST ISTA and AURORA CONSURGENS, 'who is she that cometh forth as the morning rising', Song of Songs 6:9) convey to the literate the import of the Marian image represented. But Marian symbols become less intrusive in subsequent works and are entirely absent in several late versions (1656, Prado, and 1661, church of Saint-Gervais and Saint-Protais, Langon; illus. 48), presumably because the image of the Immaculate Conception standing on the moon, stars around her head, was increasingly recognized as such and additional symbols were no longer needed. A further sign that such symbols were less central to recognizing and reinforcing the advocation are the several later works (New York, Private Collection, 1656; unknown location, 1658) in which the cherubs engage playfully with the symbols that they hold, looking into the mirror that represents her immaculacy (the *speculum sine macula*, 'unspotted mirror', of Wisdom 7:26), for example, or climbing Jacob's ladder (Genesis 28:12). These works are also a reminder that Golden Age religion was not always as austere in expression or experience as it may now appear to us.[30] Later depictions by Zurbarán also tend to show the Virgin in white tunic and blue mantle, the colours prescribed by Pacheco on the basis of Beatriz da Silva's visions that became more widely known with her beatification process of 1636.[31] In his final two versions of 1661 in Langon (illus. 48) and the Museum of Fine Arts, Budapest, the blue mantle is more fully unfurled behind her, this in particularly striking fashion in the work in Langon where the mantle's hefty, vertically zig-zagging pleats seem to concertina out sideways in parallel with the Virgin's body, Zurbarán painting for almost the last time his signature deep folds in the undulating fabric. In this work the Virgin appears simply amid golden, cloudy haze; space has dematerialized into light, but that light is rematerialized into pigment, coloured matter, through the *cartellino* illusionistically stuck on the orangey, amber haze. We will return to these *cartellini*, which figure so prominently in Zurbarán's late work, in the next chapter.

These two versions of 1661 coincided, fortuitously or not, with Pope Alexander VII's bull of 8 December of that year in favour of belief in and the cult of the Immaculate Conception, and condemning speaking or publishing against it.[32] As the chronicler Ortiz wrote, this 'filled Christendom with happiness, and especially Spain and Seville'.[33]

MURILLO, THE IMMACULATE CONCEPTION AND ZURBARÁN'S LATE STYLE

There is a fragment of an undated letter from Zurbarán in Madrid to Murillo, on the reverse of which Murillo has sketched an *Inmaculada*.[34] Both sketch and Zurbarán's location suggestively if inadvertently encapsulate Murillo's displacement of Zurbarán, for although Zurbarán's Immaculate Conceptions were popular and important in the refining of the subject, it was Murillo's that became iconic Marian images.

Zurbarán would obviously have been aware of Murillo's style, but the relationship between this and his own late style is contested. By the early to mid-1650s the features of the latter are fully evident: contours less sharply defined, palette more muted, sharp contrasts avoided. The effect is often described as vaporous.[35] Murillo's rise to prominence in Seville following his Franciscan commission of 1645–6 has often been seen as a key factor in this evolution, the older artist adapting his style to compete with changing taste.[36] Murillo conveys his subjects in a far less detached way, and one can certainly see Zurbarán's late, more emotionally engaging devotional works as in part responding to this, though sentimentalism is far less pronounced than in Murillo. But a direct and sole link between these changes and Murillo is more difficult to establish. So, for example, if we consider Zurbarán's *Annunciation* now in Philadelphia and accept Odile Delenda's date of '1650?' then, as Jonathan Brown argues, Zurbarán's

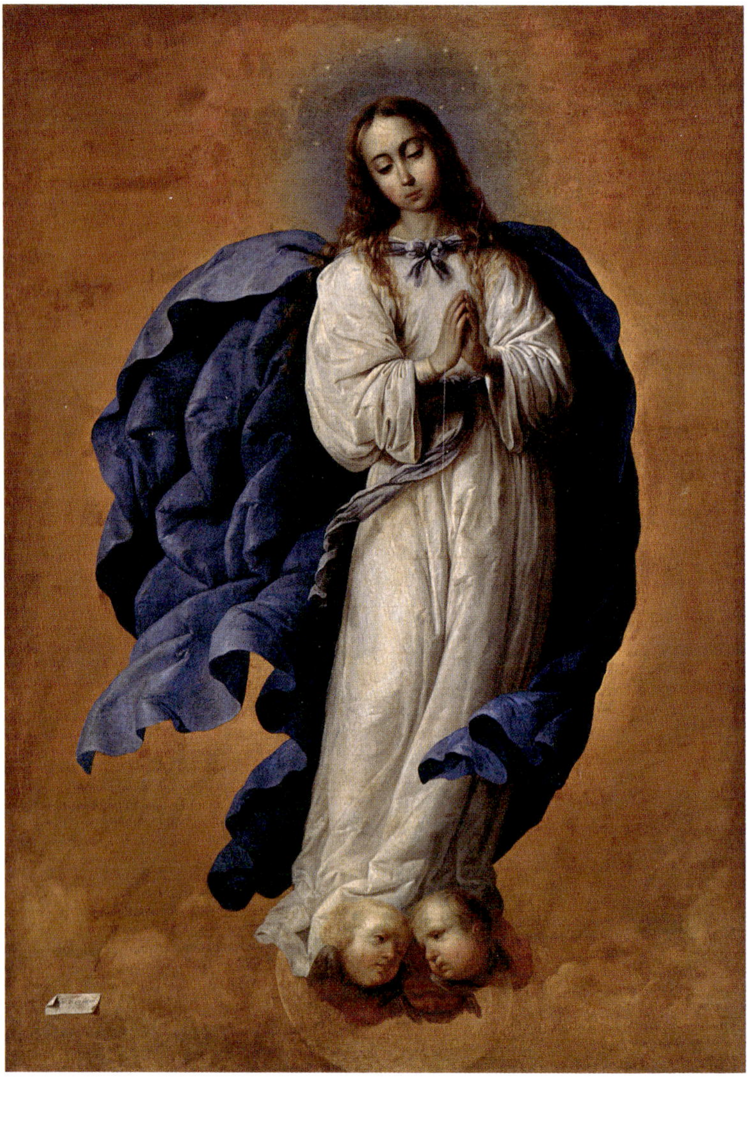

48 Francisco de Zurbarán, *Immaculate Conception*, 1661, oil on canvas.

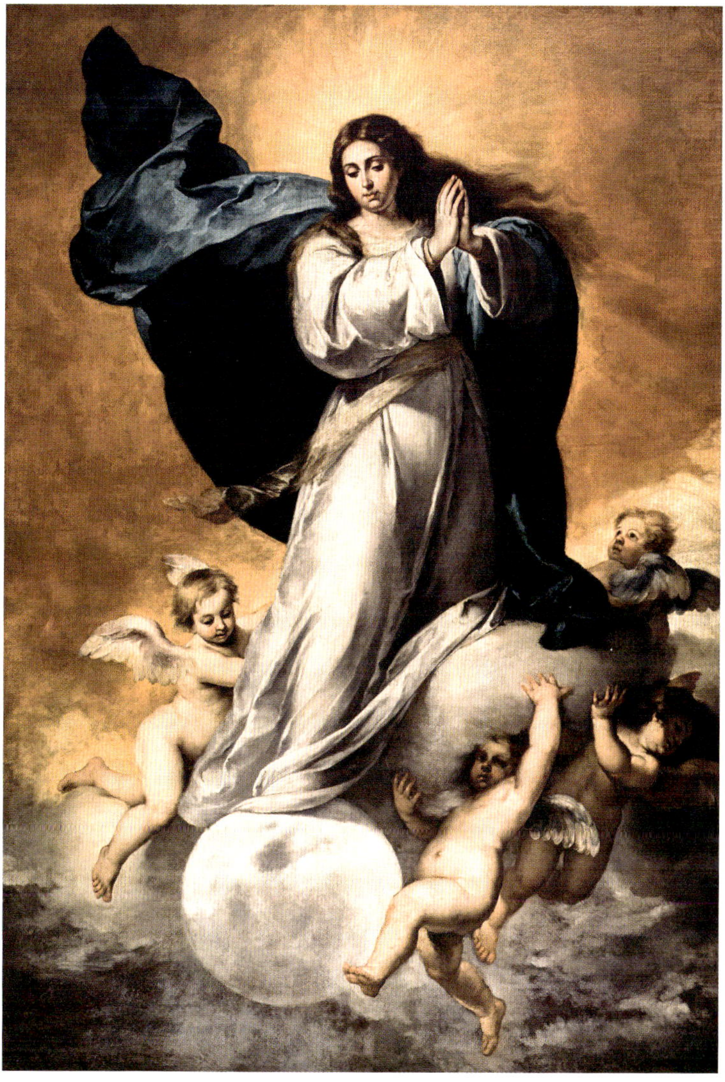

49 Bartolomé Esteban Murillo, *Immaculate Conception ('La Colosal')*, *c.* 1650 or *c.* 1652–5, oil on canvas.

> change of style appears to have been essentially accomplished by the date of this picture. If this is so, then the customary notion that Zurbarán altered his style under the influence of Murillo and the pressure of his successful rivalry must be reconsidered. This conception was, in any case, too simplistic to explain a long and thoughtful process of development during which Zurbarán selectively retained some elements of the earlier style unchanged while he modified others.[37]

Key aspects of the evolution of Zurbarán's depiction of the Immaculate Conception illustrate the complexities of this question. While the meekness characteristic of Zurbarán's *Inmaculadas* gives way in Murillo to a combination of intimacy and yet imposing majesty, and the stillness that is so characteristic of Zurbarán tends often to yield in Murillo to a greater sense of vitality, of dynamism, we might see Zurbarán reaching for this in his final 1661 versions whose voluminous and billowing mantles seem to draw on his younger colleague's iconic *Immaculate Conception ('La Colosal')* (illus. 49), for the Sevillian monastery of San Francisco (*c.* 1650 or *c.* 1652–5), though there is less sense of dynamic force conveyed in them than in Murillo where the mantle is swirled fully away from the Virgin's body both backwards and upwards.[38] However, if the date of circa 1645 is accepted for Zurbarán's *Immaculate Conception* in the Museo Cerralbo, Madrid, as well as for the version close to this in the Fundación Focus Loyola, Seville, then he had already begun to incorporate dynamism through the Virgin's mantle, albeit that this is less fully or ostentatiously extended than it will be in his 1661 versions. While there were other precedents for this more dynamic presentation of the Virgin, such as Ribera's 1635 *Immaculate Conception* for the church of the convent of the Agustinas Recoletas, Salamanca, the full emergence of this in Zurbarán's final versions may well mean that Murillo was the prompt for his further development in this direction, but so may the airborne theatricalities of High Baroque religious art taking hold in Madrid where he was based when he painted these. As part of his move from a less rigid and static presentation of the Virgin, Zurbarán also poses her from the mid-1640s with knee slightly bent, a pose used, sometimes more pronouncedly, by Murillo. This is a marked feature of Rubens's *Immaculate Conception* painted in Madrid in 1628–9 and initially hung there in the king's oratory, but the influence here may in fact have been a work then in Seville, Guido Reni's 1627 *Immaculate Conception* (Metropolitan Museum of Art). Reni's golden background is echoed in *Inmaculadas* by both Zurbarán and Murillo, and Zurbarán drew on Reni's *Coronation of the Virgin* (*c.* 1607) and/or his *Assumption and Coronation of the Virgin* (1602–3) in depicting cherubs holding a sheet of music in his 1638 *Adoration of the Shepherds* and 1656 *Immaculate Conception as a Child*. This was all part of a strong interest in Seville from around 1640 in Bolognese classicism.[39]

Murillo, of course, was not immune to Zurbarán. So although a recently discovered early Velázquez (*c.* 1618–19) shows a three- or four-year-old Mary as the Immaculate Conception, we can justifiably see Murillo's *Immaculate Conception as a Child* ('*La Niña*', *c.* 1665–6) as owing a debt to Zurbarán's affecting images of the very young virgin, including as the Immaculate Conception.[40]

THE CHILD MARY

The Spanish monarchy was not a single entity but a composite monarchy. That is to say, the monarch ruled over separate kingdoms and territories, with their own intense loyalties and histories, laws and languages, united only in his person. Since the Immaculate Conception was not linked with one order or region, it had something of a unifying effect and this precisely at a time when constituent parts of the monarchy actively sought independence or fretted at rule from Madrid. But Marian devotion was far broader and more diverse than simply devotion to the Immaculate Conception. Some popular advocations like the Virgin of Guadalupe, the Virgin of Montserrat, or Our Lady of the Pillar (the Virgen del Pilar) in Zaragoza were identified with a particular place, though not confined necessarily to that locality, while some like the Virgin of Atocha in Madrid, to whom the monarchs were devoted, or the Virgin of the Kings in Seville were focal points of more localized devotion. Other widespread advocations were associated with a particular quality of the Virgin or devotional practice, such as the Virgin of Mercy or the Virgin of the Rosary. All were depicted in images, whether sculpted, painted or engraved. And of course, Biblical episodes in which the Virgin played a central part were extremely popular subjects.

By one contemporary account Seville in the 1630s had 37 churches dedicated to the Virgin and more than five hundred altars,[41] and while Marian devotion there found intense expression in the Immaculate Conception across the seventeenth century, it was far more diversely focused, as in the rest of Spain. Based on records of art collections, for example, the four most popular Marian devotions in Seville were Nuestra Señora del Rosario (Our Lady of the Rosary), del Pópulo (of the People), de la Soledad (of Solitude) and de la Concepción. These were also the most common in New World painting shipments.[42]

Zurbarán's work involving the Virgin is diverse, numerous and spans his career, and we have already encountered works such as the *Virgin of the Carthusians*, *Christ and the Virgin in the House at Nazareth* and his Jerez de la Frontera altarpiece paintings of the *Annunciation*, *Nativity* and *Adoration*. He would produce more intimate versions of the Annunciation (1650?, *c.* 1655 and *c.* 1660), other Biblical events such as the Flight to Egypt (*c.* 1630–35) and Pentecost (*c.* 1635), numerous Holy Families (with Mary, Joseph and Jesus alone (*c.* 1655–60, *c.* 1658–60, 1659), with Mary, Jesus and the infant John the Baptist (1658, *c.* 1659–60, 1662) or with the young John the Baptist and his parents (*c.* 1630–35)), various images of the Virgin and Child (*c.* 1635–40, 1658, 1658–60, 1659, *c.* 1660), the Virgin of the Rosary (*c.* 1645–50, *c.* 1650) and works in which the Virgin protects an order or appears miraculously to individuals. But it is his depictions of the Virgin as a child that I want to discuss, since these are not only representative of the type of smaller devotional works that characterize his later output, but also innovatory subjects. We see in them the artist's pictorial imagination creating a subject that proved popular with the public.

There were a couple of subjects popular with artists that depict the Virgin as a child: the *Presentation at the Temple*, in which she is taken aged three to be raised there, and the *Education of the Virgin*, in which she is taught to read by her mother. Zurbarán adds to these with his devotional images that show the Virgin praying or asleep. Delenda has suggested their origin might lie in his *Family of the Virgin* (*c.* 1630–35), since there she is shown as a young child, seated between her parents, hands together in prayer and resting on the sewing cushion on her lap, eyes raised heavenwards.[43]

Zurbarán composed three distinct formats of the child Virgin in prayer. If the broadly accepted dates are followed for these, then the three subjects become ever more focused on just the figure of the Virgin. In all there is a certain sweetness to the young Mary that brings to mind Murillo, more known for his images of children.

The first of the three subjects, *The Young Virgin* (illus. 50), places her in one of the most 'staged' settings in Zurbarán's oeuvre. The painting has been dated as early as circa 1632–3 by Brown and the Metropolitan Museum of Art, but both Delenda and Enrique Valdivieso suggest circa 1640–45.[44] This is the busiest and compositionally 'complex' of Zurbarán's images of the young Virgin, and her pose here is the same as that in the *Family of the Virgin*. Seated on the floor, her hands are joined in prayer and

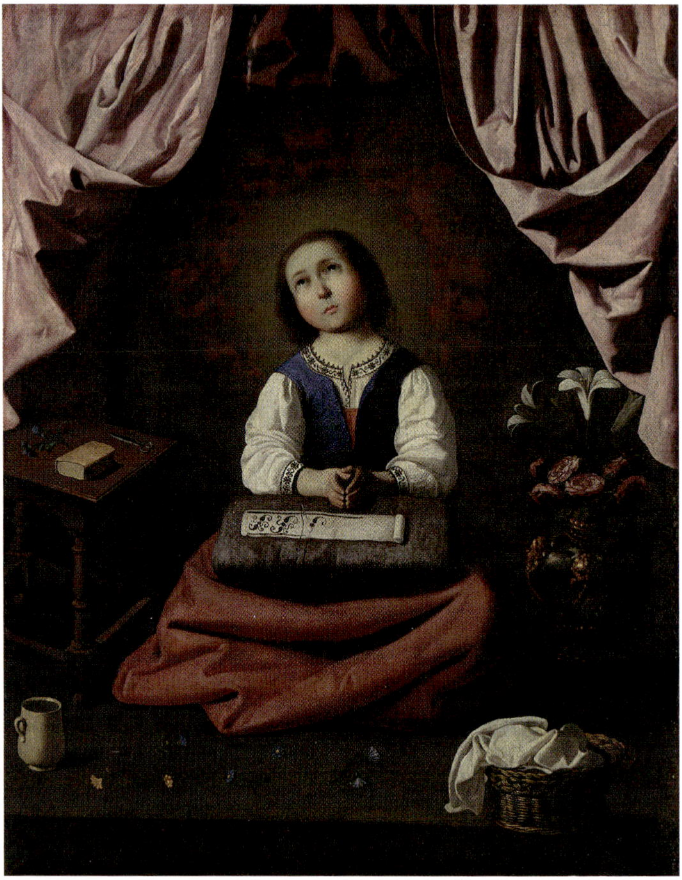

resting on her sewing cushion, into which she has inserted a black-threaded needle, indicating external activity has momentarily ceased. She looks heavenward. To the left of her, a table with scissors, a closed book and a sprig of flowers. To the right, an elaborate vase in which there are lilies and roses. Around her head a circle of cherubs' heads, all looking at her. On the ground in front of her, from left to right, a white ceramic cup of water; blue and yellow flowers, entirely separate from one another and

50 Francisco de Zurbarán, *The Young Virgin*, c. 1640–45, oil on canvas.

each precisely placed in typical Zurbarán fashion, though here with more artifice than in his other works; and a wicker basket with loosely crumpled white cloth. The overall setting, with the Virgin seated on a platform over which the basket juts and pale-mauve curtains drawn back at top left and right, has suggested both a 'theatrical tableau' with the Virgin 'on a stage' and an 'altar-like dais'.[45] While obviously true that the setting serves to 'present' a private moment of spiritual withdrawal to the viewer, the raised area probably represents a typically Spanish architectural feature, one of the many legacies of the peninsula's Islamic past, the *estrado*, a low platform in a room on which women would sit on cushions. She is certainly serially framed and variously presented (curtains-ring of cherub heads-the paler circle of light between them and her head) for the viewer in turn to meditatively consider. The painting is often called in Spanish *The Virgin in Ecstasy*, and this raises the question of whether the Virgin is praying or more specifically meditating or contemplating, possibly having reached that moment of union to which contemplation might lead. Certainly this is more than simply a prayerful life, the objects themselves and the Virgin's silent, static pose suggesting the type of withdrawn contemplation that writers saw as a possibility even within the busyness of the world.

Zurbarán then depicted the *Virgin as a Child Asleep*. There are three versions, two from circa 1655 (private collection and Banco Santander Collection, Madrid), the third circa 1655–60 (Cathedral of San Salvador, Jerez de la Frontera; illus. 51). Small variants aside, these show the Virgin seated on a cushion, eyes closed, head resting on her hand, her elbow resting on the seat of a chair; she holds a closed book, a finger inserted where she has been reading. Her pose is that of the young Jesus shown asleep within the human heart in an engraving by Anton Wierix II that Zurbarán has used here.[46] In the dark setting Zurbarán also places on the right a small table with a silvery plate on which sits a Chinese porcelain bowl with several lilies, roses and carnations. (The fashionable bowl, imported through Seville by way of the Philippines and Mexico, yet another silent reminder of global trade in Zurbarán's work.[47])

The setting is further pared back in the third subject, the *Virgin as a Child Praying*. The two versions of this subject are both dated circa 1660 (illus. 52). Here we see the Virgin seated on a small chair, hands clasped in prayer and resting on the needlework in her lap. Her head is slightly tilted upwards, her eyes open and looking heavenwards. The composition is tightly focused on the Virgin and, chair aside, there is no other spatial marker within the darkness. In the Hermitage version illustrated here, her expression has been described as one of *recogimiento*.[48] Looking at the evolution of the three variant subjects of the young Virgin, there is what we might describe as an increasing compositional withdrawal that echoes the withdrawal at the heart of *recogimiento* and of contemplation, as we saw in Chapter Four. This compositional simplicity and focus on the figure typify devotional works from Zurbarán's final years. Whether in part a consequence of working without a large workshop or for the commercial market is difficult to say, but it undoubtedly increases their devotional intensity.

In all these works showing the young Virgin, we see her life in the Temple, described as one of sewing and weaving, reading scripture and contemplation.[49] In all of them she is engaged in prayer, for even when asleep her mind was said to be meditating on what she had read and contemplated.[50] The spiritual state that Zurbarán depicts is akin to that outlined by one Jesuit:

> Through recollection [*recogimiento*], solitude, silence and stillness she would prepare for contemplation and union with God, in which she was so absorbed and enraptured, so visited and favoured by the Lord and the angels, that

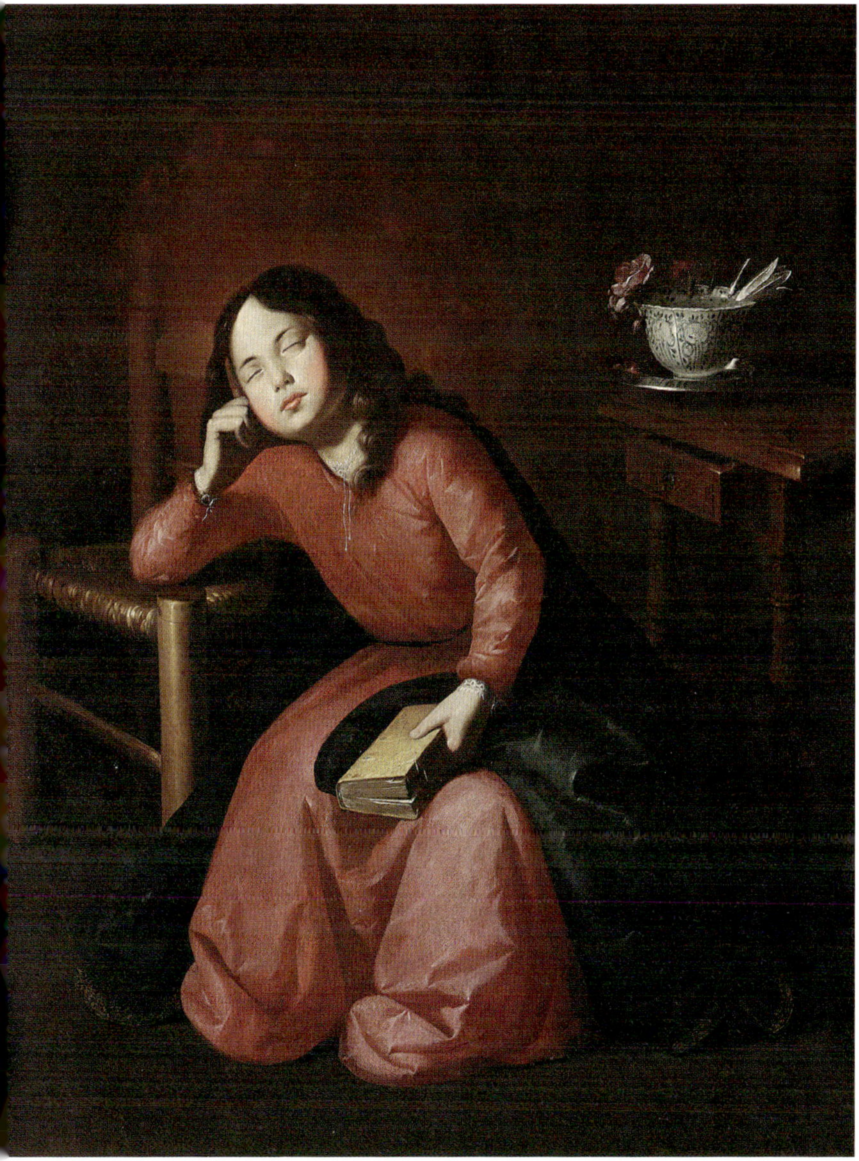

51 Francisco de Zurbarán, *Virgin as a Child Asleep*, c. 1655–60, oil on canvas.

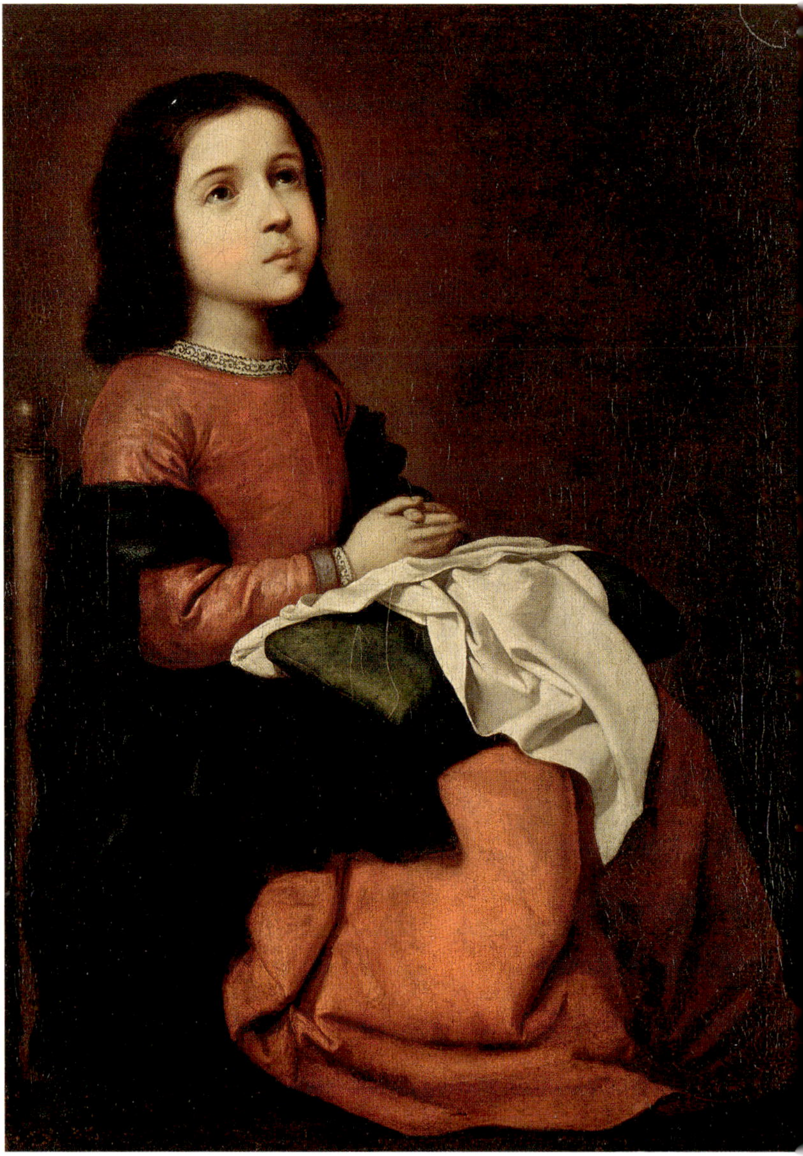

52 Francisco de Zurbarán, *Virgin as a Child Praying*, *c.* 1660, oil on canvas.

> she seemed a child from heaven rather than one raised here on earth.[51]

These depictions of the child Virgin are connected to the Immaculate Conception, not least in their combination of immanence and transcendence.[52] That combination, which Zurbarán achieves in so many of his religious works, here takes an affecting form in the young child. The contemplative state that Zurbarán conveys raises the broader question of how contemporary viewers might have engaged with his works. It is to this that we now turn.

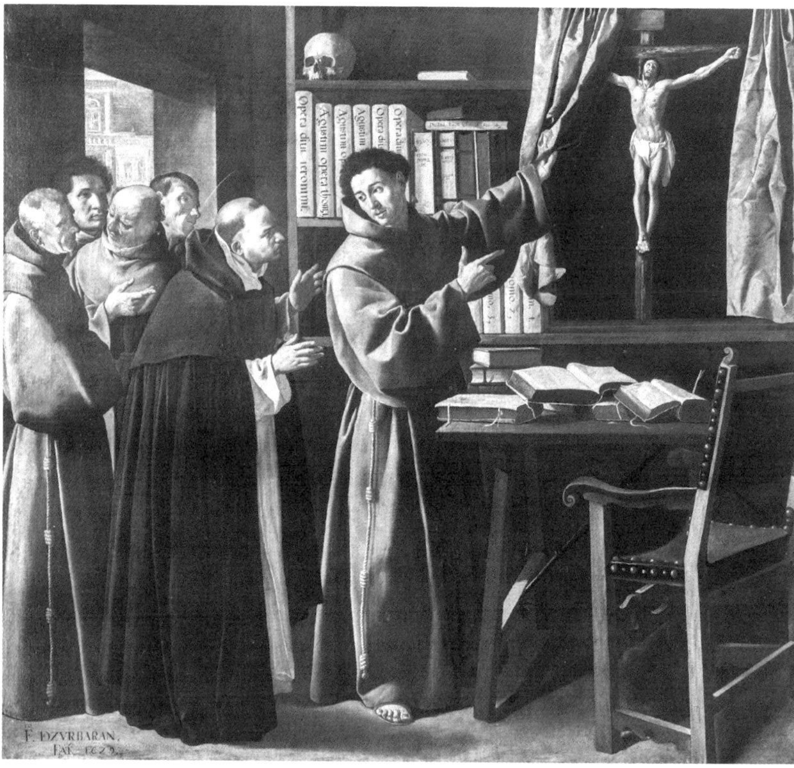
F. DZVRBARAN.

SEVEN

Images, Meditation and Meta-Images

Zurbarán's paintings are overwhelmingly religious, their range of subjects a summary of post-Tridentine Catholicism. But what was their function? How were they 'used'?

On one level their purpose was to beautify monasteries and churches and to mark their prestige. This is why commissioners employed the best artists they could. Beyond this, they self-evidently record and celebrate facets of belief held to be important at the time, Zurbarán's Immaculate Conceptions are a prime example of this. The bulk of his work for religious orders also honours and celebrates the lives of saints and figures associated with the commissioning order. On occasion this might be linked to a canonization, as with the cycle of paintings on the Mercedarian Peter Nolasco that would, like any cycle, engage a viewer both cumulatively as a series and as individual works, or to a step on the way to possible canonization, as when the Jesuit Alonso Rodríguez was declared Venerable (see illus. 57). Akin to his work for the Habsburg court, these commissions were a form of propaganda. But they also obviously functioned as examples to their viewers. Just as history was still written in the form of moral *exempla*, that is, focusing on historical figures whose actions and words were offered as positive or negative models, so Jerome, Francis, Nolasco, Alonso Rodríguez and individual Mercedarians, Hieronymites and Carthusians were put before the viewer as

53 Francisco de Zurbarán, *Visit of St Thomas Aquinas to St Bonaventure*, 1629, oil on canvas.

spiritual exemplars. This was part of a traditional view of a religious image's function that was reaffirmed in the wake of the Reformation by the Council of Trent in 1563. Following Trent, Catholic writers and art theorists rehearsed the place and utility of images in Christian life and worship and the levels of reverence due to them (*dulia*, *hyperdulia*, *latria*). The Jesuit Martín de Roa, for example, runs through how images instruct (the long-held view of them as 'books for the illiterate'), kindle love of God and the saints, and propel the viewer to imitate the virtues of those represented, all on the basis that the visual has a more immediate and emotive impact than the verbal.[1] In short they are 'necessary to move the will to devotion'.[2]

Zurbarán has a marked preference for depicting individuals in contemplation and ecstasy; that is, when the mind has moved beyond meditation, beyond word and image, to the divine itself, but in several works he depicts religious images as images for use.[3] In the *Visit of St Thomas Aquinas to St Bonaventure* (1629; illus. 53), for example, we are presented with an archetypal object of meditation, an image of Christ on the cross, which Bonaventure reveals above his desk to his visitor as the source of his knowledge, while in *St Nicholas* (*c.* 1658–60) the saint sits by a table on which rest a (devotional) book and a framed painting of the *Adoration of the Shepherds*. These indicate an important function of a religious image at the time; namely, their place in prayerful meditation, and it is this that I want to focus on. In meditation we see a major way that contemporaries would have engaged sensorially, emotionally and intellectually with many of Zurbarán's works. My purpose is not to offer a meditative 'reading' of any particular work, but to foreground this key form of pictorial engagement, sketching its contours and some of the issues it provoked, to more fully locate Zurbarán in early modern Spanish culture.

Zurbarán's images are often, and in their own way, highly self-aware and self-reflective, folding the viewer into a consideration of the work of art as art. After outlining the nature of meditative looking I will therefore turn to consider Zurbarán's paintings as meta-images, focusing on one of his most obviously meditative subjects, the Veil of Veronica, and on his *Crucifixion with a Painter* to show how self-awareness around the production of images lies at the heart of both art and the theory and practice of meditation. The consummate artist of the spiritual values of early modern Spain is also a consummate meditator in paint.

MEDITATIVE LOOKING

Ignatius of Loyola's *Spiritual Exercises* (1548) offer a codification of meditative procedures that makes them a useful guide to meditative looking. Their approach to visualizing the meditative scene has often been viewed as uniquely influential in the creation and experience of art during the period, but this emphasis on affective meditation to make what is meditated upon feel both real and present had been a common feature of devotion since the twelfth century, not least, following Bonaventure, among the Franciscans, and is found, albeit in an unsystematic way, in another hugely popular Spanish Golden Age work, the *Libro de la oración y meditación* (Book of Prayer and Meditation) by the Dominican Luis de Granada.[4] This said, the *Exercises* would have been familiar to many given the pedagogical and spiritual reach of the Jesuits, and in the seventeenth century they were a common pastoral resource and were often undertaken by other religious orders; by 1679, for example, the Dominicans required all novices to undertake them before joining the order.[5] Certainly, visualizing the meditative scene was closely associated with the Jesuits, as can be seen in the Carthusian Antonio de Molina's *Ejercicios espirituales* (Spiritual Exercises, 1615), which refer solely to Ignatius in discussing this process.[6]

Ignatius sets out as a required preliminary for each meditative exercise what he calls 'composition of place', and also describes at various points the 'application of the senses'. These are distinct, though intimately connected. Composition of place is a fixing and focusing of the mind on the subject by intensely imagining its location.[7] The application of the senses is a subsequent bringing to life of the scene by applying each sense to it. So in meditating on the nativity, the composition of place focuses on the road from Nazareth to Bethlehem, its 'length, width and whether flat or through valleys or hills', and on the cave where Jesus was born, 'how big, small, low or high and how it was laid out'. The 'application of the senses' then involves engaging with the scene sense-by-sense. So, for example, the exercitant will hear what those there 'say or may say, reflecting internally to draw some benefit from this' and, in terms of touch, 'embrace and kiss the places where those there tread and sit, always endeavouring to draw benefit from this'.[8]

What we see here is how important an imaginative, immersive and sensory engagement with the subject was held to be, even though only an initial and brief phase of the meditative exercise. Ignatius is specifically talking about internal images, but for those deficient in imagination Jesuits recommended drawing on actual paintings and images.[9] There was a very long tradition of so doing, and Ignatius himself was said to contemplate actual images before meditating on Christ's life.[10]

Several other aspects of the use of physical images can be illustrated through contemporary saints' engagement with them. Their transformative potential is exemplified in the life of Philip Neri. The founder of the Oratorians, Neri was recorded sitting in mystical ecstasy before a painting he particularly liked, Federico Barocci's *Visitation of the Virgin to St Elizabeth*, hung in a chapel of the Chiesa Nuova in Rome.[11] This illustrates that altar pieces in public churches could just as readily be the object of devotion.

But despite their wide use there was a recurrent concern over the attractive or 'worldly' appearance of religious paintings and statues, the fear being people might fixate on 'accidentals', such as their painting or adornment, rather than on who they represented, and that they may therefore not transcend them to properly focus their prayer and devotion on the 'invisible', God or the saint represented.[12] (Though Zurbarán's female saints might come to mind here, they are not indecently or gaudily dressed and adorned as some suggested the Virgin and female saints often were.[13]) Teresa de Jesús raises the question of the aesthetic quality of an image in the context of the rise of Protestantism. She says she had read it was an imperfection to have beautifully executed images, and a sign of poverty, and thus positive, to use only prints, but that she then realized that whatever awoke love for God was good and that the 'Lutherans' were lost because they had abandoned all such means. She records the message that she received: 'Daughter, my Christians must now more than ever do the opposite of what *they* do.'[14] Her mention of 'Lutherans' is telling, for it was no coincidence that religious images proliferated in Spain at this period in the wake of Protestant iconoclasm. Furthermore, and as we have seen with Alumbrado disparagement of such images, because Conversos and Moriscos (forced converts and their descendants from Judaism and Islam respectively) were held to be resistant to depictions of the divine, not using images became highly suspect; this in turn fostered their use.[15] While the quality of the image, therefore, was not a prerequisite for its meditative use since it was a means to an end, nonetheless that end might best be served by a beautiful image.

The method of the *Spiritual Exercises* could be readily extrapolated to any subject, as can be seen in the Jesuit Jerónimo Nadal's *Adnotationes et Meditationes in Evangelia* (Annotations and Meditations on the Gospels, 1595). In its more didactic expansion of the Ignatian method, we see here the contemporary meditative mind at work. Each meditation combines words and image: an engraving of an episode from Christ's life, its constituent parts clearly lettered; a Biblical quotation concerning the episode; brief notes for each lettered aspect of the image; and a meditation on the event. The result is that, as with 'composition of place' and the 'application of the senses', the reader 'first precisely situates the gospel scenes, then positions himself within the sites, finally traversing them himself in order to complete the passage from liturgical worship into private, interiorized meditative and contemplative prayer'.[16] Nadal's work was very influential, Pacheco citing him as an authoritative visual source, for example, and Zurbarán drawing on the engraving of the *Circumcision of Jesus* in his depiction of the subject for the Charterhouse in Jerez de la Frontera.[17]

After the initial affective stage the meditator would discursively ponder the subject so as to seek and commit. So, in Nadal's meditation under the *Purification of the Virgin*, he exemplifies the thoughts the meditation might encompass, presenting them as was typical in the form of a personal address between meditator and subject:

> Holy Child, You redeemed us with Your blood. Purify us, so that like Simeon, we may take You in our arms, to foster and impress You deep in our hearts. From there Your divine celestial light will flood our minds. Our darkness scattered, we will see and enjoy You. In Your presence we will grow weary of the world.[18]

What Nadal refers to as the fostering and impressing of the divine within the heart could stand as a description of meditation's aim at this time. Bringing the subject to life and bridging the gulf between the meditator and the scene meditated upon, which composition of place and the application of the senses sought to do by engaging the senses and emotions in a focused way, were seen as effective first steps towards this.

The use of an image, actual or imagined, to prompt emotional and discursive engagement with the subject need not have taken the precise form of the *Exercises*, though given the ubiquity of their usage it will often have done so, and they were in any case a systematization here of a long-recognized part of devotional life. They helpfully show how the use of an image as a meditative focus involved both an entering into a scene and the drawing out of spiritual benefit from this. Composition of place may seem less relevant when contemplating an actual image, though in Zurbarán's case his darker backgrounds leave room for engagement here and his standardly spare compositions share its goal by ensuring focused looking. His works with meditative potential range from archetypal *Andachtsbilder* like the Veil of Veronica to large-scale narrative ensembles such as the *Annunciation*, *Adoration of the Shepherds*, *Adoration of the Magi* and *Circumcision* for Jerez de la Frontera. Although these latter served a liturgical function as part of a single *retablo*, each could still be systematically 'traversed' by the mind, in the fashion of Nadal's prints, a process fostered by the young figure in both the *Circumcision* and the *Adoration of the Shepherds* who looks out and solicits the viewer's gaze and thus attention, and all four can obviously be considered together as aspects of the incarnation that was at the heart of the nativity for contemporaries. And a meditative image may be of a saint whose life, not least for a member of the relevant order, was to be entered into and reflected upon as an example to inspire, or an 'invented' scene such as *Christ and the Virgin in the House at Nazareth*, whose objects, alongside consideration of the two figures, might be pondered for their symbolic meaning.[19] With works such as the latter we encounter something of a paradox in so far as the qualities that emanate from Zurbarán's stylistic and compositional traits and that often therefore 'frame' his subjects – withdrawal, inwardness, detachment – suggest radical disengagement from the world, while affective meditation involves systematic immersion in and exploration of the pictorial world, a paradox in other words between detachment (as evoked and embodied) and engagement (in meditative use). Of course, entering into the pictorial world in this way was meant, in meditational theory, to lead rapidly to moving beyond it, as Ignatius and others emphasized, whether to prayerful consideration and application or indeed beyond there to mystical contemplation itself. Nonetheless, and while I am focusing here on the potential use of Zurbarán's images in meditation, it is worth stressing that his work is so distinctive precisely because it so often stylistically folds together what one might call the meditational and the contemplative, that is, what can be visually expressed and explored and qualities that evoke, because conditions for experiencing, what cannot, the ineffable.

The place of religious images within the spiritual life of Spanish society was significant, and in this intensely visual society their production and use were carefully considered and policed. They needed to be accurate, orthodox and approved, and their use as focal points of devotion and meditation shaped and corralled precisely because paintings and sculptures engage the senses and emotions. This was an image's power but also its potential danger, and Spanish writers were fixated on how the senses and emotions, if uncontrolled by reason, would readily lead not only to moral and epistemological error, but to sin, the strict and controlled focusing of them on the religious topic in meditation being the opposite of their superficial and wayward wandering condemned by many. While clearly those who looked at one of Zurbarán's works did not always or only do so as part of a meditation, their location in churches and monasteries, and the prevalence of prayerful meditation as an integral part of a spiritual life, would absolutely have meant that many viewers did, and not simply those in religious orders for whom meditation, contemplation and prayer were part of their lives. And the smaller-scale works that Zurbarán increasingly produced towards the end of his life speak to the market for images for private devotional use.[20]

THE VEIL OF VERONICA

One of Zurbarán's most popular devotional images was the Veil of Veronica, which he painted across his career.[21] While some may have been created for *retablos*, others will certainly have belonged to private individuals such as Sebastiana Arias Maldonado, a widow in Seville who, when remarrying, listed in 1662 as part of her dowry a framed '*Veronica* by the hand of Zurbarán', along with other devotional images by unnamed painters and sculptors.[22] They depict the cloth supposedly imprinted with an image of Christ's face after he used it to wipe his face on the road to Calvary. The imprinted image, a 'true likeness' or *vera icona*, gave the name to the woman who offered the cloth, Veronica. Several places claimed to have the actual relic, including Jaén, leading to the explanation that the cloth was folded over when Veronica gave it to Jesus and was thus imprinted with several images.[23] The relics' significance was not only that they had touched Christ's face, but more importantly, that they offered his true likeness. Significant emphasis was placed in the seventeenth century on accurately conveying a saint's true likeness if at all possible, Zurbarán's *St Dominic in Soriano*, for example, showing another miracle when an early sixteenth-century Dominican in Italy was brought a painted portrait of the order's thirteenth-century founder, Dominic, by the Virgin, St Catherine and the Magdalene.

The lifelikeness of portraits leading them to be mistaken for the actual person was a cliché of early modern discussions of portraiture. In the case of the Veronica, this is given a twist in the life of the late fifteenth-century nun Juana de la Cruz. Her father did not want her to become a nun, and she is described, after severely flagellating herself, as prostrating herself before an image of the Veronica and asking Jesus to permit her to be a nun and thus his bride. The face on the veil then became as if actually alive, and Jesus consoled her saying he would welcome her as a nun.[24]

The actual image on the veil was an *acheiropoieton*, an image not made by human hand, so that images of the veil thereby become a human image of a divine image, and the works, representations of a representation and thus a double absence. The Veronica is the most metapictorial of subjects, an occasion for artist and viewer to reflect on the creation and reception of images. The subject obviously plays to Zurbarán's artistic strengths, not least his ability to evoke material presence. He depicts the cloth with its various folds with a marked sense of *trompe l'œil*, creating in effect 'divine *trompe l'œils*'.[25] The effect is to make the cloth tangible and place it in the viewer's space as if really before us. Standardly Zurbarán shows it hanging by cords tied round its gathered upper corners with its top centre pinned up to better reveal the central image, and in many its bottom centre pinned up against the veil itself. The folds cast shadows on the veil, and the veil sometimes does on the background against which it is hung. This background is an undefined space, extremely dark in all versions except the 1658 one in Valladolid (Museo Nacional de Escultura) that is painted a deep browny-red (illus. 54).[26] The veils exhibit all the qualities of Zurbarán's depiction of fabric, perhaps best seen in the circa 1635 version in the Nationalmuseum in Stockholm (illus. 55) with its full folds where the cloth is tied or pinned and its two delicate vertical creases, one through the centre of the veil and its image, the other to the left of this. These mesmerizing creases seem to foreground the fragility of Christ and his image.

In none of his versions is Christ's face presented front on as was standard; it is shown facing left in three-quarter view with

Christ usually looking at the viewer, all of which increases the poignancy of the image. And in no version is the face forcibly present, detailed and in full colour, as was also standard. There is in fact a tendency for Zurbarán's faces to become less distinct in later versions. The Valladolid version is again the most distinctive here, Christ's face a ghostly, pink-and-ochre presence, his facial features barely discernible. In terms of the changes across the versions, it has been suggested that the cloth becomes more materially prominent, the face correspondingly less distinct, and that Zurbarán thereby juxtaposes matter and spirit, the human and the divine, such that paradoxically 'the better the material can be seen, the less the spiritual is' and vice versa.[27] Certainly, the clear distinction between the man-made (his rendering of the *trompe l'œil* veil) and the divine (Christ's miraculously produced 'self-portrait') is an expression of this distinction between irreconcilable opposites with which any artist depicting the divine had to grapple. What we see across this series with its significant variations is an artist not content to reproduce the same but varying and experimenting in distinct ways within the restricted limits of the given: a veil and an impression of a face.

The variants in the facial image have recently been explained in a very particular way; namely, that while all show Christ's face, not all show the Veronica. In this interpretation the version in Stockholm that shows Christ alive with the crown of thorns is a more traditional Veronica. The version in Bilbao (Bilboko Arte Ederren Museoa/Museo de Bellas Artes de Bilbao, *c.* 1658–60) that shows Christ with no crown of thorns and eyes closed is a post-mortem image, akin to that on the Turin shroud, and possibly meant to be the *sudarium* that had covered just Christ's head in the tomb (John 20:7). The Valladolid version, with no crown of thorns and no blood, evokes aspects of the other two possibilities but has more affinities with the Mandylion, another miraculous image created when king Abgar of Edessa wanted a portrait of

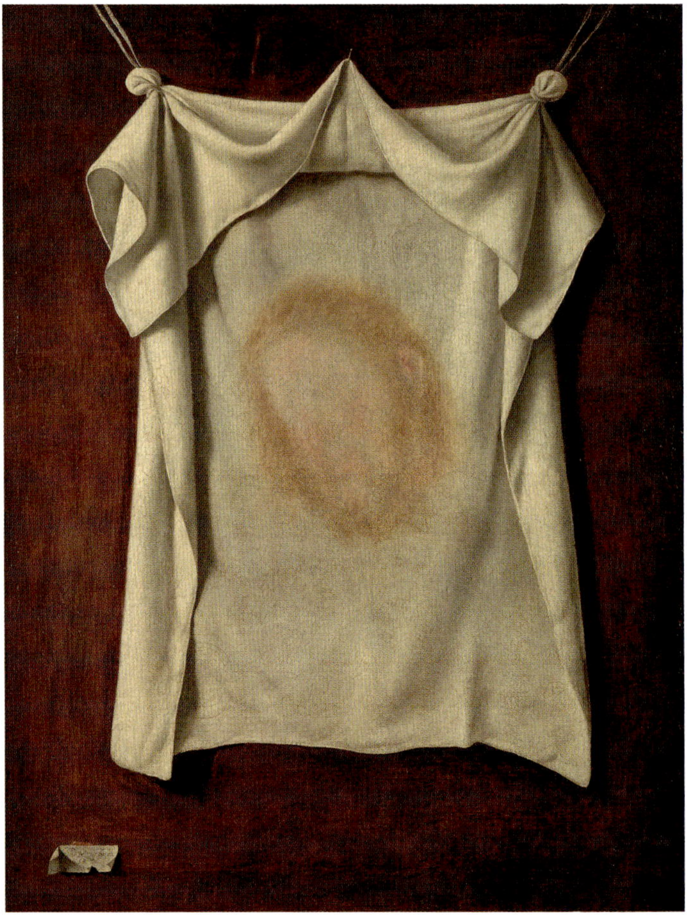

Christ but the artist that he sent found he was unable to paint Christ's face due to the 'divine splendour radiating from it', so Christ raised a damp cloth to his face leaving his image impressed on it.[28] For Felipe Pereda, Zurbarán's Veronicas thus evoke various miraculous images, but don't reproduce the standard appearance of any.[29] This said, the distinctions drawn do not always seem strongly supported by the depicted faces: though the Stockholm

54 Francisco de Zurbarán, *Veil of Veronica*, 1658, oil on canvas.

version offers a clearer facial image than the Valladolid version, for example, in neither is there any evidence of drops or streams of blood, and indeed in the Valladolid work the stronger presence of pinkish pigment obliquely evoking the face might actually be seen as more emphatically suggesting Christ's blood-and-sweat as pigment.[30]

One of the distinctively Zurbaranesque aspects of these works is the absence of elements to emphasize the narrative or

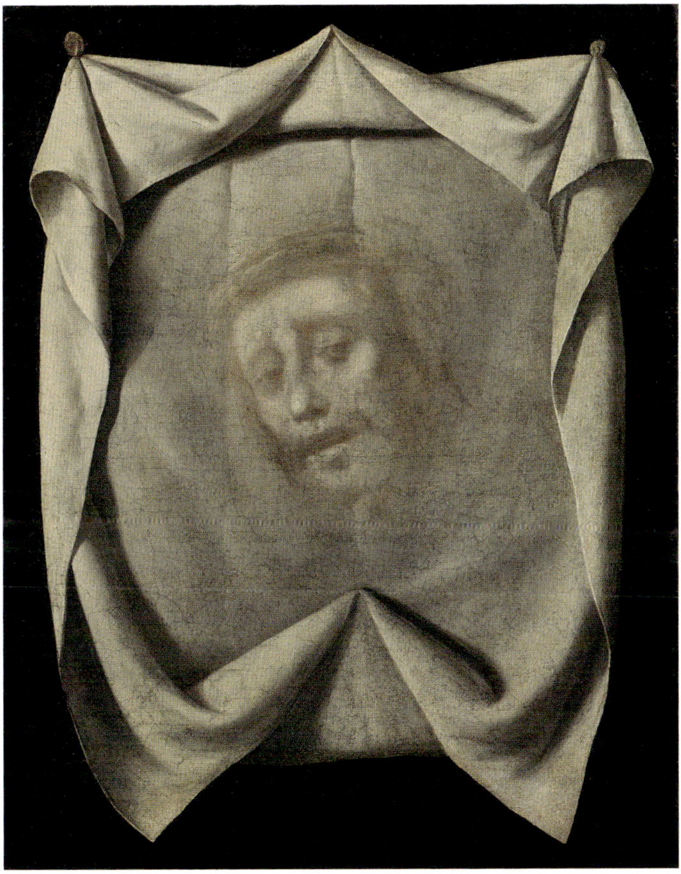

55 Francisco de Zurbarán, *Veil of Veronica*, *c.* 1635, oil on canvas.

to explicitly frame a meditative engagement: it is not held by angels (Dürer) or by Veronica herself (El Greco), and it lacks elements such as the crown of thorns resting below it on a ledge engraved with a quotation from Isaiah found in one of Philippe de Champaigne's versions (Kunsthaus, Zurich). The only extraneous element in his Veronicas is the illusionistic *cartellino* in the 1658 Valladolid version. (One other version is signed and dated 1631, in this case on the lower-right edge of the veil.) This *cartellino* appears as if affixed by wax to the actual canvas's surface, has one corner seemingly bent, another curled and a tear on its bottom edge, and reads *Fran^{co} dezurbaran. / 1658.* It is interesting because, as a *trompe l'œil* element within an already *trompe l'œil* work, it is an illusion to puncture an illusion. The *cartellino* casts a shadow in the same direction as the veil thereby seeming to reinforce the veil's 'reality' while simultaneously undermining it. Such playing with levels of illusion was characteristic of Spanish culture.

Zurbarán used *cartellini* throughout his career, but particularly in its last phase when one of their purposes, to signal the artist and his imitative skill, was particularly important following his move to Madrid and the need to develop a new client base. What may perhaps be surprising is just how prominent and intrusive these and indeed simple signatures often are in his work; they are not meant to be missed. This is perhaps most evident in some of Zurbarán's most strikingly poignant and compellingly illusionistic works such as the *Crucifixion* for San Pablo el Real and the Valladolid *Veronica*. In the *Veronica*, its disruptive presence reveals the tangibly real veil to be a painted illusion, as mentioned, intruding on a purely devotional engagement by signalling (through its *trompe l'œil* presence) and asserting (through the inscription on it) the agency of the artist, thereby setting the mind to think of art. As such it is easy to take such a *cartellino* as marking an awareness of the historical shift traced by Hans Belting from image as devotional object to image as art.[31] But in this instance, image-making also relates to the original veil. In other words, the *cartellino* brings the viewer back to the veil, art back to meditation. For both *cartellino* and veil-icon are markers of the presence of the makers of the respective images, but despite one being a miracle and the other a 'miracle' of art, neither *is* what it represents, and the veil-as-represented doubly so, of course.[32] And this is where the metapictorial element has a key place in a meditative engagement. For by forcing a reminder that an image is just an image, the viewer is reminded that all images must be surpassed. The viewer, in other words, is being prompted to move beyond representational images whose verism has now served its function to arrest the eye and focus the mind.

CRUCIFIXION WITH A PAINTER

As we have seen throughout this book, Zurbarán noticeably avoids strident depictions of pain and torment. But towards the end of his life, scenes of the Passion show Christ as a more dejected and gaunter figure and thus create a far greater sense of quiet suffering. One such is the extraordinary *Crucifixion with a Painter* (illus. 56). This is one of his works with significant variance in dating, from an early date of circa 1635, proposed on the basis of its tenebrism, to circa 1650 or 1655–60.[33]

Like the Veronica, Zurbarán painted the Crucifixion throughout his career, from his earliest dated work, the *Crucifixion* for San Pablo el Real that made such an impact on Seville, to this, his final version, circa 1655–60 being accepted. Unusually, the cross in the *Crucifixion with a Painter* has been displaced from its standardly central position.[34] As well as the more emaciated figure of Christ, emphasized further by the almost sculpturally defined loincloth that Zurbarán paints so that Christ's entire right leg is exposed, it is one of only three versions that include other figures. The first two of these depict more standard figures, one with the

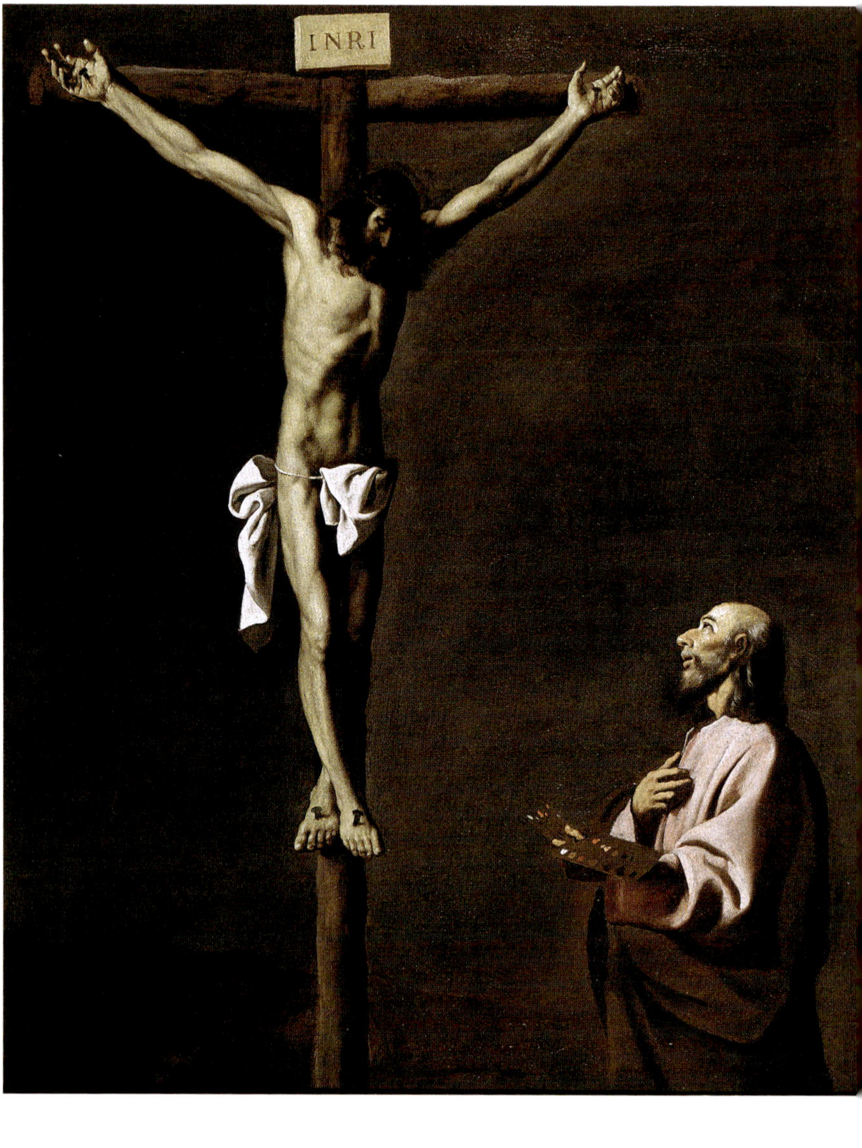

56 Francisco de Zurbarán, *Crucifixion with a Painter*, c. 1655–60, oil on canvas.

Virgin, Magdalene and the apostle John witnessing the crucifixion, the other a donor in seventeenth-century dress, his hands joined in prayer and looking not at Christ but out at the viewer. In this third version there is a middle-aged painter who is shown, three-quarter length, holding brushes and a palette with the range of colours used across the work. The painter is dressed in a mauve-pink robe and brown cloak, 'Biblical' clothing that would identify him as the evangelist St Luke, celebrated as an artist who painted a number of portraits, including the Virgin and Child.[35] It has inevitably been suggested that Zurbarán has depicted himself as Luke.[36] While this can only be speculation since there is no known image of the artist, the art of painting obviously connects Zurbarán and Luke. As Zurbarán's counterpart he discreetly signals that Zurbarán too is a 'pintor cristiano'.[37] The artist in the work becomes Zurbarán's 'spiritual self-portrait'.[38]

The inclusion of Luke with palette and brushes means the painting cannot but have a metapictorial dimension and intention, and while the engagement of the San Pablo el Real *Crucifixion* with the *paragone* between painting and sculpture highlights that Zurbarán was from the beginning a self-aware artist, the *Crucifixion with a Painter*, later date accepted, together with the *Veronica* just discussed suggests Zurbarán entered a period of sustained reflection on art and image-making in the final stage of his career, and in the same decade as his contemporary Velázquez did in the *Meninas* (1656).

Somewhat like the Veronicas with their differences from standard representations of the subject, it is difficult to pin down definitively what is represented here. Ambiguity seems deliberate. Is the artist present at the crucifixion, even though Luke is not one of the standard Biblical figures depicted in this role? For Richard Viladesau 'the primary context of the painting is theological, not visually representational,' and in theological rather than historical terms 'Luke is presented as actually being on Calvary' for

> Catholic theology taught that Jesus . . . knew each person for whom he was dying. . . . We were therefore really 'present' to him in his mind. Our prayer in the present moment thus 'reaches' him at that moment of the crucifixion, even though it is historically past. When we think of him, he . . . likewise becomes 'present' to us in that past moment, for the effects of his sacrifice continue. It is primarily the work of the sacraments to mediate this genuine presence; but sacred art also was thought to perform a kind of quasi-sacramental function in this regard.[39]

Or is he experiencing a vision?[40] If so this might be corporeal (that is, seen with the eyes) or imaginative (seen only internally), Juan de la Cruz saying the soul when it has not moved beyond word or image, beyond senses and discursive meditation to contemplation, might be granted either by God.[41] Certainly, Luke's slightly open mouth suggests a moment of visionary enthralment like Alonso Rodríguez's (illus. 57). Christ is almost imperceptibly smaller in scale than Luke, so perhaps the latter is standing in front of an image that he has created? The sketchy landscape low behind the cross might indicate that Christ on the cross here is a painting, perhaps an 'unfinished canvas'.[42] Although Luke was celebrated as a painter, Pacheco mentions a sculpted crucifix held to be by him.[43] He might therefore be before a sculpture that he has polychromed, and these were sometimes placed against painted backdrops, although in Zurbarán's *Crucifixion with a Donor* (1640) the crucifixion is unambiguously meant to be a sculpted image, since it casts a shadow against the backdrop parallel to it, as similarly does Velázquez's *Crucifixion* (*c.* 1632). Christ's crossed feet and lowered head recall the famous *Christ of Clemency* by the sculptor Martínez Montañés.[44] The contract for this required Christ to be shown as if speaking to the suppliant before him, but here Christ appears dead, his eyes seemingly closed, his body's pallor in marked contrast to Luke's vitality. If we do view Luke as contemplating something he has created, then his emotive attitude vis-à-vis the sacred image is itself a topos in accounts of artists' lives, Giorgio Vasari recording, for example, that Fra Angelico 'never painted a crucifix without the tears streaming down his cheeks'.[45]

Unsurprisingly, the issue of meditation has also been mentioned in discussions of the painting, with the suggestion that the artist shown may be meditating, indeed may have 'projected himself, as in a Spiritual Exercise, into the story of the Passion, onto Golgotha at the time of the Crucifixion'.[46] His stance conveys intense devotion as he looks directly at Christ's face, right hand touching his heart, and the size of the painting (105 × 84 centimetres ($41\tfrac{5}{16}$ × $33\tfrac{1}{16}$ in.)), the second smallest *Crucifixion* that Zurbarán painted, certainly makes the viewer's own engagement more intimate (the San Pablo el Real *Crucifixion*, in contrast, measures 290.3 × 165.5 centimetres ($114\tfrac{5}{16}$ × $65\tfrac{3}{16}$ in.)).[47] As we have seen, in affective meditation one may use an actual image or create an image in one's mind's eye, but the aim of briefly dwelling on either is to bring the scene meditated upon vividly to life and to place oneself as if present while it unfolds. The work's ambiguity is at its most deliberate here because, in terms of meditation, the status of the image is irrelevant. And this is also why the various interpretations of what we see and of the relationship between the two figures are not simply valid, but actualized: in all, Luke *is* present at the crucifixion.

A further and telling dimension here is precisely having an artist as the meditator, for the meditator had long been said to paint an image in the heart, painting and pictures wide-spread and long-standing tropes in the theory and practice of meditation.[48] This process is literalized in an engraving by Boëtius à Bolswert in the *Via vitae aeternae* (The Road to Eternal Life, 1620) by Antoine Sucquet, a Flemish Jesuit (illus. 58). This shows an

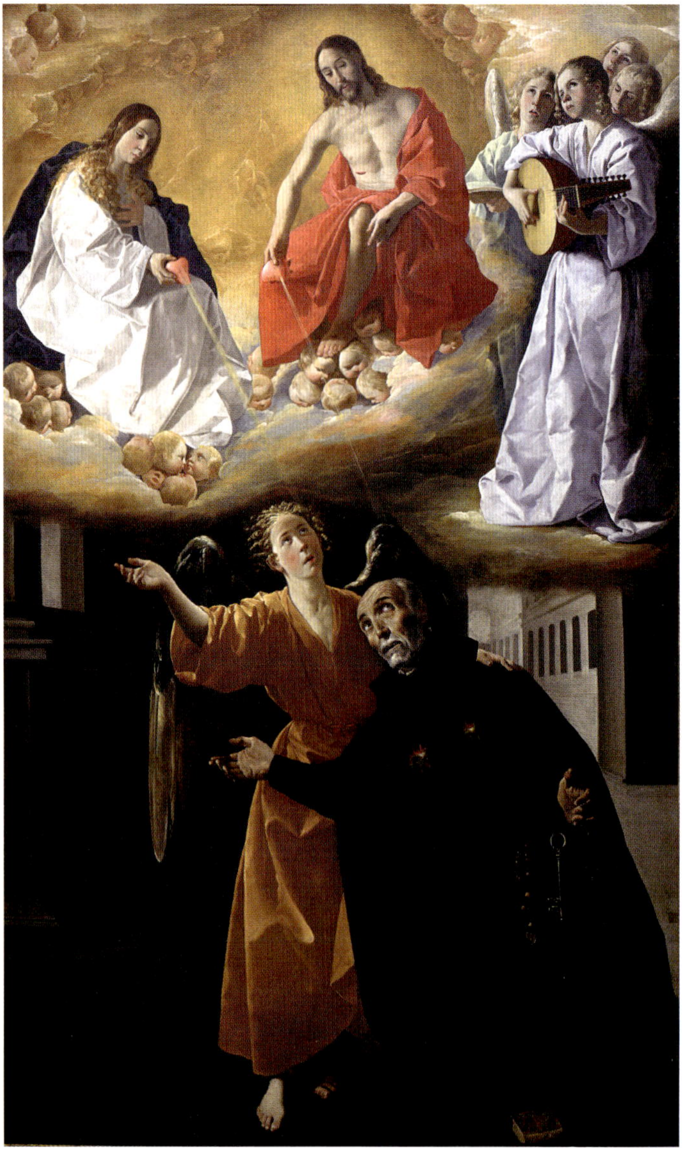

57 Francisco de Zurbarán, *Vision of St Alonso Rodríguez*, 1630, oil on canvas.

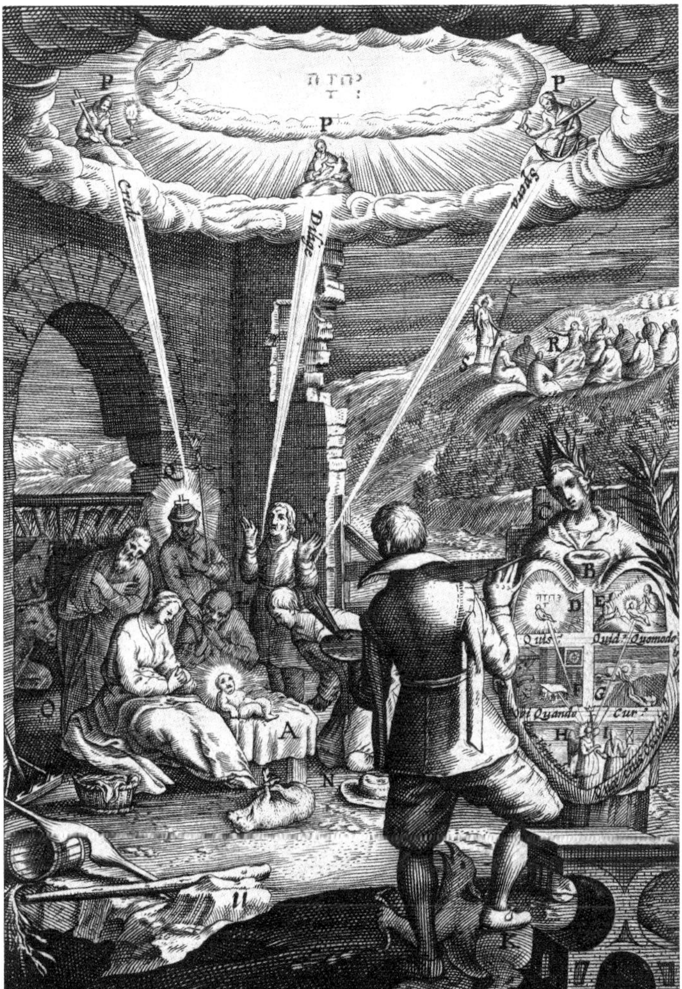

artist in seventeenth-century dress standing directly before the nativity as if actually present. Brushes and palette in hand, he has turned from his canvas to look at the scene. The canvas is heart shaped; it *is* his heart. On it he has painted aspects of the scene

58 Man meditating on the nativity, illustration by Boëtius à Bolswert from Antoine Sucquet, *Via vitae aeternae* (The Road to Eternal Life, 1620).

before him in separate compartments labelled *Quis? Quid? Quomodo? Ubi? Quando? Cur?* (who, what, how, where, when, why).[49] The text calls these 'circumstances' and they are in effect related to the 'circumstantial topics' familiar from Classical and contemporary rhetoric that were used to analyse all aspects of a subject and that are deployed here to aid the 'artist'-meditator's delving deeper into an understanding of the nativity.

What we encounter in Zurbarán's *Crucifixion with a Painter* is a sophisticated embodiment of the image in meditation and a simultaneous realization of its variants. Had an artist been asked to depict the affective dimensions of meditation, they could not have done so more fully and suggestively than Zurbarán does here, and all without the explanatory matrix of Sucquet's image and its accompanying prose text. This is an artist who has thought about images, their ontological realities, their function and purpose, and all in the context of meditation and contemplation that was at the heart of early modern Catholic spirituality and devotion.

Conclusion

At the end of the 1650s Zurbarán moved to Madrid, though precisely when is unknown. He and his household are recorded as living in Seville in the 1658 parish census, but when he gives his testimony in Madrid on 23 December 1658 as part of the investigation into the ancestry and social standing of Velázquez, who was seeking to join the Order of Santiago, he is said to have been resident in Madrid for seven months, and in the 1659 census his wife is listed as resident in Seville but his name is absent.[1] By June 1659 both are said to be 'currently' resident in Madrid.[2]

If the precise date of his move is unclear, the reasons for it are even more so. The fundamental reason adduced is Murillo's rise to prominence in Seville and Zurbarán's recognition that his style was now 'dated'. But such concerns over favour and style would equally be issues in Madrid, as Zurbarán would have known, since many artists were obviously already established in the capital and the prevailing styles there, whether the impressionistic fluidity of late Velázquez or the High Baroque dynamism and theatricality of Francisco de Herrera the Younger and Francisco Rizi, were even further from Zurbarán's style than Murillo's was. Such dynamism had in fact already made an impact in Seville in 1656–7 with Herrera the Younger's luminous and vibrant *Triumph of the Eucharist* and *St Francis in Ecstasy*, as well as Murillo's *Vision of St Anthony of Padua*, this showing that Murillo was not the only

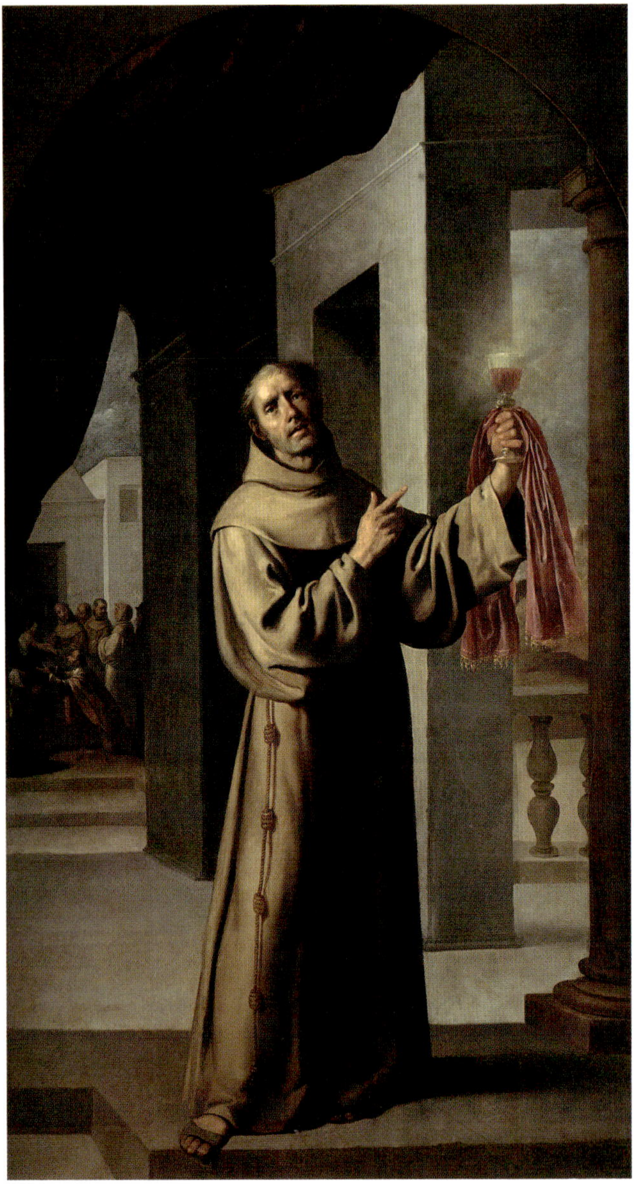

59 Francisco de Zurbarán, *St James of the Marches*, *c.* 1659–60, oil on canvas.

local rival, and perhaps unfortunately for Zurbarán, Herrera also moved to Madrid in 1660–61 having already made his mark there with his *Apotheosis of St Hermenegild*. Of course Madrid was the court, so Zurbarán may have reasoned that the market was bigger and there were more opportunities to work there than in Seville. He might also have hoped that the most favoured artist at court, his colleague Velázquez, on whose behalf he had testified in December 1658, might facilitate work and commissions. We don't know if Velázquez did do this, but his death in August 1660 removed a powerful contact, if such he was. Financial pressures were also a factor in his move. His economic position in Seville was by no means dire, but he failed to pay rent due on properties in the city in 1656 and 1659.[3] Given his involvement with the New World art market, this failure has been linked to his being financially hit by the English capture in both 1656 and 1657 of the New World treasure fleets as they returned to Seville; this would have meant the loss of remittances for his work sent to and sold in the Americas, a market he then withdrew from.[4] The loss of this market, together with the rise of other artists, Murillo especially, and thus his declining fortune in Seville, seems to have led him to seek to establish himself in Madrid. There we find him still trying to obtain the proceeds from work he had sent to Buenos Aires and that had been received there in 1649; the fact he was pursuing this eleven years later is an indication of the risks involved in transatlantic trade and his own need for money.[5]

In Madrid he primarily painted devotional subjects. A high percentage of these are signed and dated and this, together with the fact that popular subjects are repeated (for example, the *Virgin and Child*, whether alone, with St Joseph, or with the infant John the Baptist, or the *Virgin as a Child Praying*), has led to the suggestion that they were painted not on commission, but speculatively.[6] He had signed and dated works across his career, most prolifically in the 1630s, but as previously mentioned, signing works in a market where he was less well known was an effective form of advertising his skill and asserting his presence.

It is easy to get the impression of a failing artist, an impression compounded by those who view his velvety late style as less impactful than the supposedly 'virile' style of his earlier work.[7] But there are several indications that Zurbarán was not necessarily struggling.

He appears to have worked in some capacity for the palace, for in a January 1662 letter he excuses himself for not yet having fulfilled a commission for various paintings from one Jerónimo Rodríguez, now deceased, by saying that he must first finish the 'assignments from his majesty the king'.[8] The same letter mentions work for the monastery of Santo Domingo de Atocha in Madrid, the Dominicans being entrusted with the Marian image of the Virgin of Atocha that was the subject of intense devotion by the Spanish Habsburgs. He also painted *St Thomas Aquinas Visiting St Bonaventure* and *St James of the Marches* (*c.* 1659–60; illus. 59) for the chapel of St Diego of Alcalá in the Franciscan monastery in Alcalá de Henares to the northeast of Madrid. Alonso Cano had painted two works for the chapel and had seemingly been commissioned to paint more but left the contract unfulfilled, so Zurbarán was called in, an echo of how he had been hired by the Franciscans in Seville in 1629 when Herrera the Elder had been unable to fulfil contracted work – any sense of déjà vu possibly intensified by the fact that the earlier undertaking had also involved painting an occasion when Aquinas visited Bonaventure.[9] This was a prestigious assignment, for the chapel contained the remains of Diego of Alcalá, who was not only a Spanish saint but one venerated by the Habsburgs ever since his relics were held to have saved Philip II's son from dying in 1562.

The five years that he seems to have been active in Madrid thus involved more than painting private devotional works, though these did form the bulk of his output. His last known painting, a *Virgin and Child with the Infant John the Baptist* signed and dated 1662 (illus. 60), is typical of his devotional style – intimate and softly focused – and themes, a more sentimental image of the seated Virgin, prayer book in her left hand, Jesus on her lap touching the head of the kneeling John the Baptist who kisses Jesus's other hand, the Virgin obliquely glancing out towards the viewer. The work contains elements found across his oeuvre: a prominent *cartellino*; a small still life of apples and pears on a pewter or silver plate to the right behind the Virgin; and John's lamb, kneeling at front left, its tactile, knotted fleece the last Zurbarán will paint, all set against a less stridently dark background that is smoothly paler around the Virgin.

Zurbarán wrote his will on 26 August 1664 and died the next day, and since his last signed and dated work is from 1662, this may indicate that he was ill or incapacitated for a protracted period. Part of how one interprets his final years in Madrid rests on what his will and post-mortem inventory reveal about his financial status. The view that he died 'in poverty, if not misery' has rightly been replaced by one that emphasizes that he was relatively comfortably off.[10] This said, there are indications that he had little ready cash, for Leonor de Tordera, his widow, states in the post-mortem inventory that various silver items (candlesticks, a pepper pot, a sugar bowl, among other things) had been pawned to cover the costs of his illness and funeral.[11] The subsequent valuation document gives a fuller picture of the works and artistic material in his possession when he died:

a *St Peter*;
a *Custodia*;
a *Virgin and St Catherine*, framed;
a *St John*, framed;
a three-quarter length *St John*, framed;
a statue of the infant Jesus;

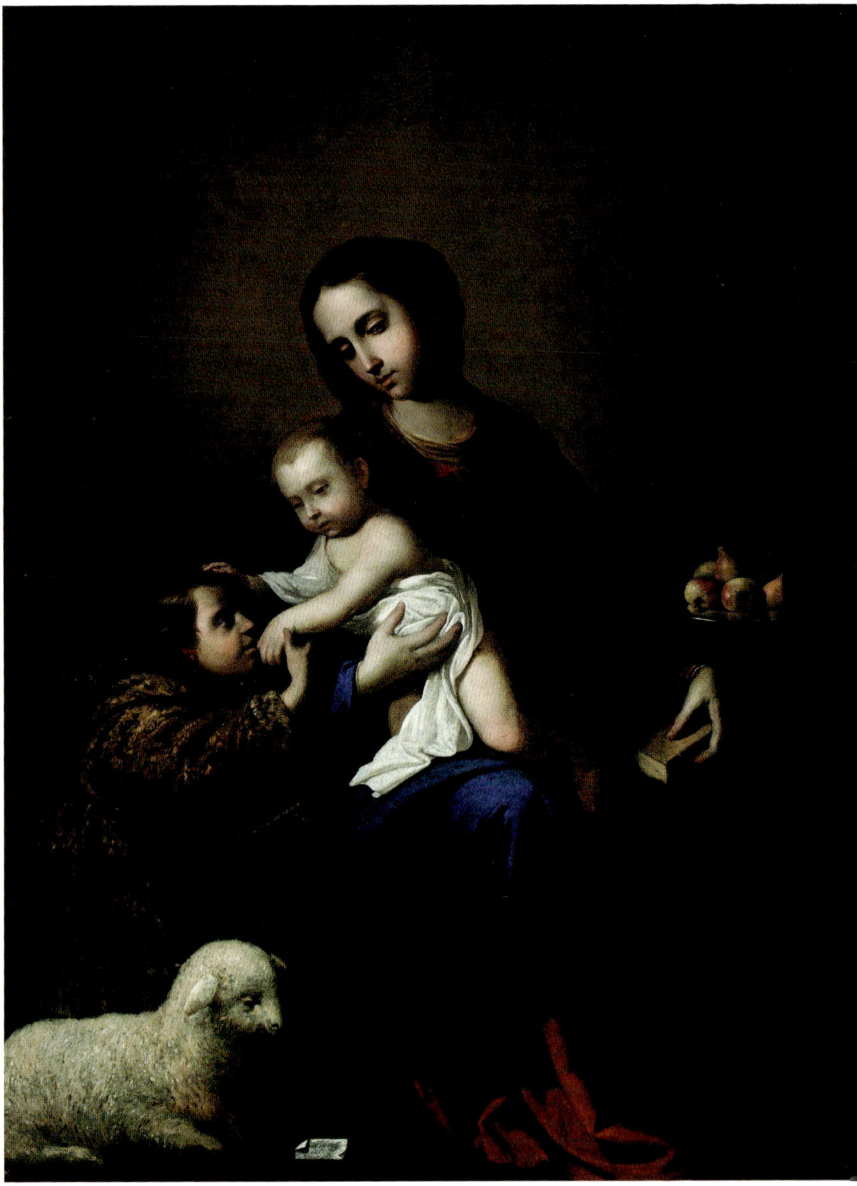

60 Francisco de Zurbarán, *Virgin and Child with the Infant John the Baptist*, 1662, oil on canvas.

a *Susanna*, framed;
a *Christ*;
an *Assumption of the Virgin*;
a *Virgin and Child with St John and St Joseph*;
four landscapes, unframed;
a portrait of a girl and boy, unframed;
12 prints of kings;
50 prints, in a book;
12 emperors on paper;
9 primed canvases;
2 easels;
a slab for grinding pigments.[12]

Aside from the paintings of habitual subjects almost certainly by him, as all the paintings mentioned may have been, several things are worth commenting on here. First, the *Susanna*. It seems impossible to imagine Zurbarán painting a *Susanna and the Elders* given its standard combination of female nudity and male voyeurism, so this may be an image of the third-century virgin martyr, though that said, María Luisa Caturla mentions that the artist Ignacio Zuloaga (1870–1945) claimed to have seen a *Susanna and the Elders* supposedly by Zurbarán but without saying where.[13] Then the landscapes. No stand-alone landscapes are known by Zurbarán, so if not a new departure they may be works that he owned or an indication he was still trading in others' work, as he had with the Flemish landscapes that were among paintings he consigned for sale in Buenos Aires in 1649. Finally, the prints that were integral to his pictorial practice across his career, here some loose, some not, some on subjects typical of the New World art trade (the series of emperors), most unidentified.

WHAT DID ZURBARÁN CREATE in his art? A singular vision of things ensouled, of the world spiritualized.

He did not just express the spirituality and mysticism of seventeenth-century Spain, the yearning for the eternal that was a driving force of its culture and an avowed part of its imperial mission to spread and defend Catholicism. Rather, to capture the spiritual and the immaterial he paradoxically captured the very materiality of things in all their textural singularity. In so doing he seems to express a sense of their individual isolation; vividly there, but all turned to eternity, not to the present they inhabit.

As an artist he is often defined by his subjects: monks and friars, saints and martyrs, and the Virgin, not least the Immaculate Conception. But it is his style and distinctive compositions in treating these that make him unique. His stylistic and compositional traits include the use of dark backgrounds, sharp contours that often make figures, and especially their hands, look as though they were separately created and then applied to the surface of the canvas, the dominance of the front plane and the placing of people and things as if each were the only person or thing present, all radically detached from one another even as they are presented within a shared space. His compositions, religious and secular, figure paintings and still lifes, present a strikingly atomized world, one not conveying any sense of alienation but rather a quietude that embraces everything. This radical atomization is occasionally a result of a certain compositional maladroitness, but even this only compounds the sense of detachment, withdrawal, stillness and absorption that defines each thing in his pictorial world. These were conditions held essential to mystical contemplation; by evoking them he seems to evoke the ineffable. It is here, perhaps more than in the actual subjects he depicts, that he embodies as no one else Golden Age spiritual life.

Alongside these qualities that emanate from his work, his paintings glory in an extraordinary use of colour and of colour combinations. His eye for colour captivates and is part of his making us linger on the surface, in defiance of his culture's strident emphasis on the need to move beyond appearances to obtain the truth beneath them. His colours may resonate symbolically, liturgical colours, for example, possibly enforcing or embodying the subject: green, Christian hope; black, sins and mourning; violet/purple, the penitential/imperial colour used during Advent and Lent; red, linked to the love of God for humankind and the spilt blood of Christ and the martyrs; white, a Marian colour alongside pink and blue, for feasts of the infancies of Jesus and the Virgin; yellow, 'symbol of divinity'.[14] But standardly, they seem part of a revelling in the beauty of the world, a beauty captured nowhere more strikingly than in his painting of fabric. Here Zurbarán combines colour with his exquisite rendering of texture, and this is as evident in his depictions of white or brown habits as in the fabulously rich clothing of a *St Apollonia* or the rustic costume of a *St Margaret of Antioch*.

As a painter he delights the eye in many ways, such as with an incidental detail, be it the inner stitching of a Dominican shoulder cape, the impasto rendering of light as it falls on an upturned bowl, the untrimmed end of a slender willow rod poking out of the weave of a wicker basket; or the moment where pigment becomes object and object pigment, as with the thin streak of white that defines the foremost lit edge of the right-hand side of Christ's loincloth as it billows in the blackness in a *Crucifixion* (*c.* 1635), the negligible dash of brighter orange against an angel's orange robe in the *Vision of St Alonso Rodríguez* (1630), a subsidiary streak of flame to create its belt; or the juxtaposition of both detail and facture, as in the *St John the Baptist* (*c.* 1638–9) where, on the left, we see a tiny piece of string holding together the two pieces of John's long cane cross, string that is carefully rendered yet barely discernible, while on the right, the loose application of broad brushstrokes of pigment to create the mountain behind the saint.

It is in such moments that we see the fabric of the world being conjured before our eyes.

CHRONOLOGY

1598	Born Fuente de Cantos
1614–17	Apprenticeship in Seville
1617	Marries María Páez, Llerena
1618	Start of pan-European Thirty Years' War
1621	Philip III dies; Philip IV becomes king
1623	María Páez dies
1625	Marries Beatriz de Morales, Llerena
1626	Contract with Dominicans in Seville for their monastery, San Pablo el Real
1627	*Crucifixion* for San Pablo el Real, Seville
1628	Contract with Calced Mercedarian monastery in Seville; resides with his team in monastery to complete commission
1629	Work for Franciscan church of the College of St Bonaventure, Seville. City council invites Zurbarán to move to Seville
1631	Altarpiece for the Dominican church of the College of Santo Tomás, Seville
1633	*Still Life with Citrons, Oranges and a Rose*
1634	Called to Madrid to work for Philip IV at the Buen Retiro
1635–59	War with France
c. 1635–40	*St Agatha*
c. 1638–9	Work for Charterhouse of Nuestra Señora de la Defensión, Jerez de la Frontera
1639	Beatriz de Morales dies. Commission from Hieronymites in Guadalupe, only major cycle still *in situ*
1640	Revolt of Catalonia. Revolt of Portugal
c. 1640–45	*St Francis* (National Gallery, London)

1643	Count-Duke of Olivares, Philip IV's favourite, dismissed
1644	Marries Leonor de Tordera, Seville
c. 1644–5	*Christ and the Virgin in the House at Nazareth* (Cleveland Museum of Art)
c. 1645–50	*St Rufina. St Margaret of Antioch*
1648	Treaty of Westphalia ends Thirty Years' War
1649	Plague in Seville; Juan de Zurbarán dies
c. 1650–55	*Still Life with Vessels*
c. 1655	Work for Charterhouse of Santa María de las Cuevas, Seville
c. 1655–60	*Crucifixion with a Painter*
1658	*Veil of Veronica* (Museo Nacional de Escultura, Valladolid)
1658–9	Zurbarán and Leonor de Tordera move to Madrid
1662	*Virgin and Child with the Infant John the Baptist*, last signed and dated work
1664	Zurbarán dies in Madrid, 27 August

REFERENCES

Contemporary documents concerning Zurbarán can be found online through the Centro de Estudios Europa Hispánica, www.ceeh.es/zurbaran-digital/introduccion; references to this database are given here as Zurbarán Digital. Documents can be found by searching place and then date, both given in references here. Those referred to were accessed 25 April 2024.

Biblical references in the text are given simply by book, chapter and verse. Those in Latin are to the *Biblia vulgata*, 9th edn (Madrid, 1994); those in English to the Douay-Rheims-Challoner version, *Holy Bible* (Baltimore, MD, 1914).

Introduction

1 Francisco Pacheco, *El arte de la pintura*, ed. Bonaventura Bassegoda i Hugas (Madrid, 1990), p. 521.
2 This is the subject of my *Incomparable Realms: Spain during the Golden Age, 1500–1700* (London, 2022).
3 Odile Delenda, *Zurbarán. Catálogo razonado y crítico*, vol. I (Madrid, 2009). For works by Zurbarán's workshop and/or followers, Odile Delenda, *Zurbarán. Catálogo razonado y crítico*, vol. II: *Los conjuntos y el obrador* (Madrid, 2010). Delenda's attributions and dating are followed, but critical divergences regarding dates, which can be significant, are raised on occasion.

1 Seville in a Time of Decline

1 Alfonso Rodríguez Grajera, 'Fuente de Cantos en tiempos de Zurbarán', in *Francisco de Zurbarán (1598–1998): su tiempo, su obra, su tierra*, ed. Felipe Lorenzana de la Puente (Fuente de Cantos, 1998), p. 28.

2 María Luisa Caturla, *Francisco de Zurbarán*, trans. and ed. Odile Delenda (Paris, 1994), doc. 17, pp. 288–9; José Lamilla Prímola, 'La familia de Francisco de Zurbarán (algunos datos históricos)', in *Francisco de Zurbarán (1598–1998)*, ed. Lorenzana de la Puente, p. 394.
3 Fernando de Herrera, *Poesía castellana original completa*, ed. Cristóbal Cuevas (Madrid, 1985), p. 807.
4 Jonathan Brown and J. H. Elliott, *A Palace for a King: The Buen Retiro and the Court of Philip IV*, revd edn (New Haven, CT, and London, 2003), p. 43.
5 Vicente Lleó Cañal, *Nueva Roma: Mitología y humanismo en el Renacimiento sevillano* (Madrid, 2012), p. 91; Antonio Domínguez Ortiz, *Orto y ocaso de Sevilla*, 3rd edn (Seville, 1981), pp. 72–3.
6 Luis Vélez de Guevara, *El diablo cojuelo*, 8th edn, ed. Enrique Rodríguez Cepeda (Madrid, 2018), p. 144; Félix Lope de Vega Carpio, *El peregrino en su patria*, ed. Julián González-Barrera (Madrid, 2016), p. 499.
7 Manuel Castillo Martos and Joaquín Rodríguez Mateos, *Sevilla Barroca y el siglo XVII*, 2nd edn (Seville, 2019), p. 165.
8 Ibid., pp. 148–50, 152–3, 162–4, 168–72.
9 Ibid., p. 376.
10 Helen Rawlings, *Church, Religion and Society in Early Modern Spain* (Basingstoke, 2002), pp. 124–5.
11 Diego Ortiz de Zúñiga, *Anales eclesiásticos y seculares de la muy noble y muy leal ciudad de Sevilla* (Madrid, 1677), pp. 713, 733, 737; Rodrigo Caro, *Antigüedades y principado de la ilustrísima ciudad de Sevilla* (Seville, 1634), fol. 63r.
12 José Fernández López in Enrique Valdivieso, *Zurbarán IV Centenario*, exh. cat., Museo de Bellas Artes (Seville, 1998), p. 30. Compare Domínguez Ortiz, *Orto*, p. 92.
13 On Fuente de Cantos and Llerena: Rodríguez Grajera, 'Fuente de Cantos', Tomás Pérez Marín, 'Llerena en la época de Zurbarán, entre la prosperidad y la decadencia' and Lamilla Prímola, 'La familia de Francisco de Zurbarán', in *Francisco de Zurbarán (1598–1998)*, ed. Lorenzana de la Puente, pp. 41, 60–61, 394.
14 David Pullins in David Pullins and Vanessa K. Valdés, eds, *Juan de Pareja: Afro-Hispanic Painter in the Age of Velázquez*, exh. cat., The Metropolitan Museum of Art, New York (New Haven, CT, and London, 2023), p. 18.
15 Luis Méndez Rodríguez in *Juan de Pareja*, ed. Pullins and Valdés, pp. 31, 33–4, 37–8.

16 Amanda Wunder, *Baroque Seville: Sacred Art in a Century of Crisis* (University Park, PA, 2017), pp. 1–5; Teofilo F. Ruiz, *Spanish Society, 1348–1700*, 2nd edn (London and New York, 2017), pp. 284–6.
17 Ortiz, *Anales*, pp. 645–6.
18 Castillo Martos and Rodríguez Mateos, *Sevilla Barroca*, pp. 97, 120–21; Wunder, *Baroque Seville*, p. 50.
19 Castillo Martos and Rodríguez Mateos, *Sevilla Barroca*, p. 103.
20 Mary Elizabeth Perry, *Gender and Disorder in Early Modern Seville* (Princeton, NJ, 1990), p. 161. Figures rose across the century and mortality rates were high: Castillo Martos and Rodríguez Mateos, *Sevilla Barroca*, pp. 335, 338.
21 Lorenzo Bautista de Zúñiga, *Anales eclesiásticos y seglares de la muy noble y muy leal ciudad de Sevilla* (Seville, *c.* 1748), unpaginated prologue under '1700'.
22 Domínguez Ortiz, *Orto*, pp. 136–42.
23 Ibid., p.144.
24 Castillo Martos and Rodríguez Mateos, *Sevilla Barroca*, pp. 66–71.
25 Brown and Elliott, *Palace*, pp. 43, 115.
26 Caturla, *Zurbarán*, docs 65, 72, pp. 297, 299; Odile Delenda in Odile Delenda and Mar Borobia, *Zurbarán: A New Perspective*, exh. cat., Museo Thyssen-Bornemisza (Madrid, 2015), pp. 16, 20.
27 Caturla, *Zurbarán*, doc. 21, p. 289.
28 Jonathan Brown, *Zurbarán* (London, 1991), p. 13; Peter Cherry, 'La formación de los pintores en los talleres sevillanos', in *Zurbarán ante su centenario (1598–1998)*, ed. Alfonso E. Pérez Sánchez (Valladolid, 1999), p. 49.
29 Ángel Aterido Fernández, ed., *Corpus velazqueño: documentos y textos*, vol. I (Madrid, 2010), pp. 28–9.
30 Antonio Palomino, *El museo pictórico y escala óptica* (Madrid, 1947), p. 937.
31 Jean Andrews, *Painting and Devotion in Golden Age Iberia: Luis de Morales* (Cardiff, 2020), p. 77.
32 Enrique Valdivieso in Alfonso E. Pérez Sánchez and Benito Navarrete Prieto, *De Herrera a Velázquez. El primer naturalismo en Sevilla*, exh. cat., Hospital de los Venerables (Seville, 2005), p. 73.
33 Rafael Japón, *The Influence of Italian Culture on the Sevillian Golden Age of Painting* (New York and London, 2022), p. 76.
34 Tanya J. Tiffany, *Diego Velázquez's Early Paintings and the Culture of Seventeenth-Century Seville* (University Park, PA, 2012), p. 136.
35 For a summary of shortcomings, Alfonso E. Pérez Sánchez, 'Torpeza y humildad de Zurbarán', *Goya*, LXIV–LXV (1965), p. 267.

36 Peter Cherry in Michael Clarke, *Velázquez in Seville*, exh. cat., National Gallery of Scotland (Edinburgh, 1996), p. 74 and 'Formación', p. 54.
37 Jusepe Martínez, *Discursos practicables del nobilísimo arte de la pintura*, ed. María Elena Manrique Ara (Madrid, 2006), p. 240.
38 José María Carrascal Muñoz, 'Visión mística y éxtasis en la pintura de Zurbarán', *Goya*, CCLVII (1997), p. 300. Also favouring conscious choice over 'ineptness', Martin S. Soria, *The Paintings of Zurbarán* (London, 1953), pp. 11, 13. Gállego suggests such 'clumsiness' may be 'to some extent intentional': Julián Gállego and José Gudiol, *Zurbarán, 1598–1664*, trans. Kenneth Lyons (London, 1987), pp. 35–6.
39 Marcia B. Hall, *The Sacred Image in the Age of Art* (New Haven, CT, and London, 2011), p. 12.
40 Pablo Hereza, *Corpus Murillo. Biografía y documentos* (Seville, 2017), p. 39.
41 Antonio Martínez Ripoll in *De Herrera a Velázquez*, ed. Pérez Sánchez and Navarrete Prieto, p. 90.
42 Miguel Ángel Melón Jiménez, 'Extremadura en el siglo XVII. Los límites de una sociedad de fronteras', in *Zurbarán ante su centenario*, ed. Pérez Sánchez, pp. 10–13.
43 Delenda and Borobia, *Zurbarán: New Perspective*, p. 16.
44 Caturla, *Zurbarán*, p. 26.
45 Odile Delenda, *Zurbarán. Catálogo razonado y crítico*, vol. I (Madrid, 2009), p. 83.
46 Jonathan Brown in *Zurbarán*, exh. cat., Museo Nacional del Prado (Madrid, 1988), p. 13.
47 Luis de Góngora, *Obras completas*, 4th edn, ed. Juan Millé y Giménez and Isabel Millé y Giménez (Madrid, 1956), p. 724.

2 Zurbarán Takes Seville

1 Contract Seville 17 January 1626 at Zurbarán Digital.
2 Odile Delenda and José Fernández López, both in Odile Delenda and Mar Borobia, *Zurbarán: A New Perspective*, exh. cat., Museo Thyssen-Bornemisza (Madrid, 2015), pp. 17, 38.
3 Odile Delenda, *Zurbarán. Catálogo razonado y crítico*, vol. II: *Los conjuntos y el obrador* (Madrid, 2010), pp. 55–6.
4 On Zurbarán's accuracy in depicting ecclesiastical vestments, Pablo Jesús Lorite Cruz, 'Liturgia estricta en la iconografía de la pintura de Francisco de Zurbarán', in XV *Jornadas de Historia de Fuente de Cantos. Zurbarán (1598–1664), 350 aniversario de su muerte* (Fuente de Cantos, 2015), pp. 167–83.

5 Antonio Palomino, *El museo pictórico y escala óptica* (Madrid, 1947), p. 937; Peter Cherry, 'La formación de los pintores en los talleres sevillanos', in *Zurbarán ante su centenario (1598–1998)*, ed. Alfonso E. Pérez Sánchez (Valladolid, 1999), p. 53. For his use of *tela encolada* to model drapery, Marjorie Trusted, *The Arts of Spain: Iberia and Latin America, 1450–1700* (London, 2007), p. 152.
6 Enrique Valdivieso, *Zurbarán IV Centenario*, exh. cat., Museo de Bellas Artes (Seville, 1998), p. 122.
7 Palomino, *Museo*, p. 938.
8 Contract Azuaga 10 August 1624 at Zurbarán Digital; Odile Delenda and Luis Garraín Villa, 'Zurbarán sculpteur: Aspects inédits de sa carrière et de sa biographie', *Gazette des Beaux-Arts*, CXXXI (1998), pp. 125–38.
9 Xavier Bray in Xavier Bray, *The Sacred Made Real: Spanish Painting and Sculpture, 1600–1700*, exh. cat., National Gallery (London, 2009), p. 18. On the influence of polychrome sculpture on painters, pp. 15–43.
10 Contract in Felipe Pereda, *Crimen e ilusión: El arte de la verdad en el Siglo de Oro* (Madrid, 2017), p. 126.
11 Bray, *Sacred Made Real*, pp. 38, 180, 182.
12 Francisco Pacheco, *El arte de la pintura*, ed. Bonaventura Bassegoda i Hugas (Madrid, 1990), pp. 713–34. Pacheco was also involved in a polemic over the *titulus* on the cross: Jonathan Brown, *Images and Ideas in Seventeenth-Century Spanish Painting* (Princeton, NJ, 1978), pp. 60–61.
13 María Luisa Caturla, *Francisco de Zurbarán*, trans. and ed. Odile Delenda (Paris, 1994), doc. 55, pp. 294–5.
14 Delenda, *Zurbarán*, vol. II, p. 76.
15 Jonathan Brown in *Zurbarán*, exh. cat., Museo Nacional del Prado (Madrid, 1988), p. 14.
16 Delenda, *Zurbarán*, vol. II, p. 19; Jesús Palomero Páramo, 'Dos pintores de Monesterio auxilian a Zurbarán en la decoración del Buen Retiro, de Madrid: Diego Muñoz Naranjo y Juan Guerra', in *Actas del Simposio Internacional Zurbarán y su época* (Torrejón de Ardoz, 1998), pp. 86–9. But on the misidentification of this Guerra, and on Muñoz Naranjo, Antonio Manuel Barragán-Lancharro, 'La familia de Francisco de Zurbarán en Monesterio', in his *Estudios de la Baja Extremadura* (Badajoz, 2009), pp. 38–45, and 'La conexión familiar del pintor Zurbarán con Monesterio', in XV *Jornadas de Historia de Fuente de Cantos. Zurbarán (1598–1664)*, pp. 114–17.
17 Caturla, *Zurbarán*, doc. 59, p. 296; Delenda, *Zurbarán*, vol. II , p. 69, n. 43; Palomero Páramo, 'Dos pintores', p. 87.

18 Caturla, *Zurbarán*, doc. 102, p. 306.
19 Jesús Palomero Páramo in Enrique Valdivieso, *Zurbarán: IV centenario del nacimiento*, exh. cat., Museo de Bellas Artes de Badajoz (Madrid, 1998), p. 22.
20 Delenda, *Zurbarán*, vol. II, pp. 20–21, 77–8, 263–5, 267, 272, 275, 321–2, 341–2.
21 Palomino, *Museo*, pp. 998, 949, 955. On workshops and their members (apprentices, *oficiales*/journeymen and master etc.) see Trusted, *The Arts of Spain*, pp. 150–52.
22 Delenda and Garraín Villa, 'Zurbarán sculpteur'.
23 Palomino, *Museo*, p. 938; Delenda, *Zurbarán: New Perspective*, p. 17.
24 Paul Guinard, *Zurbarán et les peintres espagnols de la vie monastique* (Paris, 1988), p. 94.
25 Alonso Remón, *Historia general de la Orden de Nuestra Señora de la Merced, Redención de Cautivos*, vol. I (Madrid, 1618), fol. 167r–v.
26 Ibid., fols 16r–17r, 20v–22r, 74v–75r, 172v–173r. On uncertainty regarding the Order's foundation date, Bruce Taylor, *Structures of Reform: The Mercedarian Order in the Spanish Golden Age* (Leiden, Boston, MA, and Cologne, 2000), pp. 10–13.
27 Delenda, *Zurbarán*, vol. II, pp. 131–2.
28 Taylor, *Structures of Reform*, p. 363.
29 Daniel Hershenzon, *The Captive Sea: Slavery, Communication, and Commerce in Early Modern Spain and the Mediterranean* (Philadelphia, PA, 2018), pp. 2–3, 58–9, 63–4, 193, n. 2, 215, n. 92.
30 Caturla, *Zurbarán*, docs 55 and 93, pp. 294–5, 304.
31 Document Seville 17 January 1626 at Zurbarán Digital.
32 Caturla, *Zurbarán*, doc. 72, p. 300.
33 Ibid., docs 65 and 72, pp. 297, 299.
34 Contract at Zurbarán Digital (contract is listed there as Seville 29 August 1628, but the transcribed contract is internally dated 29 July 1628). Regarding contracts, see Peter Cherry, 'The Contract for Francisco de Zurbarán's Paintings of Hieronymite Monks for the Sacristy of the Monastery of Guadalupe', *Burlington Magazine*, CXXVII/987 (1985), pp. 378–81.
35 Odile Delenda, *Zurbarán. Catálogo razonado y crítico*, vol. I (Madrid, 2009), pp. 120–21, 135 and *Zurbarán*, vol. II, p. 77.
36 Delenda, *Zurbarán*, vol. II, pp. 77–8, 80–81, 267–72; José Fernández López, *Programas iconográficos de la pintura barroca sevillana del siglo XVII*, 2nd edn (Seville, 2002), p. 278.
37 Delenda, *Zurbarán*, vol. II, p. 80.

38 Palomino, *Museo*, p. 937. On Zurbarán's white, Julián Gállego, 'El color en Zurbarán', *Goya*, LXIV–LXV (1965), p. 304.
39 Remón, *Historia*, fol. 69r–v.
40 Benito Navarrete Prieto, *La pintura andaluza del siglo XVII y sus fuentes grabadas* (Madrid, 1998), pp. 128–9, 126–7.
41 Ibid., pp. 230, 281–3, 262.
42 Ibid., pp. 166–8.
43 Ibid., p. 126.
44 Ibid., pp. 235, 285.
45 Santiago Sebastián, 'Zurbarán se inspiró en los grabados del aragonés Jusepe Martínez', *Goya*, CXXVIII (1975), pp. 82–4; Fernández López, *Programas*, pp. 265–7.
46 Navarrete Prieto, *Pintura andaluza*, pp. 33, 35.
47 Greuter's and Cobrador's prints in *Catálogo de imágenes*, vol. I: *Virgen de la Merced. Virgen del Puig. San Pedro Nolasco*: Vicent F. Zuriaga Senent, *La imagen devocional en la Orden de Nuestra Señora de la Merced, tradición, formación, continuidad y variantes*, PhD thesis, University of Valencia, 2005, pp. 483 and 503.
48 Delenda, *Zurbarán*, vol. II, p. 61.
49 Odile Delenda and Benito Navarrete Prieto in Alfonso E. Pérez Sánchez and Benito Navarrete Prieto, *De Herrera a Velázquez. El primer naturalismo en Sevilla*, exh. cat., Hospital de los Venerables (Seville, 2005), p. 109.
50 Ibid., pp. 99–122.
51 Caturla, *Zurbarán*, p. 68.
52 Palomino, *Museo*, p. 937. For Juan Agustín Ceán Bermúdez, Zurbarán was 'the Spanish Caravaggio'; *Diccionario histórico de los más ilustres profesores de las bellas artes en España*, vol. VI (Madrid, 1800), p. 44.
53 On Sevillian naturalism and Caravaggio/Caravaggism, see Navarrete Prieto and Pérez Sánchez in *De Herrera a Velázquez*, pp. 27–33; Rafael Japón, *The Influence of Italian Culture on the Sevillian Golden Age of Painting* (New York and London, 2022), pp. 105–13, 138–40.
54 Caturla, *Zurbarán*, doc. 56, p. 295.
55 For conjectures regarding the actual *retablo* paintings, and the significant involvement of his workshop, see Delenda, *Zurbarán*, vol. II, pp. 90–93.
56 David García López, *Lázaro Díaz del Valle y las Vidas de pintores de España* (Madrid, 2008), p. 334.
57 Caturla, *Zurbarán*, doc. 61, p. 296.
58 Document Seville 10 June 1630 at Zurbarán Digital.

59 Caturla, *Zurbarán*, doc. 65, p. 297.
60 On the Jesuit's vision depicted, Francisco Colin, *Vida, hechos y doctrina del venerable hermano Alonso Rodríguez, religioso de la Compañía de Jesús* (Madrid, 1652), fols 71v–72r. Rodríguez was declared Venerable shortly after his death in 1617 and canonized in 1888.
61 Regarding foundation, see Diego Ignacio de Góngora, *Historia del Colegio Mayor de Santo Tomás de Sevilla*, vol. I (Seville, 1890), pp. 81–9, 91–101; Delenda, *Zurbarán*, vol. II, p. 97.
62 Jeremy Robbins, *Incomparable Realms: Spain during the Golden Age, 1500–1700* (London, 2022), p. 25.

3 'Pintor de su Majestad': Zurbarán in Madrid

1 Jonathan Brown and J. H. Elliott, *A Palace for a King: The Buen Retiro and the Court of Philip IV*, revd edn (New Haven, CT, and London, 2003), pp. 79–81.
2 Ibid., p. 90.
3 For discussion of possible arrangements, José Álvarez Lopera in Andrés Úbeda de los Cobos, *Paintings for the Planet King: Philip IV and the Buen Retiro Palace*, exh. cat, Museo Nacional del Prado, Madrid (London, 2005), pp. 94–111.
4 The subjects of the twelve history paintings but not their artists were listed in 1635 by the secretary of the Tuscan embassy. For the Italian text, Álvarez Lopera in Úbeda de los Cobos, *Paintings for the Planet King*, p. 110, n. 87.
5 María Luisa Caturla, *Francisco de Zurbarán*, trans. and ed. Odile Delenda (Paris, 1994), doc. 70, p. 299.
6 Brown and Elliott, *Palace*, p. 281, n. 58.
7 Álvarez Lopera in Úbeda de los Cobos, *Paintings for the Planet King*, p. 137. María Luisa Caturla suggested the lost work from the hall now attributed to Cajés was in fact Zurbarán's second canvas, its subject misidentified in the 1635 Tuscan report and not, as given there, 'the expulsion of the Dutch from the island of St Martin by the Marquis of Cadereita' but rather the safe arrival in 1625 in Cadiz of the treasure fleet under Cadereita: 'Zurbarán en el Salón de Reinos', *Archivo Español de Arte*, XVIII/71 (1945), p. 299; and 'Cartas de pago de los doce cuadros de batallas para el Salón de Reinos del Buen Retiro', *Archivo Español de Arte*, XXXIII/132 (1960), pp. 334–5; also, Odile Delenda, *Zurbarán. Catálogo razonado y crítico*, vol. II: *Los conjuntos y el obrador* (Madrid, 2010), p. 156. This suggestion

is not followed by historians of the Buen Retiro, who take the hall's missing twelth canvas to be by Cajés and to depict, as in the Tuscan report, the *Recapture of St Martin*. While not hung in the hall,Zurbarán's second Cadiz canvas might still have depicted what Caturla suggested.

8 Brown and Elliott, *Palace*, pp. 178–9.

9 Fernando Marías and María Cruz de Carlos Varona in Leticia Ruiz Gómez, *Juan Bautista Maíno, 1581–1649*, exh. cat., Museo Nacional del Prado (Madrid, 2009), p. 275.

10 The palace's construction when 'soldiers were dying of hunger' was also criticized: John H. Elliott and José F. de la Peña, eds, *Memoriales y cartas del Conde Duque de Olivares*, vol. I: *Política interior: 1621–1645*, revd and expanded John H. Elliott and Fernando Negredo del Cerro (Madrid, 2013), p. 398.

11 José Pellicer de Tovar in Diego de Covarrubias y Leyva, *Elogios al Palacio Real del Buen Retiro* (Madrid, 1635), unpaginated.

12 Paul Guinard, *Zurbarán et les peintres espagnols de la vie monastique* (Paris, 1988), p. 128.

13 Álvarez Lopera in Úbeda de los Cobos, *Paintings for the Planet King*, p. 134.

14 Cited in Brown and Elliott, *Palace*, p. 180.

15 On broad affinities between Golden Age staging and Zurbarán, see Arsenio Moreno Mendoza, 'Zurbarán y el arte de la tramoya', *Goya*, CCCVII–CCCVIII (2005), pp. 249–60.

16 Manuel de Gallegos, *Obras varias al Real Palacio del Buen Retiro*, ed. Antonio Pérez y Gómez (Valencia, 1949), fol. 4r–v.

17 Juan Francisco Fernández de Heredia, *Trabajos y afanes de Hércules, floresta de sentencias y ejemplos* (Madrid, 1682).

18 Antonio Palomino, *El museo pictórico y escala óptica* (Madrid, 1947), p. 938.

19 *Zurbarán. Catálogo razonado y crítico*, vol. I (Madrid, 2009), pp. 308–9. For Guinard (*Zurbarán*, p. 130), this is Zurbarán's most Velázquez-like work.

20 Brown, *Zurbarán* (London, 1991), pp. 41, 120.

21 Valdivieso dates this Zurbarán portrait circa 1640: Enrique Valdivieso, *Zurbarán IV Centenario*, exh. cat., Museo de Bellas Artes (Seville, 1998), p. 166.

22 Delenda, *Zurbarán*, vol. I (Madrid, 2009), p. 306.

23 Brown, *Zurbarán*, p. 25; Odile Delenda in Odile Delenda and Mar Borobia, *Zurbarán: A New Perspective*, exh. cat., Museo

Thyssen-Bornemisza (Madrid, 2015), pp. 22–3. Also, Jeannine Baticle in *Zurbarán*, exh. cat., Museo Nacional del Prado (Madrid, 1988), p. 92.

24 Caturla, *Zurbarán*, p. 111.

25 On Patinir and the *St John the Baptist in a Landscape*, compare Abigail D. Newman, *Painting Flanders Abroad: Flemish Art and Artists in Seventeenth-Century Madrid* (Leiden and Boston, MA, 2022), pp. 174–5. On the miracle depicted in *St Diego of Alcalá*, see Antonio Rojo, *Historia de san Diego de Alcalá* (Madrid, 1663), pp. 121–2.

26 José Gestoso y Pérez, *El navío 'El Santo Rey D. Fernando'. Memorias históricas sevillanas del siglo XVII* (Seville, 1890), p. 26. A coda to the coda: in 1639, Zurbarán found and sent 11 gilders to Madrid at the request of the court.

4 Stilled Life and Mysticism

1 Luis Salas Almela, *The Conspiracy of the Ninth Duke of Medina Sidonia (1641): An Aristocrat in the Crisis of the Spanish Empire*, trans. Ruth MacKay (Leiden and Boston, MA, 2013).

2 Manuel Castillo Martos and Joaquín Rodríguez Mateos, *Sevilla Barroca y el siglo XVII*, 2nd edn (Seville, 2019), pp. 414–15.

3 Martín de Roa, *Santos Honorio, Eutiquio, Esteban, Patronos de Jerez de la Frontera. Nombre, sitio, antigüedad de la ciudad, valor de sus ciudadanos* (Seville, 1617), fols 46r–47v.

4 Odile Delenda, *Zurbarán. Catálogo razonado y crítico*, vol. II: *Los conjuntos y el obrador* (Madrid, 2010), pp. 171–2.

5 Delenda's *retablo* reconstruction is followed here (ibid., pp. 172–3). There is significant divergence over the location of *Lawrence* and *John the Baptist*, other proposals being over the doors to the *sagrario* either side of the altar (*Zurbarán*, exh. cat., Museo Nacional del Prado (Madrid, 1988), pp. 255–7) or either side of the crucifix at the *retablo*'s top (César Pemán, *Zurbarán y otros estudios sobre pintura del XVII español* (Madrid, 1989), pp. 95–118, 271–4).

6 Peter Cherry, 'The Contract for Francisco de Zurbarán's Paintings of Hieronymite Monks for the Sacristy of the Monastery of Guadalupe', *Burlington Magazine*, CXXVII/987 (1985), p. 377; Delenda, *Zurbarán*, vol. II, pp. 186–7.

7 On the image's discovery and the monastery's founding, Gabriel de Talavera, *Historia de Nuestra Señora de Guadalupe* (Toledo, 1597), fols 13r–16v, 19v–21r.

8 Jonathan Brown in *Zurbarán*, exh. cat., Museo Nacional del Prado, p. 23.
9 Jonathan Brown, *Images and Ideas in Seventeenth-Century Spanish Painting* (Princeton, NJ, 1978), p. 119. Delenda (*Zurbarán*, vol. II, p. 192) deems Brown's interpretation overstressed.
10 José de Sigüenza, *Historia de la Orden de San Jerónimo*, vol. I, 2nd edn (Madrid, 1907), p. 215.
11 Ibid., pp. 207, 208. A 1514 account has Christ consoling Salmerón with a vision: Odile Delenda, *Zurbarán. Catálogo razonado y crítico*, vol. I (Madrid, 2009), p. 441.
12 Sigüenza, *Historia*, pp. 421–2.
13 Ibid., pp. 175–7.
14 Ibid., pp. 429–30.
15 Delenda suggests circa 1640–43 in *Zurbarán*, vol. I, pp. 496, 499, 503 and circa 1645 in *Zurbarán*, vol. II, p. 193.
16 Letter no. XXII. Both events were part of the hagiographic tradition: see Alonso de Villegas, *Flos sanctorum e historia general de la vida y hechos de Jesús Cristo, Dios y Señor nuestro, y de todos los santos de que reza y hace fiesta la Iglesia Católica, conforme al Breviario Romano, reformado por decreto del santo Concilio Tridentino* (Madrid, 1588), fols 333r–v, 334r; Pedro de Ribadeneira, *Flos sanctorum, o Libro de las vidas de los santos*, 2nd edn (Madrid, 1604), pp. 789, 791–2.
17 Benito Navarrete Prieto, 'Aportaciones a los Zurbaranes de la Cartuja de Jerez', in *Francisco de Zurbarán (1598–1998): su tiempo, su obra, su tierra*, ed. Felipe Lorenzana de la Puente (Fuente de Cantos, 1998), pp. 154–6; Delenda, *Zurbarán*, vol. II, pp. 457–8.
18 Payment records to Zurbarán from the monastery in the mid-1640s for two works, 'the angels' and an *Archangel Michael* (María Luisa Caturla, *Francisco de Zurbarán*, trans. and ed. Odile Delenda (Paris, 1994), docs 134, 137 and 141, pp. 313–14), are deemed by Cherry ('Contract for Francisco de Zurbarán's Paintings', p. 378, n. 19) to probably refer to the sacristy's *Flagellation* and *Apotheosis*, respectively, though in the case of the *Archangel Michael*/*Apotheosis* such confusion seems strange.
19 For several other Zurbarán paintings once recorded elsewhere in the Charterhouse: Delenda, *Zurbarán*, vol. II, p. 251.
20 (1) Mid-1620s: Caturla, *Zurbarán*, pp. 29 (1624–6), 36 (1623–5); Jonathan Brown, *Zurbarán* (London, 1991), p. 48 (*c.* 1625–6). (2) Early to mid-1630s: Juan Miguel Serrera in *Zurbarán*, exh. cat., Museo Nacional del Prado, p. 316 (*c.* 1629); Paul Guinard, *Zurbarán*

et les peintres espagnols de la vie monastique (Paris, 1988), pp. 103–4, 194 (1630–35). (3) Circa 1655: Valdivieso, *Zurbarán IV Centenario*, exh. cat., Museo de Bellas Artes (Seville, 1998), pp. 216–20; Delenda, *Zurbarán*, vol. I, pp. 664, 668 and *Zurbarán*, vol. II, pp. 246–8. (Jeannine Baticle also inclines to a later date, in effect late 1640s, early 1650s: *Zurbarán*, exh. cat., Museo Nacional del Prado, pp. 300–305.) Delenda discusses documentary evidence, not contemporary, that also supports her dating (*Zurbarán*, vol. II, pp. 247–8).

21 Juan de Madariaga, *Vida del seráfico padre San Bruno, patriarca de la Cartuja* (Valencia, 1596), fols 147r–148r.

22 Ibid., fols 187r–190v; Teófanes Egido, 'La vida conventual y las devociones populares en el siglo XVII', in *Zurbarán ante su centenario (1598–1998)*, ed. Alfonso E. Pérez Sánchez (Valladolid, 1999), p. 42.

23 Luis Carlos Gutiérrez Alonso, 'Las artes decorativas en la obra de Zurbarán', *Boletín del Museo del Prado*, XIII (1992), pp. 15–16. Francisco Javier Rodríguez Viñuelas views the upturned bowl as imitation maiolica berettina ('La cerámica en la pintura de Zurbarán', in *XV Jornadas de Historia de Fuente de Cantos. Zurbarán (1598–1664), 350 aniversario de su muerte* (Fuente de Cantos, 2015), p. 236).

24 Madariaga, *Vida*, fols 36v–37r.

25 Caturla, *Zurbarán*, p. 35.

26 Delenda, *Zurbarán*, vol. II, pp. 91, 301.

27 Benito Navarrete Prieto, *La pintura andaluza del siglo XVII y sus fuentes grabadas* (Madrid, 1998), pp. 234, 300.

28 Benito Navarrete Prieto and Pedro Manuel Martínez Lara, '*Cristo servido por los ángeles* de Pablo de Céspedes y los orígenes del primer naturalismo', *Reales Sitios*, CCII (2015), pp. 36, 38.

29 Francisco Pacheco, *El arte de la pintura*, ed. Bonaventura Bassegoda i Hugas (Madrid, 1990), p. 639; Enrique Lafuente Ferrari, 'La vida de un tema iconográfico en la pintura andaluza', *Archivo Español de Arte y Arqueología*, XIII/39 (1937), pp. 249–50.

30 José María Carrascal Muñoz, who briefly uses these two terms, claims the 'dissociation of physical elements' in Zurbarán is very similar to 'that which certain alterations of consciousness produce' ('Visión mística y éxtasis en la pintura de Zurbarán', *Goya*, CCLVII (1997), p. 300).

31 Delenda, *Zurbarán*, vol. I, p. 315.

32 For these points, Alfonso E. Pérez Sánchez, *Zurbarán: La obra final, 1650–1664*, exh. cat., Museo de Bellas Artes de Bilbao (Bilbao, 2000),

pp. 65–6; Tom Lubbock, *Great Works: 50 Paintings Explored* (London, 2011), p. 19.
33 Delenda, *Zurbarán*, vol. I, p. 149. On the 'eggshell' cup, Gutiérrez Alonso, 'Artes decorativas', p. 18; Rodríguez Viñuelas, 'La cerámica', pp. 231–2.
34 Peter Cherry, 'The Hungry Eye: The Still Lifes of Juan Sánchez Cotán', *Konsthistorisk Tidskrift*, LXV/2 (1996), p. 77.
35 William B. Jordan and Peter Cherry, *Spanish Still Life from Velázquez to Goya*, exh. cat., National Gallery (London, 1995), p. 103.
36 On the Triana potteries, see Castillo Martos and Rodríguez Mateos, *Sevilla Barroca*, pp. 168–72. On these vessels, Gutiérrez Alonso, 'Artes decorativas', pp. 18–19.
37 Norman Bryson, *Looking at the Overlooked: Four Essays on Still Life Painting* (London, 1990), pp. 71–2.
38 Ibid., pp. 74–6.
39 Pemán, *Zurbarán*, p. 192; José Rogelio Buendía, 'La estela de Zurbarán en la pintura andaluza', *Goya*, LXIV–LXV (1965), p. 278.
40 For Juan de Zurbarán, see Enrique Valdivieso, *Bodegones, floreros y trampantojos en la pintura barroca sevillana* (Valencina de la Concepción, 2021), pp. 72–90; Delenda, *Zurbarán*, vol. II, pp. 275–85.
41 Guinard, *Zurbarán*, p. 21. For a much stronger statement of similarities between the two than I would make, see Emilio Orozco Díaz, 'Cotán y Zurbarán. Influjo y afinidad entre un fraile pintor y un pintor de frailes', *Goya*, LXIV–LXV (1965), pp. 224–31.
42 The 1627 *Crucifixion* is described as a 'sort of tense still life' and his circa 1640–45 *St Francis* a 'stilled St Francis': Juan José Lahuerta, 'The Crucifixions of Velázquez and Zurbarán', *RES: Anthropology and Aesthetics*, LXV–LXVI (2014/2015), p. 267; and Edward Payne, 'Surface and Depth: Zurbarán's *Saint Francis in Meditation*', *Hispanic Research Journal*, XXII/5 (2021), p. 417. Also, regarding *St Serapion*, see Julián Gállego and José Gudiol, *Zurbarán, 1598–1664*, trans. Kenneth Lyons (London, 1987), p. 51.
43 Antonio Palomino, *El museo pictórico y escala óptica* (Madrid, 1947), p. 938.
44 Gállego and Gudiol, *Zurbarán*, p. 50.
45 Compare ibid., p. 52.
46 *Zurbarán*, exh. cat., Museo Nacional del Prado, pp. 299, 304, referencing Madariaga, *Vida*, fols 130v, 168v–169v, 187r–v.
47 Odile Delenda, *Francisco de Zurbarán, Pintor, 1598–1664* (Madrid, 2007), p. 101. On solitude, Madariaga, *Vida*, fols 182v–186r.

48 Guigo II, *Ladder of Monks and Twelve Meditations*, trans. Edmund Colledge and James Walsh (n.p., 1979), p. 68.

49 Juan de la Cruz, *Obras completas*, 11th edn, ed. Lucinio Ruano de la Iglesia (Madrid, 1982), p. 54.

50 Miguel Monserrate Geli, *Libro de la vida monástica y eremítica que hicieron los antiguos padres y hacen hoy día los verdaderos ermitaños de San Pablo* (Mallorca, 1670), pp. 11–12. The work's focus is hermitical life, but these activities have broader (cenobitic) applicability. Similarly, the comments on solitude that I will cite have wider resonance, not least with Carthusian observance. For the affinity of the Jesuit *Spiritual Exercises* with the *lectio divina*, see Joseph Veale, *Manifold Gifts: Ignatian Essays on Spirituality* (Oxford, 2006), pp. 47–8.

51 Juan de la Cruz, *Subida* II.12.3–8; II.13.1; II.15.1–5; II.26.3, 5; *Noche* II.5.1, *Obras*, pp. 157–60, 160–61, 168–70, 215, 216, 361. Antonio de Molina, *Ejercicios espirituales, de las excelencias, provecho, y necesidad de la oración mental* (Burgos, 1615), pp. 43, 187–9, 206–13.

52 Pedro de Alcántara, *Tratado de la oración y meditación* (Burgos, 1579), I.12, fols 113v–115r.

53 Teresa de Jesús, *Camino de perfección* 25.2 (Valladolid MS), *Obras completas*, 9th edn, ed. Efrén de la Madre de Dios and Otger Steggink (Madrid, 2012), p. 339. This passage is cited in Molina's discussion of 'supernatural prayer'/'perfect contemplation': *Ejercicios*, pp. 211–12.

54 Stephen Haliczer, *Between Exaltation and Infamy: Female Mystics in the Golden Age of Spain* (Oxford, 2002), p. 8. For critical stances towards the religiosity underpinning this, Carlos Eire, *They Flew: A History of the Impossible* (New Haven, CT, and London, 2023), pp. 258–61.

55 Bernard McGinn, *Mysticism in the Golden Age of Spain, 1500–1650* (New York, 2017), pp. 370, 372 and *The Persistence of Mysticism in Catholic Europe: France, Italy, and Germany, 1500–1675* (New York, 2020), pp. 24–5, 533; Michel de Certeau, *The Mystic Fable*, vol. I: *The Sixteenth and Seventeenth Centuries*, trans. Michael B. Smith (Chicago, IL, and London, 1995), pp. 94–5, 101–2, 107–8, 114.

56 Terence O'Reilly, *Humanism and Religion in Early Modern Spain: John of the Cross, Francisco de Aldana, Luis de León*, ed. Stephen Boyd (London and New York, 2022), pp. 59–60.

57 For the clash of discourses when mysticism was investigated by the Inquisition, see Dale Shuger, *God Made Word: An Archaeology of Mystic Discourse in Early Modern Spain* (Toronto, 2022), pp. 150–79.

58 Teresa de Jesús, *Obras*, p.32; Carlos M. Eire, *The Life of Saint Teresa of Avila: A Biography* (Princeton, NJ, and Oxford, 2019), pp. 50–53;

María de San José Salazar, *Book for the Hour of Recreation*, intro. Alison Weber, trans. Amanda Powell (Chicago, IL, and London, 2002), p. 4.

59 On Spanish mysticism and conveying the ineffable, see my *Incomparable Realms: Spain during the Golden Age, 1500–1700* (London, 2022), pp. 165–85, some of which is expanded upon here.

60 Juan de la Cruz, *Obras*, pp. 35–7.

61 Monserrate Geli, *Libro*, pp. 10–11.

62 Francisco de Osuna, *The Third Spiritual Alphabet*, trans. Mary E. Giles (Mahwah, NJ, 1981), XXI.3–4, pp. 556–62. Also, Juan Bretón, *Mística teología y doctrina de la perfección evangélica* (Madrid, 1614), I.19, fols 140r–142r.

63 Monserrate Geli, *Libro*, introductory poem, unpaginated.

64 Osuna, *Third*, VII.8, p. 204.

65 Teresa de Jesús, *Camino de perfección* 26.3 (Valladolid MS), *Obras*, p. 341. Juan de la Cruz, *Llama* 3.44, *Obras*, p. 828. On *recogimiento*, see McGinn, *Mysticism in the Golden Age of Spain*, pp. 24–45.

66 Kevin Ingram, *Converso Non-Conformism in Early Modern Spain: Bad Blood and Faith from Alonso de Cartagena to Diego Velázquez* (Basingstoke, 2018), p. 33.

67 Terence O'Reilly, *The Spiritual Exercises of Saint Ignatius of Loyola: Contexts, Sources, Reception* (Leiden and Boston, MA, 2021), p. 94 (O'Reilly's translation). For the full 1525 Edict, see Antonio Márquez, *Los alumbrados. Orígenes y filosofía, 1525–1559* (Madrid, 1972), pp. 273–83; the tenet cited is no. 9. For a brief overview of propositions condemned, see McGinn, *Mysticism in the Golden Age of Spain*, pp. 49–50.

68 Regarding Alumbrados and *dejamiento*, see Alastair Hamilton, *Heresy and Mysticism in Sixteenth-Century Spain: The Alumbrados* (Cambridge, 1992), pp. 1–2, 29–32.

69 Alvaro Huerga, *Historia de los Alumbrados*, vol. I: *Los Alumbrados de Extremadura (1570–1582)* (Madrid, 1978), pp. 78, 397–9.

70 Hamilton, *Heresy*, pp. 117–20.

71 Ibid., p. 121.

72 Alvaro Huerga, *Historia de los Alumbrados*, vol. IV: *Los Alumbrados de Sevilla (1605–1630)* (Madrid, 1988), pp. 202–5, 211–12, 384–6, 455–6, 466. The 1525 Edict also condemned Alumbrado rejection of vocal prayer and disdain of images: Márquez, *Alumbrados*, nos 15–18, 20, 24, pp. 277, 278.

73 Huerga, *Alumbrados de Sevilla*, pp. 495–8.

74 Hamilton, *Heresy*, p. 125. Huerga, *Alumbrados de Sevilla*, pp. 242–57, 448–9.

75 Martin S. Soria, *The Paintings of Zurbarán* (London, 1953), p. 23. Gállego mentions critical suggestions of Zurbarán's 'sympathy' with Alumbradismo and suggests that this is unlikely given his many commissions from 'clergy' (Gállego and Gudiol, *Zurbarán*, pp. 11, 32). For Molinos and Alumbradismo, see Huerga, *Alumbrados de Sevilla*, pp. 349–51; Bernard McGinn, *The Crisis of Mysticism: Quietism in Seventeenth-Century Spain, Italy, and France* (New York, 2021), pp. 9, 44.

76 Osuna, *Third*, VI.2, pp. 161–5.

77 Ibid., XV.1, p. 386.

78 Ibid., XV.1 and 2, pp. 385, 390.

79 Ibid., XV.2, p. 390.

80 Ibid.

81 Pseudo-Dionysius, *Mystical Theology*, 1.1, in *Pseudo-Dionysius: The Complete Works*, trans. Colm Luibheid (New York and Mahwah, NJ, 1987), p. 135. Bonaventure, *Soul's Journey into God*, VII.5, in *The Soul's Journey into God, the Tree of Life, the Life of St. Francis*, trans. Ewert Cousins (Mahwah, NJ, 1978), pp. 114–15.

82 Juan de la Cruz, *Noche* II.5.1–3, *Obras*, pp. 361–2. Compare the Jesuit Luis de la Puente (1554–1624), *Sentimientos y avisos espirituales* (Madrid, 1876), pp. 128–33.

83 Henry Suso, *Life*, in *The Exemplar, with Two German Sermons*, ed. and trans. Frank Tobin (New York and Mahwah, NJ, 1989), p. 186.

84 Juan de la Cruz, *Noche* I.10.1–4, *Obras*, pp. 340–41.

85 Teresa de Jesús, *Vida* 18.10, *Obras*, pp. 101–2.

86 Sigüenza, *Historia*, p. 206. On being 'as if dead' at such moments, Teresa de Jesús, *Vida* 20.18 and *Cuentas de conciencia* 58.7, *Obras*, pp. 113, 626. On catalepsy and mysticism, see Eire, *They Flew*, pp. 143–4.

87 Sigüenza, *Historia*, p. 207.

88 Delenda, *Zurbarán*, vol. I, pp. 546–52.

89 Juan de la Cruz, *Cántico espiritual* [B] 1.9, *Obras*, p. 576. On self-absorption in this painting, Francisco López Estrada, 'Pintura y literatura: una consideración estética en torno de la *Santa Casa de Nazaret*, de Zurbarán', *Archivo Español de Arte*, XXXIX/153 (1966), p.36.

90 Henry S. Francis, 'Francisco de Zurbarán, *The Holy House of Nazareth*', *Bulletin of the Cleveland Museum of Art*, XLVIII/3 (1961), p. 49; López Estrada, 'Pintura y literatura', p. 39; *Zurbarán*, exh. cat., Museo Nacional del Prado, p. 377; Delenda, *Zurbarán*, vol. I, pp. 547–8.

91 Carrascal Muñoz, 'Visión mística', p. 300.

92 Castillo Martos and Rodríguez Mateos, *Sevilla Barroca*, p. 103; Antonio Domínguez Ortiz, *Orto y ocaso de Sevilla*, 3rd edn (Seville,

1981), pp. 72–3; Diego Ortiz de Zúñiga, *Anales eclesiásticos y seculares de la muy noble y muy leal ciudad de Sevilla* (Madrid, 1677), pp. 708–9.
93 Ortiz, *Anales*, p. 710.
94 Castillo Martos and Rodríguez Mateos, *Sevilla Barroca*, p. 103.
95 Amanda Wunder, *Baroque Seville: Sacred Art in a Century of Crisis* (University Park, PA, 2017), pp. 101–2.
96 On the decorative programme, Brown, *Images and Ideas*, pp. 128–46.

5 Saints and Martyrs

1 The National Gallery dates this 1635–9.
2 Alisa Luxenberg, *The Galerie Espagnole and the Museo Nacional, 1835–1853: Saving Spanish Art, or the Politics of Patrimony* (London and New York, 2016), pp. 31–2.
3 Cited by Alexandra Letvin in Susan Grace Galassi et al., eds, *Zurbarán: Jacob and His Twelve Sons. Paintings from Auckland Castle*, exh. cat., Meadows Museum, Dallas (Madrid, 2017), p. 67.
4 Pedro de Ribadeneira, *Flos sanctorum, o Libro de las vidas de los santos*, 2nd edn (Madrid, 1604), p. 831.
5 María Cruz de Carlos Varona, '"Ante Obitum Mortuus, Post Obitum Vivus". Zurbarán y la representación del cuerpo de San Francisco', *Anuario del Departamento de Historia y Teoría del Arte*, XXI (2009), pp. 179–80.
6 Odile Delenda, *Zurbarán. Catálogo razonado y crítico*, vol. I (Madrid, 2009), pp. 327–9.
7 For this last observation, Carlos Varona, '"Ante Obitum Mortuus"', p. 182.
8 In discussing darkness in what follows, I draw and expand on my *Incomparable Realms. Spain during the Golden Age, 1500–1700* (London, 2022), pp. 152–3, 194–5.
9 Antonio Palomino, *El museo pictórico y escala óptica* (Madrid, 1947), p. 937.
10 Ignatius of Loyola, *Ejercicios espirituales*, no. 79, *Obras completas*, 2nd edn, ed. Ignacio Iparraguirre (Madrid, 1963), p. 216.
11 Pseudo-Dionysius, *Pseudo-Dionysius: The Complete Works*, trans. Colm Luibheid (New York and Mahwah, NJ, 1987), p.135. *The Cloud of Unknowing and Other Works*, trans. A. C. Spearing (London, 2001), p. 26.
12 Juan de la Cruz, *Subida* I.13.1, *Obras completas*, 11th edn, ed. Lucinio Ruano de la Iglesia (Madrid, 1982), p. 122.
13 Juan de la Cruz, *Noche* I.8.2, *Obras*, p. 335.

14 Alvaro Huerga, *Historia de los Alumbrados*, vol. IV: *Los Alumbrados de Sevilla (1605–1630)* (Madrid, 1988), p. 245.
15 Juan de la Cruz, *Subida* II.1.3, *Obras*, p. 128.
16 Juan de la Cruz, *Noche* II.16.1 and *Subida* I.2.1, *Obras*, pp. 392, 94.
17 Juan de la Cruz, *Subida* I.2.5, *Obras*, p.95.
18 Teresa de Jesús, *Cuentas de conciencia* 58.3, *Obras completas*, 9th edn, ed. Efrén de la Madre de Dios and Otger Steggink (Madrid, 2012), p. 625.
19 Juan de la Cruz, *Subida* I.3.4, 4.1, *Obras*, pp. 96, 97.
20 Paolo Tanganelli in Ignacio Cano Rivero, *Zurbarán (1598–1664)*, exh. cat., Palazzo dei Diamanti (Ferrara, 2013), p. 94; Juan de la Cruz, *Llama* 3.12–14, *Obras*, pp. 808–9.
21 Robbins, *Incomparable Realms*, pp. 155–6.
22 Martin S. Soria, *The Paintings of Zurbarán* (London, 1953), pp. 13, 149. Regarding sacralization, Odile Delenda, '"En la tierra como en el cielo": la sacralización de la vida cotidiana en la obra de Zurbarán', in *Historias mortales*, ed. Noemí Sobregués (Barcelona, 2004), pp. 217–30.
23 Juan de la Cruz, *Subida* II.24.5, *Obras*, p. 212. Distinct but connected is Gregory the Great's notion of the 'flash of contemplation': Bernard McGinn, *The Growth of Mysticism: Gregory the Great Through the 12th Century* (New York, 1994), p. 67.
24 Eamon Duffy talking here of late medieval England; Eamon Duffy, *The Stripping of the Altars: Traditional Religion in England, 1400–1580* (New Haven, CT, and London, 2022), pp. 176, 175.
25 Alonso de Villegas, *Flos sanctorum e historia general de la vida y hechos de Jesús Cristo, Dios y Señor nuestro, y de todos los santos de que reza y hace fiesta la Iglesia Católica, conforme al Breviario Romano, reformado por decreto del santo Concilio Tridentino* (Madrid, 1588), fols 129r–v (separately foliated at the end of the volume).
26 Ibid., fol. 118r.
27 Ibid., fol. 118r–v.
28 Ibid., fol. 117r (Song of Songs 8:8).
29 Ribadeneira, *Flos*, p. 236.
30 Ibid., p. 234.
31 Antonio de Quintanadueñas, *Santos de la ciudad de Sevilla y su arzobispado: fiestas que su Santa Iglesia metropolitana celebra* (Seville, 1637), pp. 81–2.
32 2 Corinthians 4:7; Villegas, *Flos*, fol. 18r (separately foliated at the end of the volume).
33 Villegas, *Flos*, fol. 18r–v.

34 Ibid., fols 229v–230r.
35 Ibid., fols 230r–v.
36 Emilio Orozco Díaz, 'Para la interpretación de un tema de la pintura de Zurbarán', *Arte Español*, XIV (1942), p. 4. Against this, Soria, *Zurbarán*, p. 24.
37 Benito Navarrete Prieto, *Santas de Zurbarán: devoción y persuasión*, exh. cat., Espacio Santa Clara (Seville, 2013), p. 208.
38 Peter Cherry, ibid., p. 192.
39 Adam Jasienski, *Praying to Portraits: Audience, Identity, and the Inquisition in the Early Modern Hispanic World* (University Park, PA, 2023), pp. 29, 37.
40 Regarding processing, see Elizabeth du Gué Trapier, 'Zurbarán's Processions of Virgin Martyrs', *Apollo*, LXXXV (1967), pp. 414–19. Viewing the figures as walking, Cécile Vincent-Cassy suggests 'with their gazes, Zurbarán's saints invite the spectator to follow them on their journey to the celestial realm'; 'Francisco de Zurbarán y el retrato sacro: Las santas vírgenes y mártires del maestro y su taller', *Tiempos Modernos*, XXXIII (2016), p. 243. That his female martyrs are interpreted as 'processing' arises in part from a series by a follower that is arrayed along the nave walls of the church of Santa Clara, Carmona.
41 Amalia Descalzo Lorenzo and Javier González de Durana, both in Navarrete Prieto, *Santas de Zurbarán*, pp. 198, 201. On Golden Age women's clothing, Carmen Bernis and Amalia Descalzo, 'El traje femenino español en la época de los Austrias', in *Vestir a la española en las cortes europeas (siglos XVI y XVII)*, ed. José Luis Colomer and Amalia Descalzo, vol. I (Madrid, 2014), pp. 39–75. For royal women's fashion, Amanda Wunder, *Spanish Fashion in the Age of Velázquez: A Tailor at the Court of Philip IV* (New Haven, CT, and London, 2024).
42 Robbins, *Incomparable Realms*, p. 196.
43 Julián Gállego, *Vision et symboles dans la peinture espagnole du siècle d'or* (Paris, 1968), p. 169.
44 Robbins, *Incomparable Realms*, p. 197.
45 Jeremy Robbins, *Arts of Perception: The Epistemological Mentality of the Spanish Baroque, 1580–1720* (Abingdon, 2007).
46 Bernardino de Villegas, *La esposa de Cristo, instruida con la vida de santa Lutgarda virgen, monja de S. Bernardo* (Murcia, 1635), IV.28, p. 434.
47 Delenda, '"En la tierra como en el cielo"'.
48 On reading God in creation, see Luis de Granada, *Introducción del símbolo de la fe*, ed. Fidel Sebastián Mediavilla (Madrid, 2020), pp. 25–68. On creation's beauty, pp. 216–22.

49 As Tom Lubbock pithily notes, with Zurbarán 'everything feels seen'; *Great Works: 50 Paintings Explored* (London, 2011), p. 19. Also, Norman Bryson, *Looking at the Overlooked: Four Essays on Still Life Painting* (London, 1990), pp. 87–8.
50 Jane Bennett, *Vibrant Matter: A Political Ecology of Things* (Durham, NC, and London, 2010), pp. 4–5. Also here, Bryson, *Looking at the Overlooked*, pp. 142, 144.
51 Duncan T. Kinkead, 'Juan de Luzón and the Sevillian Painting Trade with the New World in the Second Half of the Seventeenth Century', *Art Bulletin*, LXVI/2 (1984), p. 306; Fernando Quiles García, *Sevilla y América en el barroco. Comercio, ciudad y arte* (Seville, 2009), p. 115.
52 Document Seville 22 May 1647 at Zurbarán Digital.
53 Kinkead, 'Juan de Luzón', pp. 305–6.
54 Quiles García, *Sevilla y América*, pp. 32–6.
55 Duncan T. Kinkead, 'The Last Sevillian Period of Francisco de Zurbarán', *Art Bulletin*, LXV/2 (1983), p. 307; Akemi Luisa Herráez Vossbrink and Edward Payne, both in *Zurbarán: Jacob and His Twelve Sons*, ed. Galassi et al., pp. 79, 111–12.
56 Antonio Domínguez Ortiz, *Orto y ocaso de Sevilla*, 3rd edn (Seville, 1981), p. 120. For sequestrations in 1625, 1629, 1632, 1635–7 and 1639: J. H. Elliott, *The Count-Duke of Olivares: The Statesman in an Age of Decline* (New Haven, NC, and London, 1988), pp. 245, 368, 452–3, 519, 596.
57 María Luisa Caturla, *Francisco de Zurbarán*, trans. and ed. Odile Delenda (Paris, 1994), doc. 189, p. 321–2. Spanish pigment names in Gridley McKim-Smith et al., *Examining Velázquez* (New Haven, CT, and London, 1988), pp. 97–107; and Miquel Àngel Herrero-Cortell, 'Las colores de un Imperio. Hispanic Production and International Trade of Pigments and Pictorial Materials in the Sixteenth Century', *Journal for Art Market Studies*, III/2 (2019), pp. 9–10.
58 Caturla, *Zurbarán*, docs 100–108, pp. 305–8; Lori Kata, '"With the Most Diligence Possible": Francisco de Zurbarán and the Overseas Art Trade in the Seventeenth Century', *Hispanic Research Journal*, XII/5 (2011), pp. 387–96.
59 Caturla, *Zurbarán*, doc. 147, p. 315.
60 Kinkead, 'Last Sevillian Period', p. 307; John Barton and Herráez Vossbrink, both in *Zurbarán: Jacob and His Twelve Sons*, ed. Galassi et al., pp. 42–3, 86–7, 87–8.
61 Palomino, *Museo*, p. 1031.

62 Odile Delenda, *Zurbarán. Catálogo razonado y crítico*, vol. II: *Los conjuntos y el obrador* (Madrid, 2010), p. 20.

63 Claire Barry in *Zurbarán: Jacob and His Twelve Sons*, ed. Galassi et al., p. 181; Delenda, *Zurbarán*, vol. I, p. 506.

64 Juan José Junquera y Mato, 'Zurbarán y América', in *Zurbarán ante su centenario (1598–1998)*, ed. Alfonso E. Pérez Sánchez (Valladolid, 1999), p. 153.

65 Juan Miguel Herrera in *Zurbarán*, exh. cat., Museo Nacional del Prado (Madrid, 1988), pp. 63–83.

66 Variously attributed to Zurbarán's workshop (Navarrete Prieto, *Santas de Zurbarán*, p. 212), or seven to followers and one to the circle of Zurbarán (Delenda, *Zurbarán*, vol. II, pp. 402, 404, 406, 407, 409, 410, 414, 416; for circle/follower distinction, p. 22). Delenda deems the *St Marina* I mention to be by a follower (p. 414).

67 For a recent argument that a privately owned *St Agnes* is by Zurbarán, see Jésica Martí and Ximo Company, *Francisco de Zurbarán: Santa Inés* (Lleida, 2023).

6 The Immaculate Conception and Seville

1 Diego Ortiz de Zúñiga, *Anales eclesiásticos y seculares de la muy noble y muy leal ciudad de Sevilla* (Madrid, 1677), p. 618; Antonio González Polvillo, *La Congregación de la Granada. Profecía y milenarismo en la Sevilla del Renacimiento y Barroco* (Seville, 2022), p. 302; Suzanne L. Stratton, *The Immaculate Conception in Spanish Art* (Cambridge, 1994), p. 77.

2 José Moreno Villa, 'Documentos sobre pintores recogidos en el Archivo de Palacio', *Archivo Español de Arte y Arqueología*, XII/36 (1936), p. 264.

3 For figures and inscriptions, Mª Jesús Sanz, *Fiestas sevillanas de la Inmaculada Concepción en el siglo XVII. El sentido de la celebración y su repercusión exterior* (Seville, 2008), pp. 49–53.

4 Felipe Pereda, 'Vox populi: Carnal Blood, Spiritual Milk, and the Debate Surrounding the Immaculate Conception, ca.1600', in *Interreligious Encounters in Polemics between Christians, Jews, and Muslims in Iberia and Beyond*, ed. Mercedes García-Arenal, Gerard A. Wiegers and Ryan Szpiech (Leiden and Boston, MA, 2019), pp. 318, 329; Jaime Cuadriello, in Ronda Kasl, *Sacred Spain: Art and Belief in the Spanish World*, exh. cat., Indianapolis Museum of Art (Indiana, IN, 2009), pp. 134, 139–40 for the political-theological delicacy for monarch and papacy of the Immaculist position.

5 Miguel Ruiz, *Sermón de la Inmaculada Concepción de la Virgen María* (Seville, 1616), dedication.
6 Regarding popular versus dirigiste and the Immaculate Conception, see Stratton, *Immaculate Conception*, pp. 36–7, 71. For a broader discussion, Rosilie Hernández, *Immaculate Conceptions: The Power of the Religious Imagination in Early Modern Spain* (Toronto, 2019), pp. 6–10, 13–14.
7 Anna Coreth, *Pietas Austriaca*, trans. William D. Bowman and Anna Maria Leitgeb (West Lafayette, IN, 2004); Jeremy Robbins, *Incomparable Realms: Spain during the Golden Age, 1500–1700* (London, 2022), pp. 40–47.
8 Stratton, *Immaculate Conception*, pp. 37–8.
9 Ibid., pp. 5–9; Sanz, *Fiestas sevillanas*, pp. 22–5.
10 Amanda Wunder, *Baroque Seville: Sacred Art in a Century of Crisis* (University Park, PA, 2017), p. 33. It was one of many Immaculist *fiestas* there across 1615–17: Sanz, *Fiestas sevillanas*, p. 79.
11 Ortiz, *Anales*, p. 613; José Fernández López in Enrique Valdivieso, *Zurbarán IV Centenario*, exh. cat., Museo de Bellas Artes (Seville, 1998), p. 45.
12 Stanko Vranich, 'Carta de un ciudadano de Sevilla. La guerra mariana de Sevilla en el siglo XVII', *Archivo Hispalense*, XLIV/137 (1966), p. 251.
13 González Polvillo, *Congregación de la Granada*, pp. 309–13.
14 Ibid., pp. 295–9.
15 Ibid., p. 291.
16 Ibid., p. 324ff.
17 Ibid., p. 310.
18 Stratton, *Immaculate Conception*, p. 80, 100, 103–4; Fernández López in Valdivieso, *Zurbarán IV Centenario*, p. 48.
19 Stratton, *Immaculate Conception*, p. 75.
20 María Luisa Caturla, *Francisco de Zurbarán*, trans. and ed. Odile Delenda (Paris, 1994), doc. 72, p. 299.
21 Cuadriello in Kasl, *Sacred Spain*, p. 123.
22 Stratton, *Immaculate Conception*, pp. 16–18, 23–8.
23 Ibid., p. 38. On sixteenth-century representations, Sanz, *Fiestas sevillanas*, pp. 33–8; on printed images, pp. 54–8.
24 Francisco Pacheco, *El arte de la pintura*, ed. Bonaventura Bassegoda i Hugas (Madrid, 1990), pp. 575–7.
25 Odile Delenda, *Zurbarán. Catálogo razonado y crítico*, vol. I (Madrid, 2009), p. 681.

26 Ibid., pp. 300–301.
27 For these various interpretations of the two figures, see Stratton, *Immaculate Conception*, p. 94.
28 Hernández, *Immaculate Conceptions*, pp. 137–8. She views Pacheco as a key figure in this (p. 122).
29 Ibid., pp. 132–3.
30 Robbins, *Incomparable Realms*, p. 305.
31 *Zurbarán*, exh. cat., Museo Nacional del Prado (Madrid, 1988), p. 344.
32 Stratton, *Immaculate Conception*, pp. 103–4; Wunder, *Baroque Seville*, pp. 54–5.
33 Ortiz, *Anales*, p. 764.
34 The date range 1658–64 is suggested by Diego Angulo Íñiguez, 'Murillo: varios dibujos de la *Concepción* y de *Santo Tomás de Villanueva*', *Archivo Español de Arte*, XXXV/139 (1962), p. 235; '1658?' by Pablo Hereza, *Corpus Murillo. Biografía y documentos* (Seville, 2017), p. 343.
35 Paul Guinard, *Zurbarán et les peintres espagnols de la vie monastique* (Paris, 1988), p. 59; Odile Delenda, *Francisco de Zurbarán, Pintor, 1598–1664* (Madrid, 2007), p. 52.
36 On this commission, Pablo Hereza, *Corpus Murillo. Pinturas y dibujos. Encargos* (Seville, 2019), pp. 21–81.
37 Jonathan Brown, *Zurbarán* (London, 1991), p. 114. Similarly, Valdivieso, *Zurbarán IV Centenario*, p. 172. Regarding the *Annunciation*, Brown had seen 1650 'clearly written' on its *cartellino* (*Zurbarán*, p. 114), but Delenda states this is not legible, though accepts a date of 1650 or slightly later (*Zurbarán*, vol. I, p. 610).
38 See also Murillo's *Immaculate Conception with Fray Juan de Quirós* (1652). Dates for 'La Colosal': Benito Navarrete Prieto, *Murillo y las metáforas de la imagen* (Madrid, 2017), p. 50; Hereza, *Corpus Murillo. Biografía y documentos*, p. 84.
39 Rafael Japón, *The Influence of Italian Culture on the Sevillian Golden Age of Painting* (New York and London, 2022), p. 157; for Reni, Bolognese art and Zurbarán, p. 119; Delenda, *Zurbarán, Pintor*, p. 52.
40 For '*La Niña*' circa 1665–6 date, not the standard circa 1668–9, Hereza, *Corpus Murillo. Pinturas*, p. 346. On Velázquez, Peter Cherry, 'A Newly Discovered "Immaculate Conception" by Diego Velázquez', *Burlington Magazine*, CLXII/1413 (2020), pp. 1029–37; for rare, earlier examples of the child *Inmaculada*, pp. 1034–5.
41 Rodrigo Caro, *Antigüedades y principado de la ilustrísima ciudad de Sevilla* (Seville, 1634), fol. 67v.

42 Duncan T. Kinkead, 'Juan de Luzón and the Sevillian Painting Trade with the New World in the Second Half of the Seventeenth Century', *Art Bulletin*, LXVI/2 (1984), p. 306.
43 Delenda, *Zurbarán, Pintor*, p. 121.
44 Brown, *Zurbarán*, p. 76; Valdivieso, *Zurbarán IV Centenario*, p. 174; Delenda, *Zurbarán*, vol. I, p. 524.
45 Brown, *Zurbarán*, p. 76; *Zurbarán*, exh. cat., Museo Nacional del Prado, p. 364.
46 Delenda, *Zurbarán*, vol. I, pp. 655–6; Benito Navarrete Prieto, *La pintura andaluza del siglo XVII y sus fuentes grabadas* (Madrid, 1998), p. 248.
47 Luis Carlos Gutiérrez Alonso, 'Las artes decorativas en la obra de Zurbarán', *Boletín del Museo del Prado*, XIII (1992), p. 18; Francisco Javier Rodríguez Viñuelas, 'La cerámica en la pintura de Zurbarán', in *XV Jornadas de Historia de Fuente de Cantos. Zurbarán (1598–1664), 350 aniversario de su muerte* (Fuente de Cantos, 2015), pp. 233–4.
48 Delenda, *Zurbarán*, vol. I, p. 741.
49 Francisco Arias, *De la imitación de nuestra Señora la soberana Virgen María*, in *Aprovechamiento espiritual*, 3rd edn (Seville, 1596), pp. 186, 281–2.
50 Ibid., p. 282.
51 Pedro de Ribadeneira, *Flos sanctorum, o Libro de las vidas de los santos*, 2nd edn (Madrid, 1604), p. 941.
52 Mindy Nancarrow, 'Theology and Devotion in Zurbarán's Images of the Infant Virgin in the Temple', *South Atlantic Review*, LXXII/1 (2007), p. 80; Hernández, *Immaculate Conceptions*, pp. 187, 198–9, 203.

7 Images, Meditation and Meta-Images

1 Martín de Roa, *Antigüedad, veneración y fruto de las sagradas imágenes y reliquias* (Seville, 1623), fols 42v–48v. Regarding *latria*, and so forth, fols 81r–82v.
2 Juan de la Cruz, *Subida* III.35.2, *Obras completas*, 11th edn, ed. Lucinio Ruano de la Iglesia (Madrid, 1982), p. 298.
3 For differences between union and ecstasy, Teresa de Jesús, *Vida* 20, *Obras completas*, 9th edn, ed. Efrén de la Madre de Dios and Otger Steggink (Madrid, 2012), pp. 108–16.
4 Bernard McGinn, *The Harvest of Mysticism in Medieval Germany (1300–1500)* (New York, 2005), pp. 301–3; Thomas H. Bestul, '*Meditatio*/Meditation', in *The Cambridge Companion to Christian Mysticism*, ed. Amy Hollywood and Patricia Z. Beckman (New York, 2012),

pp. 161–3; Luis de Granada, *Libro de oración*, ed. Teodoro H. Martín (Madrid, 1999), pp. 252–5, 266–9. Relevant to the *Exercises*' affective emphasis is Ignatius's debt to the Carthusian Ludolph of Saxony's *Life of Christ*.

5 Markus Friedrich, *The Jesuits: A History*, trans. John Noël Dillon (Princeton, NJ, and Oxford, 2022), pp. 151, 236–7.

6 Antonio de Molina, *Ejercicios espirituales, de las excelencias, provecho, y necesidad de la oración mental* (Burgos, 1615), pp. 247–51.

7 Loyola, *Ejercicios*, nos 47 and 49, *Obras completas*, 2nd edn, ed. Ignacio Iparraguirre (Madrid, 1963), pp. 209–10; Ignacio Iparraguirre, ed., *Directoria Exercitiorum Spiritualium (1540–1599)* (Rome, 1955), pp. 653–4; Achille Gagliardi, *Commentaire des Exercices spirituels d'Ignace de Loyola (1590)*, trans. Francis Joseph Legrand et al. (Paris, 1996), pp. 39–40.

8 *Ejercicios*, nos 112, 123, 125, *Obras*, pp. 222, 223–4.

9 Iparraguirre, *Directoria*, p. 449; Gagliardi, *Commentaire*, p. 48.

10 Alfonso Rodríguez G. de Ceballos, 'Las *Imágenes de la Historia Evangélica* del P. Jerónimo Nadal en el marco del jesuitismo y la Contrarreforma', *Traza y baza*, V (1974), p. 79.

11 Pietro Giacomo Bacci, *Vita di S. Filippo Neri* (Rome, 1642), p. 232; Jusepe Martínez, *Discursos practicables del nobilísimo arte de la pintura*, ed. María Elena Manrique Ara (Madrid, 2006), p. 189.

12 Juan de la Cruz, *Subida* III.15.2, 35.2–6, 37.2, *Obras*, pp. 259, 298–300, 303–4.

13 Bernardino de Villegas, *La esposa de Cristo, instruida con la vida de santa Lutgarda virgen, monja de S. Bernardo* (Murcia, 1635), IV.28, pp. 430–31.

14 Teresa de Jesús, *Cuentas de conciencia* 27, *Obras*, p. 604.

15 Felipe Pereda, *Images of Discord: Poetics and Politics of the Sacred Image in Fifteenth-Century Spain*, trans. Consuelo López-Morillas (Turnhout, 2018), pp. 11, 25–6, 37, 136.

16 Walter S. Melion in Jerónimo Nadal, *Annotations and Meditations on the Gospels*, vol. I: *The Infancy Narratives*, trans. Frederick A. Homann, intro. Walter Melion (Philadelphia, PA, 2003), p. 3.

17 Benito Navarrete Prieto, *La pintura andaluza del siglo XVII y sus fuentes grabadas* (Madrid, 1998), p. 50.

18 Nadal, *Annotations*, p. 173; *Adnotationes et Meditationes in Evangelia quæ in sacrosancto Missæ sacrificio toto anno leguntur* (Antwerp, 1607), p. 80.

19 For an example of using an image of a member of an order as a meditative focus, see the Jesuit Louis Richeome's meditative description aimed primarily at Jesuit novices of a painting in Rome of Stanisław Kostka: Louis Richeome, *La peinture spirituelle ou l'art*

d'admirer, aimer et louer Dieu en toutes ses œuvres, et tirer de toutes profit salutere (Lyon, 1611), pp. 47–62.

20 On religious images in houses in Seville, see Manuel Castillo Martos and Joaquín Rodríguez Mateos, *Sevilla Barroca y el siglo XVII*, 2nd edn (Seville, 2019), pp. 519–23; Joaquín González Moreno, 'Documentación sobre oratorios de los siglos XVII y XVIII', *Archivo Hispalense*, LXXXI/248 (1998), pp. 149–50.

21 Odile Delenda, 'The "Cloth of Veronica" in the Work of Zurbarán', *Buletina-Boletín-Bulletin: Bilboko Arte Ederren Museoa-Museo de Bellas Artes de Bilbao-Bilbao Fine Arts Museum*, VII (2013), pp. 125–61.

22 Document Seville 21 November 1662 in Zurbarán Digital. The signed and dated 1658 *Veronica* to be discussed here did eventually form part of a *retablo* but was probably not intended as such: *Zurbarán*, exh. cat., Museo Nacional del Prado (Madrid, 1988), pp. 388–9; Emilio Gómez Piñol, 'El velo de la Verónica en la obra de Zurbarán', *Temas de Estética y Arte*, XX (2006), pp. 115, 128.

23 Juan de Acuña del Adarve, *Discursos de las efigies y verdaderos retratos non manufactos del santo rostro y cuerpo de Cristo* (Villanueva de Andújar, 1637), fol. 218v; Francisco Pacheco, *El arte de la pintura*, ed. Bonaventura Bassegoda i Hugas (Madrid, 1990), p. 233.

24 Antonio Daza, *Historia, vida, y milagros, éxtasis y revelaciones de la bienaventurada virgen Sor Juana de la Cruz* (Lleida, 1613), fols 74v–75r; Acuña del Adarve, *Discursos*, fol. 233r.

25 María Luisa Caturla, 'La Santa Faz de Zurbarán: *trompe l'œil* "a lo divino"', *Goya*, LXIV–LXV (1965), pp. 202–5.

26 A circa 1635–40 version has a very dark maroon background: Odile Delenda, *Zurbarán. Catálogo razonado y crítico*, vol. I (Madrid, 2009), p. 296.

27 Omar Calabrese in Omar Calabrese and Victor I. Stoichita, *La Verónica de Zurbarán* (Madrid, 2015), p. 29.

28 Acuña del Adarve, *Discursos*, fol. 167r–v. For suggestions regarding different images represented, see Felipe Pereda, *Crimen e ilusión. El arte de la verdad en el Siglo de Oro* (Madrid, 2017), pp. 310–12.

29 Pereda, *Crimen*, p. 312.

30 Contrast ibid., pp. 273, 311.

31 Stoichita in Calabrese and Stoichita, *Verónica*, p. 65; Steven F. Ostrow, 'Zurbarán's *Cartellini*: Presence and the *Paragone*', *Art Bulletin*, XCIX/1 (2017), p. 87.

32 The idea of God as a painter was a topos, various writers citing the Veronica as evidence of this: Alan K. G. Paterson, 'Calderón's

"Deposición a favor de los profesores de la pintura". Comment and Text', in *Art and Literature in Spain: 1600–1800: Studies in Honour of Nigel Glendinning*, ed. Charles Davis and Paul Julian Smith (London, 1993), p. 166; Pacheco, *Arte*, pp. 231, 233; Antonio Palomino, *El museo pictórico y escala óptica* (Madrid, 1947), pp. 156–7, 159–60. Related to this conceit and Zurbarán's two signed Veronicas, Ostrow comments that 'the signatures proclaim that these images were not divinely created but were the work of a man' ('Zurbarán's *Cartellini*', p. 89).

33 (1) circa 1635: *Zurbarán*, exh. cat., Museo Nacional del Prado, p. 384; (2) circa 1650: current Prado dating; (3) circa 1655–60: Delenda, *Zurbarán*, vol. I, p. 674.

34 Susann Waldmann, *El artista y su retrato en la España del siglo XVII. Una aportación al estudio de la pintura retratista española*, trans. José Luis Gil Aristu (Madrid, 2007), p. 115.

35 Pacheco, *Arte*, pp. 229–31.

36 For example, Enrique Valdivieso, *Zurbarán IV Centenario*, exh. cat., Museo de Bellas Artes (Seville, 1998), p. 206; Delenda, *Zurbarán*, vol. I, p. 675.

37 Waldmann, *Artista*, pp. 119–20.

38 Ibid., p. 120.

39 Richard Viladesau, *The Pathos of the Cross: The Passion of Christ in Theology and the Arts, The Baroque Era* (Oxford, 2014), pp. 101–3.

40 Waldmann, *Artista*, p. 117; Lisandra Estevez, 'The Artist as Visionary in Francisco de Zurbarán's *Crucifixion with a Painter*', *Sixteenth Century Journal*, L/4 (2019), p. 1037.

41 Juan de la Cruz, *Subida* II.17.3–5, 9, *Obras*, pp. 176–8, 180.

42 Victor I. Stoichita, *Visionary Experience in the Golden Age of Spanish Art*, trans. Anne-Marie Glasheen (London, 1995), p. 74.

43 Pacheco, *Arte*, p. 494.

44 Juan José Lahuerta, 'The Crucifixions of Velázquez and Zurbarán', *RES: Anthropology and Aesthetics*, LXV–LXVI (2014/2015), p. 272.

45 Giorgio Vasari, *The Lives of the Artists*, trans. Julia Conaway Bondanella and Peter Bondanella (Oxford, 2008), p. 177.

46 Stoichita, *Visionary Experience*, p. 74. Also, Estevez, 'Artist as Visionary', p. 1049.

47 Here following measurements from the Art Institute of Chicago.

48 For example, Mary Carruthers, *The Craft of Thought: Meditation, Rhetoric, and the Making of Images, 400–1200* (Cambridge, 2008); Ralph Dekoninck, '*Ut pictura/sculptura meditatio.* La métaphore picturale

et sculpturale dans la spiritualité du XVIIe siècle', *Rivista di Storia e Letteratura Religiosa*, XLI (2006), pp. 665–94.

49 Antoine Sucquet, *Via vitae aeternae* (Antwerp, 1620), p. 358. In the subsequent meditation on the nativity, the engraving, aspects of which are lettered as in Nadal's *Adnotationes*, is the composition of place (p. 359); that is, the first step in a standard Jesuit meditation.

Conclusion

1 María Luisa Caturla, *Francisco de Zurbarán*, trans. and ed. Odile Delenda (Paris, 1994), doc. 179, p. 319; Ángel Aterido Fernández, ed., *Corpus velazqueño: documentos y textos*, vol. I (Madrid, 2010), p. 383; Caturla, *Zurbarán*, doc. 184, p. 320.

2 Caturla, *Zurbarán*, doc. 185, p. 320.

3 Duncan T. Kinkead, 'The Last Sevillian Period of Francisco de Zurbarán', *Art Bulletin*, LXV/2 (1983), pp. 305, 306–7.

4 Ibid., p. 308.

5 Caturla, *Zurbarán*, doc. 189, pp. 321–2.

6 Jonathan Brown, *Zurbarán* (London, 1991), p. 40.

7 For 'virile' applied to Zurbarán's earlier style and him as a younger artist, see Martin S. Soria, *The Paintings of Zurbarán* (London, 1953), pp. 8, 14, 20, 28; Paul Guinard, *Zurbarán et les peintres espagnols de la vie monastique* (Paris, 1988), p. 60. Also see Julián Gállego and José Gudiol, *Zurbarán, 1598–1664*, trans. Kenneth Lyons (London, 1987), pp. 8, 65.

8 Caturla, *Zurbarán*, doc. 191, p. 322.

9 On the Alcalá commission, see Antonio Palomino, *El museo pictórico y escala óptica* (Madrid, 1947), p. 988; *Zurbarán*, exh. cat., Museo Nacional del Prado (Madrid, 1988), pp. 327–34.

10 Guinard, *Zurbarán*, p. 59; Jeannine Baticle in *Zurbarán*, exh. cat., Museo Nacional del Prado, p. 105; Odile Delenda, *Francisco de Zurbarán, Pintor, 1598–1664* (Madrid, 2007), p. 55.

11 Document Madrid 3 September 1664 in Zurbarán Digital.

12 Document Madrid 12 August 1665 in Zurbarán Digital.

13 Caturla, *Zurbarán*, pp. 234, 245.

14 José de Sigüenza, *La fundación del Monasterio de El Escorial* (Madrid, 1988), pp. 499–504.

FURTHER READING

Bennett, Jane, *Vibrant Matter: A Political Ecology of Things* (Durham, NC, and London, 2010)

Brown, Jonathan, *Zurbarán* (London, 1991)

Cano Rivero, Ignacio, *Zurbarán (1598–1664)*, exh. cat., Palazzo dei Diamanti (Ferrara, 2013)

Castillo Martos, Manuel, and Joaquín Rodríguez Mateos, *Sevilla Barroca y el siglo XVII*, 2nd edn (Seville, 2019)

Caturla, María Luisa, *Francisco de Zurbarán*, trans. and ed. Odile Delenda (Paris, 1994)

Cherry, Peter, 'La formación de los pintores en los talleres sevillanos', in *Zurbarán ante su centenario (1598–1998)*, ed. Alfonso E. Pérez Sánchez (Valladolid, 1999), pp. 49–70

Delenda, Odile, *Francisco de Zurbarán, Pintor, 1598–1664* (Madrid, 2007)

—, *Zurbarán. Catálogo razonado y crítico*, vol. I (Madrid, 2009)

—, *Zurbarán. Catálogo razonado y crítico*, vol. II: *Los conjuntos y el obrador* (Madrid, 2010)

Delenda, Odile, and Mar Borobia, *Zurbarán: A New Perspective*, exh. cat., Museo Thyssen-Bornemisza (Madrid, 2015)

Fernández López, José, *Programas iconográficos de la pintura barroca sevillana del siglo XVII*, 2nd edn (Seville, 2002)

Galassi, Susan Grace, et al., *Zurbarán: Jacob and His Twelve Sons. Paintings from Auckland Castle*, exh. cat., Meadows Museum, Dallas (Madrid, 2017)

Gállego, Julián, and José Gudiol, *Zurbarán, 1598–1664*, trans. Kenneth Lyons (London, 1987)

Guinard, Paul, *Zurbarán et les peintres espagnols de la vie monastique* (Paris, 1988)

Hernández, Rosilie, *Immaculate Conceptions: The Power of the Religious Imagination in Early Modern Spain* (Toronto, 2019)

McGinn, Bernard, *Mysticism in the Golden Age of Spain, 1500–1650* (New York, 2017)

Martí, Jésica, and Ximo Company, *Francisco de Zurbarán: Santa Inés* (Lleida, 2023)

Nancarrow, Mindy, 'Theology and Devotion in Zurbarán's Images of the Infant Virgin in the Temple', *South Atlantic Review*, LXXII/1 (2007), pp. 76–92

Navarrete Prieto, Benito, *La pintura andaluza del siglo XVII y sus fuentes grabadas* (Madrid, 1998)

Pemán, César, *Zurbarán y otros estudios sobre pintura del XVII español* (Madrid, 1989)

Pérez Sánchez, Alfonso E., *Zurbarán: La obra final, 1650–1664*, exh. cat., Museo de Bellas Artes de Bilbao (Bilbao, 2000)

Pérez Sánchez, Alfonso E., and Benito Navarrete Prieto, *De Herrera a Velázquez. El primer naturalismo en Sevilla*, exh. cat., Hospital de los Venerables (Seville, 2005)

Quiles García, Fernando, *Sevilla y América en el barroco. Comercio, ciudad y arte* (Seville, 2009)

Robbins, Jeremy, *Incomparable Realms: Spain during the Golden Age, 1500–1700* (London, 2022)

Sanz, Mª Jesús, *Fiestas sevillanas de la Inmaculada Concepción en el siglo XVII. El sentido de la celebración y su repercusión exterior* (Seville, 2008)

Shuger, Dale, *God Made Word: An Archaeology of Mystic Discourse in Early Modern Spain* (Toronto, 2022)

Soria, Martin S., *The Paintings of Zurbarán* (London, 1953)

Stratton, Suzanne L., *The Immaculate Conception in Spanish Art* (Cambridge, 1994)

Valdivieso, Enrique, *Zurbarán IV Centenario*, exh. cat., Museo de Bellas Artes (Seville, 1998)

—, *Bodegones, floreros y trampantojos en la pintura barroca sevillana* (Valencina de la Concepción, 2021)

Valme Muñoz Rubio, Maria del, 'Zurbarán, uno studio della tecnica', in Ignacio Cano Rivero, *Zurbarán (1598–1664)*, exh. cat., Palazzo dei Diamanti (Ferrara, 2013), pp. 73–85

Véliz, Zahira, 'A Painter's Technique: Zurbarán's *The Holy House of Nazareth*', *Bulletin of the Cleveland Museum of Art*, LXVIII/8 (1981), pp. 271–85

Wunder, Amanda, *Baroque Seville: Sacred Art in a Century of Crisis* (University Park, PA, 2017)

Zurbarán, exh. cat., Museo Nacional del Prado (Madrid, 1988)

ACKNOWLEDGEMENTS

Zurbarán was a key figure on the Spanish Baroque course that I taught over nearly thirty years at the University of Edinburgh, and my thanks are due to the many students who studied this with me for their insightful and challenging questions that helped hone my appreciation of the artist. For conversations at various points over the years around subjects dealt with here, I would like to thank Jenny Lowe, Eric Southworth, David Howarth, Clara Marías, Celeste-Marie Bernier and, especially, Terry O'Reilly, who is greatly missed. My thanks are also due to Aurora J. Ortega López, Archivist of the Real Parroquia de Santa María Magdalena in Seville, and to Juan Ignacio Vallejo Sánchez and Jose María Jayme Castañeda at the Museo de Cádiz; their kind assistance made for memorable visits to both cities. At Reaktion I would like to thank Michael Leaman for his advice and guidance, Alex Ciobanu for his sharp and expert eye and for undertaking all image acquisitions and rights, Miren Lopategui for her proofreading, Emma Devlin for her guidance through the editorial process, and the series editor, François Quiviger, for his close reading and invaluable suggestions. The person-without-whom has always been David Ingham, and I owe more than I can say to his insights and willingness to pursue works by Zurbarán. This book, as always, is for him, with love.

PHOTO ACKNOWLEDGEMENTS

The author and publishers wish to express their thanks to the sources listed below for illustrative material and/or permission to reproduce it. Locations of artworks are also given below, in the interest of brevity:

Art Institute of Chicago: 7; Catedral de Jerez de la Frontera: 51 (Album/Alamy Stock Photo); Catedral de Sevilla: 8 (Album/Alamy Stock Photo), 46 (The Picture Art Collection/Alamy Stock Photo); The Cleveland Museum of Art, OH: 36; Église Saint-Gervais-Saint-Protais, Langon, photo © RMN-Grand Palais/Jean-Pierre Lagiewski/Dist. Foto SCALA, Florence: 48; Gemäldegalerie, Staatliche Museen zu Berlin/Gustav Schwarz (presumably destroyed in May 1945): 53; Gemäldegalerie Alte Meister, Staatliche Kunstsammlungen Dresden: 12 (Bridgeman Images); Isabella Stewart Gardner Museum, Boston: 18 (Bridgeman Images); The Metropolitan Museum of Art, New York: 50; Musée des Beaux-Arts de Lyon (Inv. A 115), image © Lyon MBA – photo Martial Couderette: 38; Musée Fabre, Montpellier: 41 (Heritage Images/Fine Art Images/akg-images); Musée de Grenoble, photos © RMN-Grand Palais/Daniel Arnaudet/Dist. Fotos SCALA, Florence: 22, 23, 24, 25; Musée du Louvre, Paris: 13 (Bridgeman Images); Museo de América, Madrid: 2 (Artexplorer/Alamy Stock Photo); Museo de Bellas Artes, Bilbao: 44 (Heritage Image Partnership Ltd/Alamy Stock Photo), 60 (Art Collection 2/Alamy Stock Photo); Museo de Bellas Artes, Seville: 4 (Bridgeman Images), 5 (akg-images/Album/Oronoz), 14 (Bridgeman Images), 20 (Peter van Evert/Alamy Stock Photo), 29 (akg-images/Joseph Martin), 30 (Bridgeman Images), 31, 49 (Heritage Image Partnership Ltd/Alamy Stock Photo); Museo de Cádiz: 40 (Artefact/Alamy Stock Photo); Museo Lázaro Galdiano, Madrid: 21 (Artexplorer/Alamy Stock Photo); Museu Nacional d'Art de Catalunya, Barcelona/www.museunacional.cat (CC BY-NC-SA 3.0): 47; Museo Nacional de Escultura, Valladolid: 45 (Heritage

Images/Fine Art Images/akg-images), 54 (Album/Alamy Stock Photo); Museo Nacional del Prado, Madrid: 3 (Album/Alamy Stock Photo), 11 (Impaint/Alamy Stock Photo), 15 (akg-images/Erich Lessing), 16 (akg-images/Album/Oronoz), 17 (Bridgeman Images), 19 (akg-images), 33 (akg-images/Erich Lessing), 39 (Album/Alamy Stock Photo), 56 (Bridgeman Images), 59 (Impaint/Alamy Stock Photo); The National Gallery, London: 1, 34 and 37 (Heritage Images/Fine Art Images/akg-images), 43 (Bridgeman Images); National Gallery of Ireland, Dublin (CC BY 4.0): 42; Nationalmuseum, Stockholm, photo Anna Danielsson: 55; Norton Simon Museum, Pasadena, CA (Acc. no. F.1972.06.P), photo © The Norton Simon Foundation: 32; Real Academia de Bellas Artes de San Fernando, Madrid, photos Heritage Image Partnership Ltd/Alamy Stock Photo: 10, 57; Real Monasterio de Santa María de Guadalupe, photos Album/Alamy Stock Photo: 26, 27, 28, 35; Real Parroquia de Santa María Magdalena, Seville: 6 (Album/Alamy Stock Photo); Rijksmuseum, Amsterdam: 58; The State Hermitage Museum, St Petersburg: 52 (photo Wikimedia Commons, public domain); Wadsworth Atheneum Museum of Art, Hartford, CT: 9 (NPL – De Agostini Picture Library/Bridgeman Images).

INDEX

Illustration numbers are indicated by *italics*